FREUD'S PHILOSOPHY OF THE UNCONSCIOUS

FREUD'S PHILOSOPHY OF THE UNCONSCIOUS

by

DAVID LIVINGSTONE SMITH

SPRINGER-SCIENCE+BUSINESS MEDIA, B.V.

A C.I.P. Catalogue record for this book is available from the Library of Congress.

ISBN 978-90-481-5289-6 ISBN 978-94-017-1611-6 (eBook)
DOI 10.1007/978-94-017-1611-6

Printed on acid-free paper

To my wife Subrena for the blessing of her love. The sweetness of the present, the vitality of the future.

Although psycho-analysis is in no sense itself a philosophy, an interpretation of life, it does bring to the solution of philosophical questions a wealth of new and suggestive data.

Israel Levine, *The Unconscious*

TABLE OF CONTENTS

SERIES PREFACE

This series will include monographs and collections of studies devoted to the investigation and exploration of knowledge, information, and data-processing systems of all kinds, no matter whether human, (other) animal, or machine. Its scope is intended to span the full range of interests from classical problems in the philosophy of mind and philosophical psychology through issues in cognitive psychology and sociobiology (regarding the mental abilities of other species) to ideas related to artificial intelligence and computer science.

While emphasis will be placed upon theoretical, conceptual, and epistemological aspects of these problems and domains, empirical, experimental, and methodological studies will also appear from time to time.

Confusion between philosophy and psychology commonly occurs among those who are neither philosophers nor psychologists, less frequently among those who are. Some philosophers excuse themselves from taking Freud seriously by viewing him merely as a psychologist, while some psychologists excuse themselves by viewing him merely as a philosopher. Anyone who has ever adopted such an attitude toward Freud should find this work a repository of refutations, for Freud's work--as David Smith amply displays--abounds with insights--both philosophical and psychological--about the nature of the mind, especially the existence of mentality without consciousness.

This rich historical and analytical study demonstrates Freud's enduring significance for contemporary debates within both of these domains.

J.H.F.

PREFACE

The literature on Freud and his theory of the 'dynamic' unconscious is gargantuan and still burgeoning, if only because of post-Freudian object relations theory, Kohutian self-psychology and Hartmannian ego-psychology, not to speak of Lacanian variants. Yet, to the best of my knowledge as a critic of psychoanalytic theory and therapy for over two decades, there has been no book elucidating the intersection of contemporary philosophy of mind, Freud's intellectual odyssey in the philosophy of mind and his negative stance toward philosophy and metaphysics.

In this excellent study, David Smith weaves a rich, conceptually penetrating and historically sophisticated tapestry in just that area. The book will be much welcomed by philosophers of mind, cognitive psychologists and any reader who has a scholarly interest in Freud.

Adolf Grünbaum
Andrew Mellon Professor of Philosophy of Science,
Research Professor of Psychiatry,
Chairman, Center for Philosophy of Science,
University of Pittsburgh.

ACKNOWLEDGEMENTS

My deepest thanks go to Dr James Hopkins for taking on the formidable task of my philosophical education.

I also owe a profound debt of gratitude to Professor Adolf Grünbaum, whose rock-solid support and encouragement have made a huge difference in my attitude towards my own work.

I would like to thank Mr. Keith Davies of the Freud Museum, London, who generously allowed me access to the index of Sigmund Freud's library.

I owe a huge debt to my son Benjamin for his expert and generous technical assistance during the preparation of this manuscript. Both Benjamin and my daughter Sasha have shown amazing resilience and forbearance during the turbulent period when this work was being researched and written. Thanks.

Thanks also to Ms. Anna David, Mrs. Hilde Rapp and Dr. Ulrich Berns, who have provided me with essential assistance translating passages from Freud's German original and patiently answering my questions about the use of German terms.

Special thanks are owed to Marsha Taylor who bravely accepted the challenge of proofreading and editing the manuscript in the face of my appalling spelling and grammar.

I would like to thank the multitalented Mr. Brett Kahr for his benign obsessionality when checking my list of references.

Finally I would like to thank Dr. Harry Schlepperman, who has generously shared with me his encyclopedic knowledge of the history of psychoanalytic thought.

INTRODUCTION

FREUD AND PHILOSOPHY

The present work is an attempt to set out Sigmund Freud's contributions to the philosophy of mind, to defend Freud's contributions against some recent philosophical criticisms and to provide additional justification for aspects of Freud's theory of mind.

This project may seem perverse, given Freud's notoriously anti-philosophical reputation.[1] Notwithstanding this reputation, Freud was not hostile to philosophy *per se* but, like the logical positivists, his Viennese contemporaries, he was critical of the philosophical orthodoxy of his day.[2] I will show that Freud was alive to many of the philosophical ramifications of his work, and go a long way towards justifying Glymour's (1991) claim that:

> Freud's writings contain a philosophy of mind, and indeed a philosophy of mind that addresses many of the issues about the mental that nowadays concern philosophers and ought to concern psychologists. Freud's thinking about the issues in the philosophy of mind is better than much of what goes on in contemporary philosophy, and it is sometimes as good as the best....Even when Freud had the wrong answer to a question, or refused to give an answer, he knew what the question was and what was at stake in it. And when he was deeply wrong it was often for reasons that still make parts of cognitive psychology wrong (46).

In short, I will take issue with the claim by Quinton that 'Freud was not a philosopher' (1972: 72).

While a student at the University of Vienna, the adolescent Freud was strongly influenced by the philosopher Franz Brentano, who became something of a mentor to him, and even contemplated doing a joint doctorate in philosophy and zoology. Referring in a letter to Wilhelm Fliess dated 1 January 1896 to this period of his life he admitted to secretly nourishing the hope of returning to 'my original goal of philosophy'.[3] Three months later he informed Fliess that: 'As a young person I knew no other longing than that for philosophical knowledge and now I am about to fulfil it as I move from medicine to psychology'.[4] Later, Freud became a member of the Society for Positivist Philosophy, which also included Einstein and Mach[5] amongst its members. Freud was highly critical of the neo-Cartesian tradition in the philosophy of mind with its metaphysical dualism, anti-naturalism, introspectionism and rationalism, which was dominant during his lifetime. What Lyons (1986) calls the 'golden age of introspection' extended from about 1637 - the year that Descartes published his *Discourse* - until the first decade of the twentieth century. The Cartesian emphasis on consciousness had been underscored in Germany by Reinhold. Reinhold's ideas were taken up by Fichte, Mehmel, Fortlage and others and incorporated into nineteenth century psychology (Leary, 1980).

Many of Freud's ostensibly hostile remarks about philosophy are specifically directed against the dualism and introspectionism that saturated the philosophy of mind during much of his lifetime.

He writes, for example, that:

> To most people who have been educated in philosophy the idea of anything psychical which is not also conscious is so inconceivable that it seems to them absurd (1923b: 13).

The truth of Freud's claim is underwritten by the work of authors who were his contemporaries. Baldwin's authoritative *Dictionary of Psychology* (1901), for example, stated that consciousness is generally taken to be 'the point of division between mind and not-mind' and is 'the distinctive character of whatever can be called mental life' (216; cited in Güzeldere,1995a).

Freud held that insofar as the dualists foreclosed the possibility of unconscious mental events and situated the mental in a non-natural order they were philosophical enemies of psychoanalysis and of scientific psychology.

> It is easy to understand why doctors...should have no liking for psycho-analysis.... But as a compensation it might be supposed that the new theory would be all the more likely to meet with applause from philosophers.[6] For philosophers were accustomed to putting abstract concepts (or, as unkind tongues would say, hazy words[7]) in the forefront of their explanations of the universe, and it would be impossible that they should object to the extension of the sphere of psychology for which psycho-analysis had paved the way. But here another obstacle arose. The philoso-

> phers' idea of what is mental was not that of psycho-analysis. The overwhelming majority of philosophers regard as mental only the phenomena of consciousness. For them the world of consciousness coincides with the sphere of what is mental. Everything else that may take place within the "mind"- an entity so hard to grasp - is relegated by them to the organic determinants of mental processes or to processes parallel to mental ones. Or, more strictly speaking, the mind has no contents other than the phenomena of consciousness, and consequently psychology, the science of the mind, has no other subject-matter (1925b:216).[8]

And later...

> The reasons for this hostility were to be found...from the philosophical point of view, in its assuming as an underlying postulate the concept of unconscious mental activity (1926c:269).

A typical Freudian attack on philosophical rationalism[9] can be found in his 'New introductory lectures on psycho-analysis'' (1933a).

> Philosophy is not opposed to science; it gives itself the airs of a science, works partly with the same methods[10], but parts company with it by clinging to the illusion that it offer a gapless and coherent world picture which, however, must collapse every time our knowledge makes some new progress. In its method it is mistaken insofar as it overestimates the cognitive value of our logical operations [i.e., is rationalistic] and sometimes also acknowledges other sources of knowledge, like the intuition (cited and translated by Kaufmann, 1980:19).

Freud's materialism entailed the theory of 'psychical determinism', that is, Freud believed that if the mind is identical to a physical object – the brain – then mental events must be nomologically ordered just as all material events are. This doctrine was deeply antagonistic to the voluntarist beliefs promulgated by post-Kantian idealists and Romantic philosophers which later found expression in the writings of the existentialists. Indeed, well into the twentieth century Freud was criticized for denying agent causation (e.g., Sartre, 1943).

A good deal of the intellectual opposition to psychoanalysis in the German-speaking world sprang from a philosophical source: the prevalence of post-Kantian idealism in the late nineteenth and early twentieth centuries (Decker, 1977).

> A "science" of human psychology was impossible because no one could really know the mind of another. To make generalizations and on that basis construct a "system" of the mind was therefore impossible. The "soul" was not explainable or reducible

> and therefore could not be "analyzed". Every psyche was unique, and the best that could be done was to examine its phenomena individually (324).

Freud's desire to subsume his psychology under the umbrella of natural science, a desire stemming from his allegiance to Mach's doctrine of the unity of science, ran contrary to the dualistic epistemological zeitgeist. This epistemological dualism was nested within an ontological dualism that was virtually taken for granted by the educated German-speaking public; from this vantage point, Freud's monism was regarded as deeply counter-intuitive.

> Late nineteenth-century scientists received justification...from their philosophical education, which had stressed the basic duality of mind and body. Thus it was epistemologically legitimate to concentrate on mind or matter and leave the other out of consideration.... Freud's monism was a sharp intruder in the midst of all this protective dualism (Decker, 326-327).

In the world of psychology, Freud was confronted with Wundt's introspectionism. Introspectionism dominated psychology until the second decade of the twentieth century, when behaviorism usurped its position. As its name implies, introspectionism sought to confine psychology to the study of conscious experiences. As such, it was hostile to the invocation of theoretical entities (e.g., Titchener, 1917). Introspectionism was hospitable to the prevailing idealist trend.

Behaviorism developed as a reaction against the Cartesian approach typified by introspectionism. It is therefore not surprising that early behaviorist writings have certain features in common with the writings of Freud. The following excerpt from Watson's classic 'Psychology as the behaviorist views it' (1913) has an uncannily Freudian ring:

> The time seems to have come when psychology must discard all reference to consciousness.... The suggested elimination of states of consciousness as proper objects of investigation in themselves will remove the barrier which exists between it and the other sciences (177).

However, like the introspectionists, Watson (1927) equated consciousness with mentality, reasoning that if there is no such thing as mind it follows that there are no such things as unconscious mental processes.

The new hegemonies of logical empiricism and behaviorism, which formed a natural alliance (Smith, 1986), were also inhospitable to psychoanalysis in part because of the latter's invocation of theoretical entities. Freud's psychology of unconscious mental processes was, as Glymour (1991) and Erdelyi (1985) have claimed, an early form of cognitivism, a theoretical movement conventionally regarded as having been initiated by the publication of Neisser's *Cognitive Psychology* (1967).

The most important evidence concerning Freud's attitude towards philosophy comes from his own philosophical efforts. In spite of his self-diagnosis as 'lacking talent for philosophy by nature' (cited in Gay, 1988:46n), Freud's writings show him to be a philosopher of considerable finesse who confronts issues in a strikingly contemporary fashion.[11] Freud was fully aware that his work had important ramifications for the philosophy of mind.

> Philosophy...will be unable to avoid taking the psycho-analytic contributions to psychology fully into account.... In particular, the setting up of the hypothesis of unconscious mental activities must compel philosophy to decide one way or the other and, if it accepts the idea, to modify its own views on the relation of mind to body so that they may conform to the new knowledge (1913: 178).

Although a few philosophers published work dealing with or touching on psychoanalytic topics in the 1920s (e.g., Russell, 1921; Field, 1922; Levine, 1923; Broad, 1925), within the analytical tradition serious philosophical attention to Freudian thought seems to have begun in the 1930s with Wittgenstein's lectures at Cambridge. Wittgenstein inspired a number of philosophers to write about what they took to be Freud's confusion between causal and rational explanations of mental events. This trend culminated in MacIntyre's *The Unconscious* (1958). In the early 1960s, however, Donald Davidson's groundbreaking work was beginning to undermine the orthodoxy that causal and rational explanations should be sharply demarcated from one another. Simultaneously, in the late 1950s and early 1960s, the groundwork for a new naturalistic consensus was laid by the work of Place (1956), Smart (1959) and others advocating the identity theory of mind-brain relationship, aided and abetted by the rise of cognitive science and the work of Sellars (1956, 1963) and Feyerabend (1963) on the theoretical nature of folk-psychology. Putnam's (1960) functionalism and externalism (1975) completed the picture. By the early 1980s materialism and anti-introspectionism were commonplace, while cognitive scientists such as Marr (1982) were unashamedly offering principled explanations of mental events relying on hypothetical unconscious processes. More recently, philosophers such as Dennett (1987, 1992), Dretske (1995) and Millikan (1984, 1993) have moved in the direction of neo-Darwinian accounts of mental phenomena. The philosophical climate has never been more congenial to Freudian thinking. In spite of this, there has not yet been a comprehensive reassessment of Freudian thought in light of the new philosophy of mind. Such a reassessment would, at the very least, show Freud to have been a precursor of contemporary philosophical writers and also might reveal that he has something fresh to add to the current debates.

In the first eleven chapters of this book, I will use Freud's writings to establish the nature of his views on several topics of concern to contemporary philosophy of mind. Chapter One documents Freud's initiation into the world of philosophy at the University of Vienna by his tutor, Professor Franz Brentano. Chapter Two discusses Freud's relationship with the ideas of Theodor Lipps and Friedrich Nietzsche, showing that Lipps' direct impact on Freud was probably profound and Nietzsche's negligible. Chapter Three charts Freud's philosophical trajectory from psychophysical dualism to a very contemporary materialism. Because there is little scholarly consensus on Freud's position with regard to the mind-body problem, Chapter Four is devoted to a critical analysis of rival interpretations of Freud's stance on the mind-body problem. Chapter Five discusses Freud's radical theory of unconscious mental events against the background of his materialism, and shows how he attempted to neutralize two rival accounts of unconscious mental events: the dissociationist and the neurophysiological dispositionalist approaches. Chapter Six describes Freud's use of what I call the 'Continuity argument' to defend his thesis of unconscious mental events and shows how this argument is bound up with his materialism. Chapter Seven considers Freud's work in relation to the philosophical concepts of the English neuroscientist John Hughlings Jackson, as well as Freud's philosophical and psychological concerns in the context of nineteenth century developments in neuroscience, and discusses an important source of Freud's philosophical ideas. Chapter Eight gives an account of Freud's naturalistic theory of consciousness, and describes his views on the role played by language in the functioning of the mental apparatus. Chapter Nine broaches the difficult and hitherto uninvestigated topic of Freud's views on the theoretical of folk-psychological items, tracing out his ideas about the nature of folk-psychology and scientific psychology. Chapter Ten explores Freud's attitudes towards what are now called homuncular and causal role functionalist concepts of mind. Chapter Eleven examines problems implicitly raised by Freud's account of the special characteristics of certain forms of unconscious thinking.

The next five chapters deal with selected philosophical criticisms of Freud's work and attempts to philosophically underwrite Freudian claims. Chapter Twelve concentrates on the contributions of Wittgenstein and MacIntyre, Chapters Thirteen and Fourteen critically examine recent work by John Searle. Chapters Fifteen and Sixteen survey Donald Davidson's attempts to underwrite philosophically certain aspects of Freud's theory of mind. Chapter Seventeen succinctly summarizes the main conclusions of the work.

During the years of research leading up to the publication of this monograph I have had innumerable conversations with psychoanalysts and Freud scholars regarding Freud's philosophy of mind. I have been consistently surprised by the extent to which even experts in the field are largely unaware of Freud's philosophical commitments and their implications for his psychology. As I will show, one's understanding of many of Freud's psychoanalytical doctrines is condemned to being impoverished without the benefit of an understanding of their position within the philosophical context of his thinking.

It is not only psychoanalysts and Freud scholars who have failed to properly estimate Freud's standing as a philosopher. On the whole, philosophers have failed to come to grips with Freud. The infrequent references to Freud to be found in the philosophical literature are usually either ill-informed efforts to philosophically underwrite what the author takes to be Freud's psychological doctrines, ill-informed philosophical criticism of those doctrines, or attempts to recruit Freud in support of philosophical beliefs with which he would never have agreed.

Coming at a time when criticism of Freud is widespread within the academic community, it is hoped that the present text will encourage the reassessment of his intellectual standing. In light of the widespread skepticism to be found within even the profession of psychoanalysis, not to mention psychology and psychiatry more generally, regarding many of his psychological theories, Freud's contributions to cognitive science and the philosophy of mind may prove to be amongst his most significant gifts to the twenty-first century.

I

FREUD'S CONTACT WITH BRENTANO

Freud's correspondence with his friend Eduard Silberstein provides a glimpse into his encounter with Franz Brentano and philosophy at the University of Vienna.[12]

Freud's first serious reference to philosophy in the correspondence, in the letter of 22-23 October 1874, mentions that:

> Brentano is running two courses, selected metaphysical problems on Wednesday and Saturday evenings, and a text by Mill on the utilitarian principle on Fridays, both of which we attend regularly (66).

Freud elected to take Brentano's courses. Philosophy had not been a required part of the medical curriculum for two years (Quinton, 1972).

There are several references in the correspondence to Freud's fellow philosophical students: Richard Wahle, Sigfried Lipiner and Joseph Paneth. Wahle later became professor of philosophy at Czernowitz and Vienna. Lipiner, a minor poet, became a personal friend of Friedrich Nietzsche. Paneth, later a University lecturer, was closest to Freud. Freud wrote to Silberstein on 8 November:

> I should be sorry...if you...were to neglect philosophy altogether, while I, the godless medical man and empiricist, am attending two courses in philosophy and reading Feuerbach in Paneth's company. One of these courses - listen and marvel! - deals with the existence of God, and Prof. Brentano, who gives the lectures, is a splendid man, a scholar and philosopher, even though he deems it necessary to support the existence of God with his own expositions. I shall let you know just as soon as one of his arguments gets to the point (we have not yet progressed beyond the preliminary problems), lest your path to salvation in the faith be cut off (71-72).

On 6 December Freud mentions a philosophical journal that he and his friends had produced, stating that:

> The second issue of our journal has just appeared and contains a critique of Lipiner's article on the teleological argument autore me [by me], "The foundations of

materialist ethics" by Paneth, and On Spinoza's Proof of God's Existence by Emanuel Loewy (73).

On 7 March 1875 Freud returns to the subject of Brentano

Prof. Brentano continues to lecture until Saturday, and on every day, no less, to make good the lacunae caused by his illness. The two of us (Paneth and I) have established closer contact with him; we sent him a letter containing some objections and he invited us to his home, refuting them, and seemed to take some interest in us, asked Wahle about us...and now that we have sent him a second letter of objections, has summoned us again. When you and I meet I shall tell you more about this remarkable man (a believer, a teleologist!) and a Darwinian and a damned clever fellow, a genius in fact), who is, in many respects, an ideal human being. For now just the news that under Brentano's fruitful influence I have arrived at the decision to take my Ph.D. in philosophy and zoology; further negotiations about my admission to the philosophical faculty either next term or next year are in progress (94-95).

And on 13 March:

My report that I intended to change over to the philosophical faculty must be amended inasmuch as it was my original plan to combine attendance at two faculties and to take both doctorates in three to four years. This, however is impossible, at least the first part; I shall have to make closer inquiries about the second. In any case, I am free to take zoology, my main subject, in the philosophical faculty and to attend philosophy lectures whenever I please, which is what will happen next semester. Naturally, a Ph.D. examination remains a possibility and tomorrow I and Paneth, who is involved in these plans, will be seeking Brentano's advice (101).

Freud records in the same letter that, he had registered for a (twice weekly) course on logic and a course on philosophy, both taught by Brentano. He concludes as follows:

"And thus we live, thus fortune guides our steps," though Fried. Nietzsche took David Strauss to task in Strasbourg for this philistine dictum in 1873. Of my relationship to Brentano which you may be imagining is closer than it really is, and of the philosophical outlook I have derived from it, I shall write to you tomorrow, when our visit to him, at ten o'clock, is over (102).

The next letter, that of 15 March, gives a lengthy summary of the meeting:

He brought out our letter and wanted to refute our objections, which was still necessary only in one case however. Then he made a few quite favorable remarks about our endeavors....He complained that philosophy was in absolute chaos here, whereupon Paneth, who had attended Zimmerman's lectures, made some highly dispar-

> aging remarks about the latter, thus forcing Brentano to pronounce upon Herbart. He utterly condemned his a priori constructions in psychology, thought it unforgivable that Herbart had never deigned to consult experience or experiment to check whether these agreed with his arbitrary assumptions, declared himself unreservedly a follower of the empiricist school which applies the method of science to philosophy and to psychology (in fact this is the main advantage of his philosophy, which alone renders it tolerable for me), and mentioned a few remarkable psychological observations that demonstrate the untenability of Herbart's speculations (102).

Zimmerman, a rival professor of philosophy at the University of Vienna, advocated the ideas of Johann Friedrich Herbart, a psychologist and philosopher best known for his theory of unconscious mental events. Herbart's thesis continued that of Leibniz (1711). According to Herbart (1824), unconscious ideas are ideas that are too weak to remain above the threshold of consciousness. Although individually weak, the aggregate '*Vorstellungsmassen*') of unconscious items could, according to Herbart, influence conscious mental life. In light of this passage from Freud's youthful correspondence, it is ironical that Dorer (1932) has argued that Herbart was one of the most important intellectual influences on Freud's creation of psychoanalysis.[13]

> There was much greater need for research into individual questions, the better to arrive at reliable individual conclusions, than for attempts to tie up the whole of philosophy, which was futile because philosophy and psychology were but young sciences and could expect no support from physiology in particular (Ibid.).

Brentano's empiricist slant and his view on the relationship between philosophy and science were evidently congenial to Freud's intellectual temperament and may have influenced his subsequent work. Brentano was committed to 'the austere ideal of rigorous philosophical science' (Husserl, 1919: 50), and his emphasis on empiricism, logic and the natural scientific ideal helped lay the groundwork for the emergence of logical positivism in Vienna.

> When we asked for personal advice, he told us that it was quite feasible and a good idea for us to attempt a doctorate in philosophy as well as in medicine, and that this was not unprecedented - *Loetze* had done just that and had then opted for philosophy. We would do well to specialize in a philosophical subject; the Minister had enjoined him to train lecturers in philosophy. (Though we are unlikely to take him up on this) (Ibid.).

Brentano went on to divulge his opinions on the value of the work of various philosophers, apparently with the intention of pointing out useful lines of investigation for Freud and Paneth.

> From among philosophical writers he selected some he advised us to read and took the rest to task mercilessly. We ought to start with Descartes, and study all his writings because he had given philosophy a new impetus. Of his successors, Geulincx, Malebranche and Spinoza none was worth reading. All of them had picked up the wrong end of Descartes' philosophy, his complete separation of body and soul (103).

Brentano thus encouraged Freud to criticize substance dualism, at least in its interactionist form, although he himself did not advocate a materialist position.

> Spinoza indulged in pure sophisms; he was to be trusted least of all. *Locke* and *Leibniz*, by contrast, were indispensable, the first being a most brilliant thinker, the second not fully satisfactory only because he tended to dissipate his strength. These two were succeeded by the popular philosophers, who were of purely cultural and historical, not philosophical interest. By contrast, two figures from the skeptical period, *Hume* and Kant, were indispensable, *Hume* being the most precise thinker and the most perfect writer of all philosophers (Ibid.).

Freud purchased Hume's *Essays* in 1879 and Locke's *Essay on Human Understanding* in 1882. He purchased Kant's *Critique of Pure Reason* in 1882, owned the two volumes of Kant's *Writings on Natural Philosophy*, owned but did not read Kant's *Anthropology* and owned Kant's *On the Power of the Mind to Master One's Morbid Feelings* (Davies & Fichtner, forthcoming).

> Kant, for his part, did not at all deserve the great reputation he enjoys; he was full of sophisms and was an intolerable pedant, childishly delighted whenever he could divide anything into three or four parts, which explains the inventions and fictions in his schemata, what people praise in him Brentano was ready to credit to *Hume*, what is entirely Kant's own he rejected as harmful and untrue. In short, Kant come off very badly in Brentano's eyes; what makes Kant important is his successors, Schelling, Fichte and Hegel, whom Brentano dismisses as swindlers[14] (you can see how close he comes to the materialists in this regard; he told us how discouraged he felt in his youth, when he started to read philosophers, how he nearly despaired of his philosophical talent until he was made aware of his abilities by [?] an older philosopher (103-104).

Brentano evidently hoped that Freud and Paneth would not be similarly discouraged. It is perhaps noteworthy that there is no record of

Freud having owned works by the philosophers of whom Brentano unequivocally disapproved: Geulincx, Malebranche, Spinoza, Fichte, Schelling and Hegel, although he did possess a copy of Fischer's 1897 book on *Spinoza's Life, Work and Teachings*.

> "And so you want to let us off without reading them?" I asked. More than that, I want to warn you against reading them; do not set out on these slippery paths of reason - you might fare like doctors at insane asylums, who start out thinking people there are quite mad but later get used to it and not infrequently pick up a bit of dottiness themselves (104).

These views certainly cohere with Freud's distrust of metaphysics, and his proto-logical positivist claim that metaphysics is an abuse of thinking .

> Of the most recent philosophers he then recommended August Comte, whose life he described to us, and he was about to go on to the English philosophers when Prof. Simony turned up and we were packed off, with permission to call again during the "vacation" and to fetch him for a walk.

Freud makes it clear to Silberstein that, despite appearances, Brentano had not singled he and Paneth out as promising philosophers.

> So far, so good, and you might flatter yourself on having a friend thought worthy of the company of so excellent a man, were it not that thousands of others had been invited to his home, or to converse with him, which greatly detracts from our distinction. He came here to found a school and to gain disciples, and hence proffers his friendship and time to all who need it. For all that, I have not escaped from his influence - I am not capable of refuting a simple theistic argument that constitutes the crown of his deliberations. His great distinction is that he abhors all glib phrases, all emotionality and all intolerance of other views. He demonstrates the existence of God with as little bias and as much precision as another might argue the advantage of the wave over the emission theory (Ibid.).[15]

Freud also makes it clear that his own metaphysical convictions tended towards materialism.

> Needless to say, I am only a theist by necessity, and am honest enough to confess my helplessness in the face of his argument; however, I have no intention of surrendering so quickly or completely. Over the next few semesters, I intend to make a thorough study of his philosophy, and meanwhile reserve judgment and the choice between theism and materialism. For the time being I have ceased to be a materialist and am not yet a theist (104-105).

It is perhaps significant in light of this passage that Freud owned a copy of Lange's (1873-75) *History of Materialism.*

By 27 March Freud seems to have formed an uncomplimentary assessment of Kant, describing a group of homeopaths as 'great metaphysicians, and Kantians in particular, which is most laudable but perhaps unhealthy' (106). With the help of Silberstein's intervention, Freud begins tentatively to criticize Brentano's theological conceptions.

> Ever since Brentano adduced such ridiculously simple arguments in favor of his God, I have been afraid that one fine day I will be taken in by the scientific proofs of the validity of spiritualism, homeopathy, by Louise Lateau, etc. In short, I have been too little of the dogmatist, adhering to all I believed in out of logical conviction alone.
>
> Your appreciation of Brentano is uncommonly good.... Indeed, his God is a mere logical principle and I have accepted it as such. He repudiates any direct intervention by God on the grounds that it would be dysteleological. How far he allows regard for God to affect life is still unclear, though as far as I remember he once hinted at something like that in ethics. And I still have to find out what he thinks of ritual and a thousand other things that are more important in practice than his empty God. Unfortunately, when we allow the God concept we start down a slippery path. We shall have to wait and see how far we fall. Since he claims that man knows very little of the world, perhaps stopping short at the Dubois-Reymond limits of cognition, he may be forgiven for crediting God with even less knowledge. Man lacks a proper conception of God and can approach it only by analogy; it cannot be reached by human calculation. Confusing though it all seems, it is nevertheless closely reasoned, and madly methodical. In short, Brentano cannot possibly be refuted before one has heard or studied him and plundered his stores of knowledge. So sharp a dialectician requires one to hone one's own wits on his before challenging him (106-107).

The distinction between the God of ritual worship and the abstract philosophical God finds an echo many years later in Freud's (1927) The future of an illusion'.

On 11 April Freud continues to be troubled by Brentano's argument.

> For the time being I have to confess that I badly mistook the basic questions that agitate me, and that I was completely lacking in philosophical insight. The rueful confession of a former swashbuckling, stubborn materialist! But even in my new coat I feel anything but comfortable, and have thought it best to defer a final decision until such time as I may be more versed in philosophy and more mature in science (109-110).

The remainder of the letter is largely taken up with Freud's struggle with Brentano's arguments on behalf of deism.

Freud's experiences at university clearly had a strong impact upon his philosophical development. Freud's positivism found support in the work of Brentano who had strong intellectual links with French positivism and British empiricism. Brentano, one of the philosophers who laid the groundwork for Viennese logical positivism, believed that 'the true method of philosophy is none other than that of natural science' (cited in Spiegelberg, 1982:31). He believed that the future of philosophy was contingent upon its embracing a natural-scientific attitude (Gilson, 1976).

Freud followed Brentano in the belief that 'psychology was to be the proper lever for the necessary reform of philosophy and the restoration of a scientific metaphysics' (Spiegelberg, 1982) and intended his metapsychology as the realization of this project. Although he rejected Brentano's ontological dualism, Freud retained his commitment to methodological dualism.[16]

II

FREUD, LIPPS AND NIETZSCHE

Freud explicitly acknowledged the impact of several philosophical thinkers upon his work.[17] One of the main philosophical influences on the development of Freud's psychoanalytical ideas was Theodor Lipps, an early exponent of phenomenology. In the present chapter I will briefly evaluate Lipps' influence on Freud and then go on to discuss critically the claim made by a number of historians of depth psychology that Nietzsche had a direct and insufficiently acknowledged impact on Freud's intellectual development.

FREUD AND LIPPS

Theodor Lipps was a psychologist and philosopher who influenced the development of the phenomenological movement and was an early advocate of experimental psychology (Ellenberger, 1970; Spiegelberg, 1982; Flügel and West, 1964). Freud refers approvingly to Lipps at several points in his writings. Lipps influenced Freud in at least two ways. First and most importantly, Lipps was a proponent of the theory of unconscious mental events. Second, Lipps' work on humor inspired Freud's own investigations into this subject.

While on holiday in Aussee, Freud wrote to Fliess on 26 August, 1896 that:

> I have set myself the task of building a bridge between my germinating metapsychology and that contained in the literature and have therefore immersed myself in the study of Lipps, who I suspect has the clearest mind among present-day philosophical writers (1887-1904: 324).

In his next letter to Fliess, five days later, Freud wrote:

> I found the substance of my insights stated quite clearly in Lipps, perhaps rather more so than I would like.... Consciousness is only a sense organ; all psychic content is only a representation; all psychic processes are unconscious. The correspondence

> [of our ideas] is close in details as well; perhaps the bifurcation from which my own ideas can branch off will come later (325).

And on 27 September[18]: 'Who is Lipps? A professor in Munich, and in his terminology he says exactly what I arrived at in my speculations about consciousness, quality and so forth' (329). (Freud is here alluding to his work in the 'Project for a scientific psychology' which will be discussed more fully in subsequent chapters). The paper by Lipps to which he refers was presented at the Third International Congress for Psychology held in Munich in 1896. This congress included presentations by many of the leading philosophers, psychologists and psychotherapists of the day (Ellenberger, 1972). At least some of the presentations, of which Lipps' was one, discussed notions of unconscious mental events. Lipps argued against the neurophysiological dispositionalist thesis (described in Chapter Five below) in favor of the concept of occurrent unconscious mental states (Ellenberger, Ibid.). Freud did not attend the congress.

Freud refers to Lipps twice in his discussion of the concept of the unconscious in 'The interpretation of dreams' (1900) and twice in the 'Outline of psycho-analysis' (1940a). The fact that Freud referred to Lipps' writings in publications dating from the beginning and from the end of his psychoanalytic career suggests a strong and sustained interest in his work. This is confirmed by that fact that Freud's personal library in London, which includes only those books that he thought worth retaining in his flight from Nazi persecution, contains no less than ten of Lipps' books, at least one of which was purchased as late as 1919.[19]

According to Decker (1977), Lipps' 'belief in the unconscious gradually becomes less clear and emphatic if one compares his unambiguous statements in the *Grundtatsachen des Seelenlebens* (1883) with those in his *Leitfaden der Psychologie* (1903)' (260).

FREUD AND NIETZSCHE

There has been considerable controversy about the nature and extent of Freud's intellectual debt to Nietzsche (Scavio, Cooper & Clift, 1993; Lehrer, 1995). Freud would have been exposed to Nietzsche's thought during the years of his membership of the Reading Society of the German Students of Vienna, a society largely devoted to the discussion of Nietzschian ideas. Two of Freud's university friends, Josef Paneth and Siegfried Lipiner, had a particular interest in Nieztsche's philosophy (McGrath, 1967). In 1900 Freud purchased a set of Nietzsche's *Collected Works* and he was given a second set by Otto Rank on the occasion of his 70th birthday (Jones, 1953). Ellenberger (1970), Esterson (1993), Sulloway (1979) and others describe Nietzsche as a major source for Freud's psychological ideas to whom Freud himself avoided giving full and appropriate acknowledgement.

Freud wrote in his 'Autobiographical study' (1925a) that he had long avoided reading Nietzsche because the amazing confluence in their thinking might have deflected Freud from independent development of his ideas. This reaffirms of a statement recorded in the *Minutes of the Vienna Psychoanalytic Society* made by Freud on 1 April 1908 (Nunberg and Federn, 1962). An entry in the *Minutes* dated 28 October 1908 repeats this. Freud states that he had never read more than half a page of Nietzsche here and there. In a letter from Freud to Lothar Bickel dated 28 June 1931 Freud states that he rejected the study of Nietzsche for the reasons already mentioned (Gay, 1988). We know From a letter to Arnold Zweig dated 28 April 1934 (Freud, 1873-1939; also cited in Kaufmann, 1980) that Freud says that he admired Nietzsche in his youth, but later became critical of him. We also know from Freud's letter to Fliess of 1 February 1900 that Freud had not read Nietzsche before having purchased the *Collected Works* in 1900. Freud remarks in the letter that he had not yet opened the Nietzsche books and there is no reference to his reading Nietzsche in the remainder of the correspondence. This is consistent with views expressed by Rank, who wrote to George Wilbur on 21 January 1931:

> Don't overlook the tremendous influence he [Nietzsche] had on Freud inasmuch as he influenced all European thinking (Freud read Nietzsche only in his later years but was spiritually under his influence from the beginning...) (Kaufmann, 1980:269)

Rank was intimately conversant with the work of both Freud and Nietzsche. He had also been close to Freud for many years but by 1931 was estranged from him. His remarks should therefore be given considerable weight. All of the available evidence therefore suggests that Nietzsche's influence on Freud was of a vague and second-hand nature -

and that Freud did not study Nietzsche until relatively late in life, and that the charges against Freud of unacknowledged influence or outright plagiarism are not corroborated. Kaufmann (1980) suggests that Freud's remarks recorded in the *Minutes* in 1908 can be taken to imply that Freud began reading Nietzsche seriously in 1908 by way of preparation for the two meetings of the Vienna Psychoanalytic Society dealing with Nietzsche's *Genealogy of Morals* and *Ecce Homo*. Kaufmann's argument is speculative, as is his assertion that Freud's relationship with Lou Andreas-Salomé (who had been a confidante of Nietzsche and wrote a book about him) stimulated Freud to study Nietzsche after 1912. Kaufmann's claim conflicts with Freud's assertion in the 'Autobiographical Study' that he had not yet read Nietzsche.

Using the available evidence we can arrive at a more plausible conjecture about the period when Freud began to study Nietzsche. Rank, writing in 1931, said that Freud read Nietzsche only late in life. As Rank's final estrangement from Freud occurred in April 1926, Freud must have begun reading Nietzsche before that date. The 'Autobiographical study' was written in the autumn of 1924. If we take both Freud and Rank at their word, Freud must have begun to read Nietzsche at some point during the intervening period. Perhaps Freud's mention of Nietzsche in the autobiography was sparked by a growing interest in the philosopher. This might explain why Rank chose to give Freud a set of Nietzsche's *Collected Works* for his birthday in May 1926.

Freud owned a 1928 English translation of *The Antichrist*, a copy of Challaye's (1933) *Nietzsche* and a copy of Lindsay's (no date) *Dionysos, Nietzsche contra Nietzsche*. Both were evidently gifts from the authors. He also possessed Meyer's (1913) book on *Nietzsche's Life and Work* (Davies and Fichtner, forthcoming).

III

FREUD AND THE MIND-BODY PROBLEM

There is little consensus in the scholarly literature on Freud's position concerning the mind-body problem. Opinion is divided as to whether Freud was a dualist or a materialist. Amongst the advocates of the dualist interpretation, some scholars hold that Freud advanced an epiphenominalist view of the mind.[20] Others claim that he was a psychophysical interactionist.[21] Still others take Freud to have been a psychophysical parallelist[22]. Amongst advocates of the materialist interpretation, most describe Freud as an identity theorist of an unspecified kind.[23] Others describe him as having settled on a token identity theory.[24] A few argue that Freud's position shifted over time.[25]

An understanding of Freud's position concerning the mind-body problem is central to an appreciation of the development of his philosophical and scientific thought. In the present chapter I will show that it is possible to reach reasonably clear and definite conclusions about Freud's metaphysical commitments with regard to this issue through examining his comments on the mind-body relationship chronologically and within the broader context of his work.

DUALISM AND MATERIALISM IN THE NINETEENTH CENTURY

The intellectual community within which Freud began to carve a niche in the 1880s was deeply concerned with and deeply confused about the relationship between mind and body. As early as the seventeenth century thinkers such as Arnauld and Lock e had challenged Descartes' psychophysical dualism in favor of a physicalist theory, arguing that the intuition of the mind's non-extension in space is simply an illusion. As Locke put it in his *Essay Concerning Human Understanding*[26]:

> We have the ideas of matter and thinking, but possibly shall never be able to know whether any mere material being thinks or no; it being impossible for us...to discover

> whether omnipotency has not given to some systems of matter, fitly disposed, a power to perceive and think, or else joined or fixed to matter, so disposed, a thinking immaterial substance (Locke, cited in Vesey, 1965: 22).

Notwithstanding these and other criticisms, substance dualism (in its interactionist and parallelist forms) had been the dominant approach to the mind-body problem for three centuries. Dualism established separate domains for body and mind and allowed the science of physiology to develop without posing any challenge to religious beliefs about the nature of the soul. However, by the second half of the nineteenth century, the traditional forms of dualism were becoming increasingly difficult to sustain coherently. The independent discovery of the law of the conservation of energy by Mayer, Helmholz and Joule in 1847 scientifically undermined interactionist claims.[27] Ten years later Darwin demonstrated the continuity between human beings and other creatures, and attributed human evolution to the operation of purely physical selection pressures. Perhaps most significantly, a flourishing new discipline of neuroscience could not ignore the intimate relationship between mental and neurophysiological events. One philosophical response to these pressures was to advocate forms of epiphenominalism (Huxley, 1874), which understood mind as 'the smoke above the factory' of brain. Epiphenominalism became increasingly popular amongst philosophers and scientists during the closing decade of the nineteenth century (Bradley, 1895) as it allowed that mental events were somehow dependent upon neurophysiological events in the brain. According to this doctrine, the brain has causal powers to produce mental events and that mental events themselves possess no causal powers. Epiphenomenalism thus provided a framework in which dualist intuitions about the mental and physical domains could be reconciled with the fruits of scientific progress, but it did so in a manner that conceded so much to materialism that some writers (e.g., MacDougall, 1911) described it as a materialist thesis. Of course, epiphenominalism also contravened the dualist intuition of mental causation.

There were other even less satisfactory 'solutions' to the mind-body problem current during the late nineteenth century. Lewes (1877) preferred variants on Spinoza's dual-aspect monism or neo-Kantian phenomenalistic parallelism (Spencer, 1855), types of property dualism that invoked a mysterious underlying substance supporting physical and mental properties. Still others, such as Fechner (1848, 1851) and Clifford (1878) invoked the strange and ultimately question-begging doctrines of panpsychism. Idealist monism, the view that consciousness is the 'thing in itself' of which the body is a mere appearance, was also widely embraced. The sophisticated contemporary physicalist alternatives, which sharply distinguish between the concepts of token and type identity and allow for supervenient dependence of mental properties upon neurophysiological properties whilst retaining a notion of mental causation, were quite difficult to entertain in the nineteenth century.

There were earlier philosophical doctrines described as 'identity theories' but these were rather different from the identity theory as we know it today and were often forms of dualism.[28] The Romantic philosopher Schelling, for example, claimed that the structure of the mind was reflected in the structure of the brain. Schelling inspired Burdach to base his psychology on a neo-Spinozic dual-aspect monism (Leary, 1980). However, the earliest unambiguous statement of contemporary psychophysical identity theory that I have been able to locate is found in Schlick (1925): even well into the twentieth century one finds that definite claims on behalf of mind-brain identity are quite infrequent. In the absence of sophisticated symbol-manipulating machines, it was very difficult to envisage how a purely physical system could perform mental operations.[29]

During the eighteenth century, materialist doctrines had been espoused by La Mettrie and D'Holbach. The rise of materialism was underpinned by developments in the science of physiology, beginning with Harvey's discovery of the circulation of blood in 1628. In the Netherlands, Johannes Sylvius formed the first school of chemical physiology. In Italy Borelli, a mathematician, described the physiology of respiration in purely mechanical terms, while in England Hook, Lower and Mayow made important discoveries concerning the chemical physiology of respiration and circulation. By the middle of the eighteenth century an exciting new synthesis of cutting-edge developments of mechanical physiology had been forged by Boerhaave and Haller. Although opposed by conservative vitalists such as Stahl and Müller, materialism was on the rise.

The forms of materialism that surfaced in the eighteenth century and gained momentum in the nineteenth were rather different from the materialist doctrines popular today. These early materialists were in fact often panpsychists. 'They were,' writes MacDougall (1911: 98), 'concerned to show that matter consists not merely of inert solid particles...but that it is rather endowed with intrinsic powers of activity, of which thought and feeling are special developments.'

Concern with the mind-body problem was particularly acute in the disciplines of scientific psychology and neuroscience, where it had an impact upon everyday scientific activity. There was considerable confusion about how the relationship between mental and neural events should be conceptualized, and there were no agreed guidelines for the principled regimentation of psychological and neurophysiological vocabularies. Many writers advocated a vague methodological psychophysical parallelism, or 'epistemological' parallelism' as Schlick (1925) called it, claiming only that there exists some correspondence between chains of mental events and chains of neurophysiological events. Neuroscientists often used physiological and psychological predicates interchangeably (Amacher, 1962; Sulloway, 1979), straining against the epiphenominalist dictum that mental events possess no causal powers.

FREUDIAN DUALISM (1888-1895)

It is hardly surprising, then, that those of Freud's writings touching on the nature of the mind/brain relation that were composed early in his career express a dualist position.[30] One of the most important documents in this connection is his 1888 article on the brain known under its German title 'Gehirn'[31] written for Villaret's *Handwörterbuch der gesamten Medizin* (1888/1891).

Although Freud scholars agree that 'Gehirn' was written from a dualist perspective, there is some debate about exactly how this dualism should be construed. Andersson (1962) argues that Freud gives an epiphenominalist account, Silverstein (1985) claims it was interactionist, while Solms and Saling (1990) are in favor of a parallelist interpretation. Silverstein's thesis is incompatible with Freud's claim in the article that the brain is the organ of mental activity. As Solms and Saling mention, the fact that 'Gehirn' contains no references to mental events possessing causal powers also counts against the interactionist interpretation (although not decisively). Solms and Saling's parallelist case suffers from the same two defects[32] as well as the fact that Freud describes the causal power of neural states to bring about mental states.

We are thus left with Andersson's claim. However, Solms and Saling raise an objection against it, which requires consideration. The argument turns on an issue exemplified in the following passage:

> We have no reason whatsoever to assume that any segment of the material process needs to be shaped differently depending on [whether] the sensation, perception or idea corresponding to it enters consciousness or not (Freud, 1888: 64).[33]

This passage can be interpreted in several different ways. Solms and Saling seem to take Freud to be asserting that material processes in one's central nervous system do not determine whether one is conscious or unconscious of a 'corresponding' mental token occurring in one's mind. In other words, they take Freud to be claiming that it is something outside the central nervous system that determines this. Given that Solms and Saling argue for a parallelist interpretation of Freud's philosophy of mind, this is taken to be just an instance of the more general dictum that neurophysiological events are causally irrelevant to mental phenomena.

Solms and Saling emphasize that the plausibility of their interpretation of this passage is contingent upon whether or not Freud in 1888 held that there can be unconscious mental contents. They offer several passages from 'Gehirn' in support of this thesis.

> If the same brain element undergoes the same change in state at different times, then the corresponding mental process can be linked with it on one occasion (it can cross the threshold of consciousness [at] another time not (62).

And...

> If all segments of the chain cross the threshold of consciousness, the psychical process is shaped in its simplest form. However it may, on the one hand, become complicated by complications of ethical and other nature, and, on the other hand; several or even more segments of the [psychical] process can remain under the threshold of consciousness whereby nothing needs to be changed in the form of external effects ....The conviction of having voluntarily executed a movement may arise if at least the idea of the aim [of the movement] has entered consciousness (this happens most

clearly when several aims have entered into competition and a conscious motive has given the ruling) (63-64).

Solms and Saling interpret the locution 'threshold of consciousness' in the first of these passages as referring to transitions between unconscious mental and conscious states of an idea, but this is not necessarily the case. The 'threshold' mentioned by Freud may be understood as a hypothetical threshold between neurophysiological events and their (conscious) mental consequences. Concerning the second passage, the fact that the editors have interpolated and italicized the term 'psychical' renders its invocation somewhat question-begging. The ethical considerations mentioned by Freud might just as well be understood as interfering with the process by means of which neural states are transformed into conscious states.

There is also evidence of a more positive nature showing that Solms and Saling's conjecture does violence to Freud's position. Consider the following comments, taken from the same paragraph as the original contentious remarks.

> If a specific change in the material state of a specific brain element connects with a change in the state of our consciousness, then the latter is entirely specific as well; however it is not dependent on the change in the material state alone whether or not this connection occurs. If the same brain element undergoes the same change at different times, then the corresponding mental process can be linked with it on one occasion (it can cross the threshold of consciousness), [at] another time not (62).

Freud implicitly equates the process of coming into consciousness with that of coming into mind. The statement that the mental effect of a neural state does not depend upon the corresponding neural state alone sounds like an appeal to non-physical causation. However, Freud goes on to say that:

> For the present we are unable to formulate the ruling over the laws governing this [any] closer. We do not know whether or not the ruling only depends, apart from [depending on] the change in the state of the considered elements, upon the simultaneous states and changes in the state of the other brain elements, or, moreover depends upon still something else (62-63).

The fact that Freud believes that whether or not a neural process issues in a mental event may be determined by additional neural processes 'other brain elements') decisively refutes the claim that he was committed to psychophysical parallelism in 1888, although he did not actively rule out the possibility of non-physical causation ('still something else'). This sounds very much like Freud's later distinction in the 'Project for a scientific psychology' between content-bearing and consciousness-generating neural states.

Two years after 'Gehirn', Freud wrote in 'Psychical (or mental) treatment' (1890), that:

> Modern medicine, it is true, had reason enough for studying the indisputable connection between the body and the mind; but it never ceased to represent mental events as determined by physical ones and dependent on them. Thus stress was laid on the fact that intellectual functioning was conditional upon the presence of a normally developed and sufficiently nourished brain that any disease of that organ led to disturbances of intellectual functioning, that the introduction of toxic substances into the circulation could produce certain states of mental illness or - to descend to more trivial matters - that dreams could be modified by stimuli brought to bear upon a sleeper for experimental purposes.
>
> The relation between body and mind (in animals no less than human beings) is a reciprocal one; but in earlier times the other side of this relation, the effect of the mind upon the body, found little favour in the eyes of the physicians. They seemed to be afraid of granting mental life any independence, for fear of that implying an abandonment of the scientific ground on which they stood (294).[34]

This seems unambiguously interactionist if interpreted literally.

We find Freud making the claim in his book *On Aphasia* that 'the psychical is a process parallel to the physiological' (Freud, 1891:55, also Freud, 1915a:207) which, if not intended in a merely methodological context, is compatible with parallelism and epiphenominalism but incompatible with materialism and interactionism. Freud conjectures in 'The neuro-psychoses of defence' (1894) of apparently unconscious mental processes that:

> Perhaps it would be more correct to say that these processes are not of a psychical nature at all, that they are physical processes whose psychical consequences present themselves as if what is expressed by the terms "separation of the idea from its affect" and "false connection" of the latter had really taken placed (53).

Freud seems to be implicitly giving an epiphenominalist or interactionist account. Later, after his conversion to the identity theory, he would take great pains to show the implausibility of such a view.

FREUDIAN MATERIALISM (1895 -1939)

Freud's 1895 manuscript now called the 'Project for a scientific psychology' marked a turning point in his philosophy of mind. It is in the 'Project' that he first espoused the identity theory. The opening paragraph of this work announces Freud's new philosophical program.

> The intention is to furnish a psychology that shall be a natural science: that is, to represent psychical processes as quantitatively determinate states of specifiable material particles, thus making those processes perspicuous and free from contradiction (1950: 295).

That Freud is unambiguously and unequivocally presenting a physicalist theory of mind is made clear from his remarks about consciousness.

> A word on the relation of this theory of consciousness to others. According to an advanced mechanical theory, consciousness is a mere appendage to physiologico-psychical processes and its omission would make no alteration in the psychical passage [of events]. According to another theory, consciousness is the subjective side of all psychical events and is thus inseparable from the physiological mental process. The theory developed here lies between these two. Here consciousness is the subjective side of one part of the physical processes in the nervous system, namely of the ω processes; and the omission of consciousness does not leave psychical events unaltered but involves the omission of the contribution from ω (1950: 311).

Freud thus distances himself from epiphenomenalism on one hand and the identification of consciousness with all neural processes on the other. He identifies consciousness with a particular (hypothetical) functional unit of the central nervous system that he designates by the Greek letter ω. Güzeldere (1995b) refers to this kind of theory as 'consciousness modularism' (129), a thesis which has more recently endorsed by such cognitive scientists as Schacter (1988) and Shallice (1992).[35] Freud did not attempt to specify by virtue of what ω produced consciousness, a fact which has perhaps led some mistakenly to attribute a dualist perspective to him. The problem of explaining just how neural wetware can produce consciousness, David Chalmers' (1996) notorious 'hard problem', is still with us.

One objection to a physicalist reading of the 'Project', first voiced by Friedman and Alexander (1983), claims that Freud used neurophysiology as a mere metaphor to illustrate his purely mentalistic conceptions and that his relationship to natural science was 'ironical at best and, at times, even "subversive"' (303). They argue that this is clearly implied by the opening paragraph of the project, in which Freud states that he will 'represent' mental processes physicalistically. Surely, they argue, if Freud is merely 'representing' the mind as a material system he is using neurophysiology merely figuratively. Unfortunately for these authors, their argument turns on a translation ambiguity: Freud's term '*darzustellen*' can translated as 'present', 'depict', 'delineate' or 'represent'. There is nothing in the context of the 'Project' that would lead one to favor Friedman and Alexander's rendering over an interpretation of Freud as setting out to present mental phenomena in physicalist terms.

I have found only one passage in Freud's post-Project writings that might legitimately cast doubt on his adherence to the identity theory. This passage appears in the posthumously published 'An outline of psycho-analysis' (1940a), which Freud wrote at the end of his life.

> Many people, both inside and outside [psychological] science are satisfied with the assumption that consciousness alone is psychical; in that case nothing remains for psychology but to discriminate among psychical phenomena between perceptions, feelings, thought-processes and volitions. It is generally agreed, however, that these conscious processes do not form unbroken sequences which are complete in themselves; there would be no alternative left to assuming that there are physical or somatic processes which are concomitant with the psychical ones and which we should necessarily have to recognise as more complete than the psychical sequences, since some of them would have conscious processes parallel to them but others would not. If so, it of course becomes plausible to lay the stress in psychology on these somatic processes, to see in them the true essence of what is psychical and to look for some other assessment of the conscious processes. The majority of philosophers, however, as well as many other people, dispute this and declare that the idea of something psychical being unconscious is self-contradictory.
>
> But that is precisely what psycho-analysis is obliged to assert, and this is its second fundamental hypothesis. It explains the supposedly somatic concomitant phenomena as being what is truly psychical and thus in the first instance disregards the quality of consciousness (157-158).

At first blush Freud may seem to be saying that the unconscious processes which supply continuity to sequences of apparently disconnected mental events are just supposedly somatic, i.e., they are actually mental rather than somatic. On this interpretation, Freud seems to be reverting to a parallelist position.

There are good reasons to doubt the fidelity of the published version of the 'Outline'. Archival research by Grubrich-Simitis (1993) has revealed that the 'Outline' was never taken beyond the draft stage by Freud. She has shown that the editors had to take considerable liberties in order to produce the present version of the text and has remarked upon numerous significant errors in transcription; Strachey points out in his introduction to the work that 'the editing is at certain points a little free' (142).[36]

The German version of the relevant passage from the 'Outline' is somewhat less ambiguous.

> Den Ausgang für diese Untersuchung gibt die unvergleichliche, jeder Erklärung und Beschreibung trotzende Tatsache des Bewusstseins. Spricht man von Bewusstsein, so weiss man trotzdem unmittlebar aus eigenster Erfahrung, was damit gemeint ist. Vielen innerhalb wie ausserhalb der Wissenschaft genügt es anzunehmen, das Bewusstsein sei allein das Psychische und dann bleibt in der Psychologie nichts anderes zu tun, als innerhalb Denkvorgänge und Willensakte zu unterscheiden. Diese bewussten Vorgänge bilden aber nach allgemeiner Übereinstimmung keine lücklosen, in sich abgeschlossenen Reihen, so das nichts anderes übrig bleibe als psychische oder somatische Begleitvorgänge des Psychischen anzunehmen, dennen man eine grössere Vollständigkeit als den psychischen Reihen zugestehen muss, da einige von ihnen bewusste Parallelvorgänge haben, andere aber nicht. Es liegt dann, natürlich nahe, in der Psychologie den Akzent auf diese somatischen Vorgänge zu legen, in ihnen das eigentlich Psychische anzuerkennen und für die bewussten Vorgänge eine andere Würdigung zu suchen . Dagegen sträuben sich nun die meisten Philosophen sowie viele andere und erklären ein unbewusst Psychisches für einen Widersinn.
>
> Gerade das is es, was die Psychoanalyse tun muss und dies ist ihre zweite fundamentale Annahme. Sie erklärt die vorgeblichen somatischen Begleitvorgänge für das eigentliche Psychische, sieht dabei zunächst von der Qualität des Bewusstseins ab (1940b: 79-80).

Literally rendered, this passage reads as follows:

> The starting point for this investigation is the unique fact of consciousness, which lies beyond explanation or description. If one talks of "consciousness" one knows immediately from one's own experience what is meant. Many within and outside of the scientific community consider it sufficient that "consciousness" only means "the psyche" which would mean that psychology's only function is to distinguish within psychic phenomenology between perception, emotion, thought processes and willful acts. However, as is generally accepted, these conscious processes do not form gapless, complete series within themselves. It therefore follows to presume that physiological or somatic processes accompany the psychical ones. One thus has to

> admit that the physiological or somatic processes are more complete than the psychical ones, because some of them have conscious parallel processes while others do not. It suggests itself, therefore, to emphasise in psychology these somatic processes and to see in them the true psyche. As regards conscious processes, one should seek a different appreciation. Most philosophers, among others, resist this hypothesis and believe that [the concept of] unconscious psychic processes is absurd.
>
> This is exactly what psycho-analysis must do, and this is its second fundamental assumption. Psycho-analysis believes the alleged somatic accompanying processes to be the real psychic ones and refrains initially from looking at the quality of consciousness.

On a materialist interpretation, Freud should be taken to refer to 'supposedly (just) somatic concomitant phenomena'; i.e., he should be taken as arguing against the proposition that the continuity-supplying neural processes are non-mental, an argument that will be described more fully in Chapter Six. This interpretation seems warranted by the next sentence in Freud's text, which does not affirm that those unconscious phenomena concomitant with conscious mental events are non-neural 'supposedly somatic'). Instead, it asserts the precise opposite: the psychoanalytic assertion that the somatic (neural) processes are 'the true essence of what is psychical' (157). Although the scope of 'allegedly' ('*vorgeblichen*') remains ambiguous in the German text, the remainder of this literal rendering supports the materialist thesis more strongly than the standard translation. This is particularly evident in the case of the crucial concluding sentence. Whereas the *Standard Edition* says that psychoanalysis 'explains the supposedly somatic concomitant phenomena as being what is truly psychical', which might be read as stating that 'those phenomena alleged by others to be somatic have been shown by psychoanalysis to be truly psychical rather than somatic', the fresh translation states: 'Psychoanalysis believes the alleged somatic accompanying processes to be the real psychic ones' thus claiming a relation of identity between somatic and mental events.

Freud never published the 'Project' and, after producing several revisions, abandoned it.[37] According to Chessick (1980):

> It was the subject of psycho-physical parallelism on which Freud...foundered, and which caused him to abandon the "Project". For example, he explains that the starting point of the investigation into the psyche "is provided by a fact without parallel, which defies all explanation or description - the fact of consciousness", which Freud's early neurological theory had absolutely no means of explaining (265).

It is true that Freud did not claim to be able to explain just how it is that neural activity gives rise to consciousness, but this has no bearing on the fact that the 'Project' is Freud's attempt to overcome the problems inherent in mind-body dualism and gives a solution to which Freud continued to adhere for the remainder of his life.

Freud was well aware that philosophers both preceding and contemporaneous with him had speculated about the nature of unconscious mental events. He took issue with these views on the grounds of their dependence on a dualist conception of the mind-brain relation. Within the dualist framework unconscious mental processes were seen as both non-physical and, therefore, ultimately mystical in nature, or they were relegated to the non-mental world of purely physical dispositions.[38]

> It is true that philosophy has repeatedly dealt with the problem of the unconscious, but, with few exceptions, philosophers have taken up one or other of the two following positions. Either their unconscious has been something mystical, something intangible and undemonstrable, whose relation to the mind has remained obscure,[39] or they have identified the mental with the conscious and have proceeded to infer from this definition that what is unconscious cannot be mental or a subject for psychology (1913:178).

The philosophical thrust of Freud's theorizing is well summarized in a passage from 'An outline of psycho-analysis' (1940a):

> Psycho-analysis makes a basic assumption, the discussion of which is reserved for philosophical thought but the justification of which lies in its results. We know two kinds of things about what we call our psyche (or mental life): firstly its bodily organ and scene of action, the brain (or nervous system) and, on the other hand, our acts of consciousness, which are immediate data and cannot be further explained by any sort of description. Everything that lies between is unknown to us, and the data do not include any direct relation between these two terminal points of our knowledge (144-145).

He goes on to remark that:

> If it [knowledge of how conscious mental events correspond to neural events] existed, it would at the most afford an exact localisation of the processes of consciousness and would give us no help towards understanding them (Ibid.).

In other words, the reliable correlation of mental event types with neural event types would, if possible, leave untouched the problem of just what it is that gives neural events their mental properties. Frattaroli

(1992:57) astonishingly describes this passage as 'unambiguously dualistic'.

In 'Some elementary lessons on psycho-analysis' (1940c), another posthumously published work, Freud carries the analysis further.

> The equation of what is mental with what is conscious had the unwelcome result of divorcing psychical processes from the general context of events in the universe and of setting them in complete contrast to all others (283).

The equation has this result if it is embedded within a dualist framework, giving bleak prospects for any hope of a scientific psychology.

> But this would not do, since the fact could not be long overlooked that psychical phenomena are to a high degree dependent upon somatic influences and on their side have the most powerful effect upon somatic processes. If ever human thought found itself at an impasse it was here (Ibid.).

Res extensa causally interacts with *res cogitans*. But how?

> To find a way out, the philosophers at least were obliged to assume that there were organic processes parallel to the conscious psychical ones, related to them in a manner that was hard to explain, which acted as intermediaries in the reciprocal relations between "body and mind", and which served to re-insert the psychical into the texture of life. But this solution remained unsatisfactory (Ibid.).

As Freud was aware, no amount of invoking intermediaries can enable dualism to explain the apparent causal interaction between body and mind. He then goes on to state quite baldly that psychoanalysis offers a workable approach to the mind-body problem, namely that:

> The psychical, whatever its nature may be, is in itself unconscious and probably similar in kind to all other natural processes of which we have obtained knowledge (284).

IV

OTHER VIEWS OF FREUD'S POSITION ON THE MIND-BODY PROBLEM

I will now undertake the review of the literature on Freud's philosophy of the mind-body relation that was promised in Chapter Three. Andersson (1962) states that Freud was an epiphenominalist in 1888 and that by 1892-93 he was compelled by his clinical work to speak in terms of psychical causality which conflicts with the epiphenomenalist position. Andersson believes that Freud probably understood his mentalistic accounts of causation as provisional models ('*Vorlaufigkeiten*') necessitated by the relatively primitive state of neurological knowledge. Andersson cites the passage from 'Gehirn' (which I have reproduced earlier in Chapter Three) in which Freud states that whether or not an item enters consciousness involves no difference in the neural processes giving rise to that mental item. Of course, such a description is compatible with epiphenomenalism, but it is also compatible with other forms of dualism.

Solms and Saling (1990) claim that as early as 1888 Freud regarded consciousness as epiphenomenal with respect to unconscious mental processes rather than with respect to physical (neural) processes. Indeed, Solms and Saling (1984) believe that:

> Because he did not believe that the psychological structure of consciousness was determined by a chain of physiological events he postulated a psychological unconscious (409).

This is incorrect. As I have shown, Freud's concept of unconscious mental items was born from his need to transcend his earlier dualism. Unconscious mental items are, for Freud, identical with neural events and all mental events are unconscious under their neuroscientific descriptions. Certainly Freud was a dualist of some description prior to his 'turn' of 1895. However, the remarks contained in 'Psychical (or mental) treatment' (1890) seem to show conclusively that as early as 1890 he was strongly opposed to epiphenominalism,.

Silverstein (1985, 1989) argues that Freud was a psycho-physical interactionist, basing his argument on several passages in Freud's early writings. First, a passage from 'Gehirn' (1888):

> Although the mechanical process is not understood, it is the actual presence of this coupling of material changes of conditions in the brain with changes in the state of the conscious mind which makes the brain a center of psychic activity. Although the essence of this coupling is incomprehensible to us, it is not haphazard, and on the basis of combinations of experiences of the outer senses on the one hand and introspection on the other we can determine something about the laws that govern this coupling (cited in Silverstein, 1985:209).

This passage certainly establishes that Freud was a dualist, in 1888. Silverstein understands mind-brain 'coupling' as synonymous with mind-brain interaction - an assumption that does not seem to be warranted. The passage, also mentioned by Silverstein, from the same work dealing with the difference between voluntary and reflexive movement (quoted in Chapter Three) is similarly opaque. Silverstein is on firmer ground when he draws on 'On psychical (or mental) treatment' (1890). He also presents the following passage from 'Hysteria' (Freud, 1888c):

> The psychical changes which must be postulated as being the foundation of the hysterical status take place wholly in the sphere of unconscious, automatic cerebral activity. It may, perhaps, further be emphasised that in hysteria the influence of psychical processes on physical processes in the organism (as in all neuroses) is increased (49).

Silverstein goes on to comment that:

> Thus, in hysteria, psychical processes not under conscious control and not within the sphere of conscious awareness play a determining role in symptom formation. Here we can see Freud's dilemma that leads him to develop metapsychological models. How could he discuss and describe unobservable psychical processes and distinguish them from what was physical? How did they interact to produce neurotic symptoms? (211).

In spite of first impressions (and in spite of my sympathy with Silverstein's general thesis) I do not think that this passage supports the interactionist case. One must bear in mind the larger context in which the passage is embedded. The article is an account of hysteria, a neurotic disorder characterized by bodily symptoms. The bulk of the article is taken up with a description of such symptoms. In this context it seems likely that Freud uses the terms 'psychical processes' and 'physical processes in the organism' to denote 'central nervous system processes' and 'psychical processes occurring outside the central nervous system' respectively, an interpretation with which Wallace (1992) concurs. This would explain why Freud - a dualist in 1888 - describes the relevant 'psychical' processes as occurring 'in the sphere of unconscious, automatic cerebral activity'. This interpretation finds support in the contemporaneous 'Gehirn' where Freud uses the terms 'brain' and 'mind' (in contradistinction to 'mind' and 'body') when discussing the philosophical issue. In the opening passages of 'Hysteria', too, Freud writes that:

> Hysteria is a neurosis in the strictest sense of the word - that is to say, not only have no perceptible changes in the nervous system been found in this illness, but it is not to be expected that any refinement of anatomical techniques would reveal any such changes. Hysteria is based wholly and entirely on physiological modifications of the nervous system and its essence should be expressed in a formula which took account of the conditions of excitability in the different parts of the nervous system (41).

It follows that Silverstein's reflections about Freud's supposed difficulties demarcating neural from mental influences on symptom formation are not really to the point. As I have shown, Freud's development of metapsychological models had nothing whatsoever to do with his early dualism. Freud's metapsychology was based firmly on his materialism.

A case for Freudian interactionism can be made on the basis of 'Hysteria' but it rests on the notion of the causal impact of brain upon mind rather than the converse, and is therefore also compatible with epiphenominalism. Freud writes that:

> Alongside the physical symptoms of hysteria, a number of psychical disturbances are to be observed, in which at some future time the changes characteristic of hysteria will no doubt be found but the analysis of which has hitherto scarcely been begun. These are changes in the passage and in the association of ideas, inhibitions of the activity of the will, magnification and suppression of feelings, etc. - which may be summarized as changes in the normal distribution over the nervous system of the stable amounts of excitation (49).

In other words, the functional disorders of the nervous system characteristic of hysteria influence the mind as well as the body.

We encounter many of the same confusions in a later paper on Freud's purported psycho-physical interactionism (Silverstein, 1989). He writes, for example, that:

> It was Freud's dualistic interactionism which allowed him to the develop the idea of "conversion" in explaining hysteria, the concept that psychical conflicts could be symbolically represented in motor or sensory manifestations (1093).

This is manifestly incorrect. Freud's concept of hysterical conversion - the 'puzzling leap from the mental to the physical' (Freud, 1916-17:258) - was a concept of how cortical events (corresponding, in one fashion or another, to mental events) influence physiological processes external to the central nervous system. Freud's references to the reciprocal relationship between body and mind in the context of discussions of hysterical conversion (with the exception of the 1890 paper on 'Psychical (or mental) treatment') are best understood along these lines (Wallace, 1992).

Silverstein (1989) goes on to mention Freud's remark, recorded in the *Minutes of the Vienna Psychoanalytic Society* in 1912, that:

> If the present speaker had to choose among the views of the philosophers, he could characterize himself as a dualist. No monism succeeds in doing away with the distinction between ideas and the objects they represent (Nunberg and Federn, 1975:136).

This statement by Freud merely expresses his commitment to realism and opposition to idealism, and has no bearing on the case at hand. Silverstein seems to be trading on the ambiguity of the term 'dualism'. Freud's realism is in no way entailed by his alleged psychophysical interactionism, as Silverstein seems to imply. Freud's distinction offered in the 1919 edition of 'The interpretation of dreams' (1900) between 'psychical reality' and 'material reality' (620) also has nothing to do (contra Silverstein) with mind-body dualism. This Freudian distinction refers specifically to the correspondence or lack of correspondence between mental representations and the states of affairs that they represent: the representations (psychical reality) may or may not accurately portray actual states of affairs (material reality).

Silverstein (1989) quotes Freud as saying that 'What is psychical is something so unique and peculiar to itself that no one comparison can reflect its nature' (1919:161) as evidence for ontological dualism, but a scrutiny of the context in which the sentence occurs shows that, far from announcing an ontological position, it refers to a rather trivial terminological dispute about the connotations of the word 'psychoanalysis'.

Silverstein (1989) also states that:

> Freud might resort to physicalistic metaphors, such as the "cathexis of psychical paths" to portray the intentional quality of unconscious mental processes (wishes), but when he did so, he insisted that 'psychical paths' were not to be equated with neuronal structures in the material brain (1094).

The passage that Silverstein takes to exemplify this stance contains the following remarks:

> I am making no attempt to claim that the cells and nerve fibres, or the systems of neurones which are taking their place today, are these psychical paths, even though it would have to be possible in some manner which cannot yet be indicated to represent such paths by organic elements of the nervous system (1905:148; emphasis added).

Far from promoting dualism, Freud appears to be advocating a token identity theory.

Such is Silverstein's commitment to interactionism that he even interprets Freud's objection to the linguistic argument against the notion of unconscious mental items as flowing from his dualism. He believes that Freud, in his opposition to the linguistic argument, rejected the notion that unconscious items were physical, whereas I have shown that what Freud rejected was the thesis that they are merely physical (physical and non-mental). Ironically, in opposing the linguistic argument, Freud opposed the very interactionist framework with which Silverstein saddles him.

Finally, Silverstein mentions a letter written by Freud in 1931 to Alexander Lipschutz:

> I am very pleased...that you are not among those who place psycho-analysis in opposition to endocrinology, as though psychic processes could be explained directly by glandular functions, or as though the understanding of psychical mechanism could replace the knowledge of the underlying chemical process (Freud, 1873-1939: 406).

But Freud's opposition to an extremely implausible endocrinological eliminativism[40] does not go anywhere towards establishing his dualist credentials.

Amacher (1965), basing his argument largely on the 'Project', argues that Freud was an identity theorist.[41] From the opening passage on it is quite clear that the 'Project' was based on the metaphysical foundation of the identity theory.

> The intention of this project is to furnish us with a psychology which shall be a natural science; its aim, that is, is to represent psychical processes as quantitatively determined states of specifiable material particles and so to make them plain and void of contradictions (355).

Amacher errs, however, in attributing this metaphysical slant to the influence of Freud's teachers (Meynert, Brücke, Exner and others) and therefore implies that Freud adhered to the identity theory from the beginning of his career. This is, of course, untrue: the 'Project' was Freud's first identity theory-based writing. Solms and Saling (1985) refute Amacher by citing the passage from *On Aphasia* - quoted above - which they regard as explicitly parallelist. In a later work (1990) they use dualist passages from 'Gehirn' to contradict Amacher. This approach is quite a reasonable response to Amacher's inappropriate extrapolations from the position expressed in the 'Project' to Freud's pre-1895 metaphysics. However, in neither text do Solms and Saling concede that the 'Project' and all of Freud's later writings are based on the identity theory.

Natsoulas (1984) also realizes that Freud was a materialist/identity theorist.

> Freud was a materialist, just as most psychologists nowadays are. In his view the mind or psychical apparatus was a certain physical system rather than something mental, which stood to the human body in a parallel, epiphenominal, or interactive relation. The mind-body dualism that some people detect in Freud's...later work is actually a methodological rather than substantive one (197).

It is unclear whether or not Natsoulas realizes that Freud had earlier espoused a dualist position.

Mackay's (1989) view on these matters seems somewhat inconsistent. On the one hand he states, with Amacher, that Freud's 'general physicalism' was carried over from various nineteenth-century thinkers, including Brücke, Meynert and Exner from the earliest 'pre-psychoanalytic' period of his career onwards. The evidence marshaled to support this thesis succeeds only in showing that Freud believed the nervous system to be a wholly physical system explicable in terms of electrochemical processes and that this physical system is somehow correlated with mental events, a view which is quite compatible with psychophysical parallelism and epiphenominalism. However, later in the same book, Mackay states that Freud's teachers were psycho-physical parallelists and that Freud initially took over this position as well! He includes a passage from the 'Project' to illustrate Freud's supposed adherence to parallelism in 1895:

> No attempt, of course, can be made to explain how it is that excitatory processes in the ω neurones bring consciousness along with them. It is only a question of establishing a coincidence between the characteristics of consciousness that are known to us and the processes in the ω neurones which vary in parallel with them (311).

I have already demonstrated that the 'Project' was Freud's first work informed by the identity theory. In the passage cited above Freud seems to be using the term 'parallel' in a methodological rather than a metaphysical sense. His desire to 'establish a coincidence' is based on scientific constraints - he does not possess a neuroscientific explanation of the nature of consciousness (i.e., he cannot explain why it is that the stimulation of the ω neurons gives rise to just this effect) rather than because of a commitment to dualism. Mackay writes that: 'By the time of the topographical formulation, Freud has explicitly abandoned psychophysical parallelism'. I am not entirely certain of the date to which Mackay assigns this transition. The time of the topographical formulation begins around the year 1899; however, the quotation that Mackay uses to substantiate his thesis is taken from a topographical paper of 1915 (Freud, 1915a). In any case, I am in general agreement with Mackay's second position - that Freud moved from dualism to physicalism but I dispute his dating of the shift.

Solomon (1974a) also argues that Freud was an identity theorist, showing that the 'Project' advances an identity-theoretical stance that this stance was retained throughout Freud's later career. Although Solomon does not concern himself with the pre-'Project' period, I can find little to fault in his discussion of Freud as an identity theorist.

Like Amacher, Flanagan (1984) argues that Freud's materialism was carried over from his teachers and mentors, especially Brücke, and that the 'Project for a scientific psychology' expressed this materialism in the form of a type identity theory. Indeed, the theoretical reduction at which Freud was aiming is announced in the opening passage of the 'Project': Freud hoped to find a (superior) neuroscientific vocabulary to replace the mentalistic vocabulary of folk-psychology.

> The justification Freud recommends in the "Project" for urging reduction in the direction of neuroscience is that by representing psychical processes in terms of specific material particles, we will make these processes "perspicuous and free from contradiction." His rationale for reductionism is that ordinary psychological vocabulary is vague and imprecise and this imprecision limits our understanding of the psychological phenomena (59).

Although Flanagan is mistaken about Freud's pre-1895 metaphysical commitments, he was the first to claim that the 'Project' expressed a type identity theory. Flanagan goes on to observe that:

> The remarkable thing from the perspective of the philosophy of mind and the philosophy of the history of science is that Freud no sooner announced the program of materialism with reductionism than he abandoned it (60).

According to Flanagan, Freud moved from type identity theoretic reductionism to a form of methodological dualism, which he [Flanagan] calls the 'Thesis of the Autonomy of Psychological Explanation'. So, after 1895 Freud was a methodological dualist. Was he, according to Flanagan, an ontological dualist as well? Flanagan criticizes Jones (1953) for describing Freud as a psychophysical parallelist, stating that 'it is...implausible to regard Freud as an advocate of any kind of metaphysical dualism'(64). He believes that there are only two plausible readings of Freud's position: a neutral, agnostic position on one hand, or a non-reductive token identity theory on the other. Jones is cited as a supporter of the former possibility (inconsistently in light of his dualist interpretation of Freud mentioned above), stating (1953) that Freud regarded the essential nature of both mind and matter as unknown. This is undoubtedly correct, but has little bearing on the question of mind-brain identity.[42] Flanagan regards the second alternative as the most likely.

Flanagan seems to infer that Freud shifted from a type identity theory to a token identity theory after 1895 on the basis of the fact that he revoked the 'Project' and never subsequently elaborated a reductive neuroscientific model. The absence of explicitly neuroscientific models in Freud's work after 1895 need not be attributed to his changing ontological commitments. It may well have been that Freud retained his faith in type identity whilst not having the resources to devise a type-reductive scheme. There are a number of passages in Freud's works which indicate that he hoped that such a reduction might one day be made and was only hindered by a lack of neuroscientific knowledge. In 1905, for example, Freud wrote that:

> I am making no attempt to proclaim that the cells and nerve fibres, or the systems of neurones which are taking their place today, are...psychical paths, even though it would have to be possible in some manner which cannot yet be indicated to represent such paths by organic elements of the nervous system (148).

Freud seems to be saying that, although the semantic links between mental items are not identical to synaptic links between individual neurons or tracts linking neural systems, there must in principle be some way of specifying the neural correlates of these links. Similarly, Freud wrote in 1915 that:

> Every attempt...to discover a localisation of mental processes, every endeavor to think of ideas as stored up in nerve-cells and of excitations as travelling along nerve-fibres, has miscarried completely....our psychical topography has for the present nothing to do with anatomy (174-175).

Finally, in 1939:

> The psychical topography that I have developed...has nothing to do with the anatomy of the brain, and actually only touches it at one point. What is unsatisfactory in this picture - and I am aware of it as clearly as anyone - is due to our complete ignorance of the dynamic [neurophysiological] nature of the mental process (1939:97).

Lest the reader feel that my interpolation of the word 'neurophysiological' is tendentious, he or she may refer to Solms and Saling (1986) who interpret this passage in a similar manner.

Wallace (1992) advances the theses that (a) Freud was never an ontological dualist, (b) that his dualism was always of a purely methodological character and that Freud was an ontological materialist from at least 1888 onwards.

Certainly, many of the statements that I have construed as expressing an attitude of ontological dualism are compatible with methodological dualism as well. Wallace quotes several such passages from Freud's early writings whilst ignoring passages from the same period that show unequivocally Freud's commitment to ontological dualism. He first mentions the passage from 'Hysteria' (Freud, 1888, quoted above) which Silverstein (1985) uses to support the interactionist case. As I averred in my critique of Silverstein, Freud's statements in 'Hysteria' dealing with the neural concomitants of the psychical characteristics of hysteria are best understood as statements about the neural events which are causally necessary for the production of certain mental events. They point toward the impact of the body upon the mind. Wallace next moves on to Freud's 'Preface to the translation of Bernheim's *Suggestion*' (1888d), a document which discusses rival psychological and physiological accounts of the nature of suggestion. Freud's solution to this problem is that suggestion involves both 'psychical' and 'physiological' components (cortical and subcortical regions of the central nervous system). Whereas Wallace takes these remarks to reflect an ontological materialism, they can equally be understood as referring to the neural causes of hypnotic events, and therefore as compatible with interactionism and epiphenominalism. Wallace's interpretation is quite plausible if taken in isolation from less ambiguous passages roughly contemporary with the 'Preface to Bernheim' (such as the account of mind-brain 'coupling' in 'Gehirn' mentioned by Silverstein). Indeed, a passage appearing near the end of the 'Preface' and which is mentioned by Wallace seems to hint at Freud's dualist leanings:

> We possess no criterion which enables us to distinguish exactly between a psychical and a physiological one, between an act occurring in the cerebral cortex and one occurring in the subcortical substance; for "consciousness", whatever that may be, is not attached to every activity of the cerebral cortex, nor is it always attached in an equal degree to any one of its particular activities; it is not a thing which is bound up with any locality in the nervous system (84).

Wallace writes that:

> In deeming psychical activities to be cerebral cortical activities, Freud avoided metaphysical dualism...Any dualism was hence that between cerebral cortical functioning ("psychical") and that of the rest of the human organism ("physiological")....By re-

fusing to localize anatomically such items as consciousness, viewed as properties, not substances Freud declared himself a functionalist (242).

Wallace ignores Freud's notion of the 'attachment' of consciousness to the cerebral cortex, (we do not normally speak of the 'attachment' of a property to its object). Wallace provides no evidence to support his contention that during this period Freud understood consciousness to be a property rather than a substance, and he neglects the similarity between the talk of 'attachment' in the 'Preface to Bernheim' and the blatantly dualist account of mind-body 'coupling' in 'Gehirn'. The assertion that Freud's *prima facie* ontologically dualist statements merely express the divide between the cerebral cortex and the rest of the human organism (or, more accurately, the subcortical regions of the central nervous system) is sharply contradicted by, for example, Freud's discussion of mind-body interactionism in 'On psychical (or mental) treatment' (1890) in which talk of mind and body cannot reasonably be construed as shorthand for the cortical-subcortical distinction.

Wallace next considers the passage in *On Aphasia* (1891) to which I have referred earlier in the present work. In full, the passage runs as follows:

> Is it justified to immerse a nerve fibre, which over the whole length of its course has been only a purely physiological structure subject to physiological modifications, with its end in the psyche and to furnish this end with an idea or a memory? Now that "will" and "intelligence," etc. have been recognized as psychological technical terms referring to very complicated physiological states, can one be quite sure that the simple "sensory presentation" can be anything else but another such technical term? The relationship between the chain of physiologic events in the nervous system and the mental process is probably not one of cause and effect. The former do not cease when the latter set in; they tend to continue but, from a certain moment, a mental phenomenon corresponds to each part of the chain, or to several parts. The psychic is, therefore, a process parallel to the physiological, a "dependent concomitant" (55).

Although it is possible to read this as a materialistic appeal to the concept of supervenience, a close analysis shows this to be unlikely. Freud is attempting both to combat the neuro-anatomical localizationism proposed by scientists such as Wernicke and especially Meynert and to advance a position on the mind-brain relation. On both matters he adheres to Jackson's position, and even includes a passage from Jackson to illustrate this. Some authors (e.g., Silverstein, 1989) regard Jackson's dualism as purely methodological while others (e.g., Angel, 1961; Marx, 1967)) see it as metaphysical as well. Jackson (1875, cited in Marx 1967) declared himself opposed to the theory of mind-brain identity. It is clear from Jackson's writing that he was in the first instance an ontological dualist but was prepared to fall back on a merely methodological dualism should the identity theory prove to be correct.

> The doctrine I hold is this: first, that states of consciousness (or, synonymously, states of mind) are utterly different from nervous states; second, that the two things occur together - that for every mental state there is a correlative nervous state; third, that, although the two things occur in parallelism, there is no interference of one from the other. This may be called the doctrine of Concomitance. Thus, in the case of visual perception, there is an unbroken physical circuit.... The visual image, a purely mental state, occurs in parallelism with - arises during (not from) - the activities of the two highest link of this purely physical chain: so to speak it 'stands outside' those links (Jackson, 1884:72)

And three years later:

> A critic of my Croonian Lectures...says that I state this doctrine in order to evade the charge of materialism....The critic referred to says that the doctrine of concomitance is Leibniz's "two clock theory". It may be; it matters nothing for medical purposes whether it is or is not.

Jackson continues:

> To put the matter in another way, let it be granted for the sake of argument that the separation into states of the highest centres [of the brain], and what we called the utterly different and yet concomitant states of consciousness, is known to be erroneous and that the...[identity theory] is ascertained to be the true one. I then ask that the doctrine of concomitance be provisionally accepted as an artifice, in order that we may study the most complex diseases of the nervous system more easily (Jackson, 1887:84-85).

In *On Aphasia* Freud approvingly quotes Jackson's remark that 'physical states in lower centres [do not] fine away into psychical states in higher centres' (Jackson, 1878-79:156; Freud, 1891:56n). If we examine the context of these remarks, we find that they are part of an argument that psychological and neuroscientific modes of discourse should be kept separate – an argument which, in turn, is based on the metaphysical proposition that mental events do not cause physical events. Thus, if Jackson were driven to fall back upon an identity theoretic position, he would probably assert (like Davidson) that mental events can only bring about physical events by virtue of their physical realization.

Wallace admits that a parallelist interpretation of *On Aphasia* cannot be ruled out, although he believes that the evidence of other passages of the book renders this implausible and that *On Aphasia* was written from a materialist (identity theoretic or dual-aspect monistic) position. He also states that although the notion of psychoneural 'concomitance' is Jacksonian, the term 'dependent concomitant' is a Freudian coinage suggesting, perhaps, a modification of Jackson's metaphysics. Other writers (e.g., Angel, 1961; Solms & Saling, 1990; Sulloway, 1979) claim that the term 'dependent concomitant' does come from Jackson.

A summary of 'the accepted doctrine' by Jackson's pupil the philosopher and psychologist Charles Mercier (1888) suggests that Jackson believed mental events supervened upon neural events.

> When the rearrangement of the molecules takes place in the higher regions of the brain, a change of consciousness simultaneously occurs. The two changes are concomitant. The change of consciousness never takes place without the change in the brain; the change in the brain never takes place under the same conditions without the change in consciousness (10).

In either case, the fact that Freud gave the phrase in English and placed it within quotation marks suggests that he at the very least believed himself to be using a Jacksonian concept. Although the term 'dependent concomitant', if indeed a Freudian innovation, might be taken to suggest either the doctrine of epiphenominalism or some concept of psychoneural supervenience, the fact that Freud makes no effort to demarcate his metaphysics from that of Jackson strongly militates against this hypothesis.

According to Wallace, the following passage from *On Aphasia* expresses a materialist rather than a dualist ontology.

> What, then, is the physiological correlate of the simple idea emerging or re-emerging? Obviously nothing static, but something in the nature of a process. This process is not incompatible with localization. It starts at a specific point in the cortex and from there spreads over the whole cortex and along certain pathways. When this event has taken place it leaves behind a modification, with the possibility of a

memory, in the part of the cortex affected. Whenever the same cortical state is elicited again, the previous psychic event re-emerges as a memory (55).

Wallace is correct to say that this does not square with a parallelist stance. It is, however, consistent with the interactional dualism that I have imputed to Freud. Marx (1967) draws our attention to the fact that Freud goes on to doubt the existence of any mental item corresponding to the latent modification in the cortex: 'our consciousness does not show anything like it which would deserve the name of "latent memory image" in the psyche' (58), which along with the evidence of other Freudian texts from this period decisively refutes Wallace's hypothesis. Marx (1967) notes that Freud, unlike other aphasiologists such as Küssmaul (1885) with whose work Freud was familiar, was reluctant to accept notions of unconscious mental correlates corresponding to the hypothesized latent modifications of the cortex, a reluctance which flows naturally from Freud's ontological dualism. Wallace does not provide any additional evidence to support his materialist interpretation of *On Aphasia*.

Wallace next moves on to a consideration of the 'Project', correctly describing it as a materialist document. More specifically, following Flanagan (1986) he concludes that the 'Project' was written from a type identity theoretic position. The movement to type identity theory is, in part, a consequence of the move to a greater neuroanatomical (as opposed to neurophysiological) emphasis.

For example, the class of events characterized mentalistically as "perception" is identical to the neurological class of φ neurons, that of memory to the ψ neurons, and that of consciousness to ω neurons (Wallace, 1992:249).

Although it is more correct to say that Freud regarded psychological items as identical to processes within the hypothetical neuronal systems, the general point does hold. It is because Freud embraces this kind of identity theory that he can pursue the aim of reducing psychological to neural events (Wallace, 1992; Flanagan, 1986). With regard to Freud's post-'Project' materialism, Wallace states that:

It is hard to know conclusively whether Freud's subsequently untrammeled methodological dualism was held provisionally, in the hope of eventual neurobiological reduction - or whether it reflected a token-token identity theory (Flanagan, 1986:59) or a dual-aspect monism, either of which permits a materialistic metaphysic and an

> open-ended methodological interactional-dualism (Wallace, 1988a; 1988b; 1989; 1990). Of these three possibilities, I lean toward dual-aspect monism (Wallace, 1992: 249).

In conclusion, each of the authors who have written about Freud's approach to the mind-body problem have managed to identify a bit of the truth about his philosophy of mind. None of them identifies the whole truth, however, through failing to attend to Freud's changes of mind, particularly the 'turn' of 1895. According to the available documentary evidence Freud was a dualist from 1888 until 1895. From 1888 to 1890 he was a psychophysical parallelist or epiphenominalist. In 1890 'On psychical (or mental) treatment', Freud flirted with interactionism and explicitly rejected epiphenominalism. *On Aphasia* shows him to be a parallelist or epiphenominalist again in 1891, a perspective that he retained until the period of the composition of the 'Project' in 1895. Freud remained an identity theorist from 1895 until his death in 1939.

V

THE UNCONSCIOUS

Concepts of unconscious mental states were widely discussed during the second half of the nineteenth century. Before this period, the concept of the unconscious had primarily fallen within the mystical domain of the Romantic Movement. Indeed, even well into the nineteenth century writers like von Hartmann (as summarized in Eisler's *Wörterbuch der Philosophie*) could claim that the unconscious is:

> The absolute principle, active in all things, the force which is operative in the inorganic, organic and mental alike, yet not revealed in consciousness....The unconscious exists independently of space, time and individual existence, timeless before the being of the world....For us it is unconscious, in itself it is superconscious (cited in Baldwin (Ed.), 1902:725).

For the first time, notions of unconscious mental events were becoming part of science: the new sciences of psychology and neurology (Ellenberger, 1970; Decker, 1977; Whyte, 1979).[43] The widespread use of the terms 'unconscious' or 'subconscious' easily obscures the diversity of concepts covered by these terms[44] and the vagueness with which they were often formulated. A few generalizations can, however, be made about nineteenth-century concepts of the unconscious, which reflect the prevailing approaches. Nineteenth-century concepts of the unconscious were consistent with the philosophy of mind in which they were imbedded, i.e. they tended to accord with dualistic conceptions of the mind-body relationship.

There was an important epistemological constraint placed upon theories of mind by virtue of their dualistic context. Cartesian doctrines of mental self-transparency dominated psychology from the seventeenth century until well into the twentieth, posing obvious problems for any conception of unconscious mental events. If the mind is transparent to itself - inevitably and incorrigibly aware of its own contents - how is it possible to be unconscious of one's own mental states? There were two widely accepted strategies for dealing with this dilemma.

One possibility was to treat unconscious mental states as just the neurophysiological causal basis for conscious mental states. Baldwin, writing in his classic *Dictionary of Philosophy and Psychology* (1902) defined 'mind' as 'The individual's conscious process, together with the dispositions and predispositions which condition it' (83). Mind may not be strictly identical with consciousness insofar as some have advanced 'the hypothesis of unconscious mental modifications, dispositions, &c.' (Ibid.). In the entry for 'the unconscious' written by Titchener for the *Dictionary*, we find the general (psychological) meaning of 'unconscious' described as 'not conscious, non-mental; not possessed of mind or consciousness' and that the term is sometimes used in a more specialized sense to denote 'psychophysical (i.e., presumably cortical) processes which, for various reasons, lack their normal conscious correlates' (724).

So conceived, unconscious mental states are only apparently mental: they are more accurately described as neurophysiological dispositions for (by definition, conscious) mental states. A second possibility was to grant the genuinely mental character of unconscious states, but to describe such states as instances of divided, split or dissociated[45] consciousness.[46] Within this framework unconscious states were conceptualized as something like conscious states in other minds. Each sub-mind could then be transparent to itself without this carrying over to the mind taken as a whole.[47]

FREUD'S PRE-TOPOGRAPHICAL PHASE

Herzog (1991) seems to have been the first scholar to claim that Freud did not employ a concept of the mental unconscious before the 1895 'Project'. She calls this the 'pre-topographical' phase of Freud's work, a term that I shall adopt. The material presented in Chapter Three suggests why this might have been the case. So long as Freud operated within a dualistic philosophical context it was difficult, if not impossible, for him to conceive of unconscious mental states as anything other than neurophysiological dispositions or instances of divided consciousness.[48] I will argue that Herzog's thesis is indeed true and will go on to propose that Freud's advocacy of the notion of a mental unconscious from the writing of the 'Project' onwards was conceptually contingent upon his simultaneous conversion to the identity theory.

In support of Herzog, I have been unable to find any unambiguous reference to the concept of a mental unconscious in Freud's writings composed prior to the 'Project', in striking contrast to his work from the 'Project' onwards. There are, however, explicit descriptions of the dispositional and split-consciousness theories.[49]

The dispositional theory was discussed by a number of psychologists and philosophers during the latter part of the nineteenth century. Amongst these was Franz Brentano. Brentano considered the dispositional theory in his main work, *Psychology from an Empirical Standpoint* (1874), with which Freud must have been familiar. He wrote, in the context of an argument intended to refute Maudsley's thesis of unconscious mental events that:

> There are undoubtedly habitual dispositions resulting from previous actions....If we want to admit generally that it is certain that these acquired aptitudes and dispositions are tied up with real things (and I, at least, do not hesitate to do so, although there are other metaphysicians, John Stuart Mill for example, who would have reservations), we must also grant that they are not mental phenomena, because otherwise, as we shall show, they would be conscious. Psychological reflection informs us only that they are causes, unknown in themselves, which influence the rise of subsequent mental phenomena, as well as that they are in themselves unknown effects of previous mental phenomena. In either case psychological reflection can prove in isolated instances that they exist; but it can never in any way give us knowledge of what they are (60).

In fact, 1893, Maudsley was a dispositionalist.[50]

> Another objection to the doctrine of unconscious ideas, is that we only know ideas through consciousness, and consciousness through ideas; the expression "unconscious idea" is as absurd, therefore, as that of unconscious consciousness....It is this which is the absurdity; for the idea, like the definite movement of muscle, is the function not the structure, not the statical element, but the element in action; we might as well speak of the movement of blowing the nose as being laid up inactive in the muscles of their nerve-centres...as talk of unconscious ideas stored up in the mind (Maudsley; cited in Klein, 1977).

Gustav Fechner, creator of the science of psychophysics, whom Freud read and admired, also propounded the dispositional theory.

> Sensations, ideas, have, of course, ceased actually to exist in the state of unconsciousness, insofar as we consider them apart from their substructure. Nevertheless something persists within us, i.e., the psychophysical activity of which they are a function, and which makes possible the reappearance of sensation, etc. (Fechner, cited in Brentano, 1874: 104).

John Hughlings Jackson, whose ideas I have discussed briefly in Chapter Four and will examine in greater detail in Chapter Seven, wrote in a paper with which Freud was familiar that:

> I take consciousness and mind to be synonymous terms...if all consciousness is lost all mind is lost.... Unconscious states of mind are sometimes spoken of, which seems to me to involve a contradiction. That there may be activities of lower nervous arrangements of the highest centres, which have no attendant psychical states, and which yet lead to next activities of the very highest nervous arrangements of those centres whose activities have attendant psychical states, I can easily understand. But these prior activities are states of the nervous system, not any sort of states of mind (1887: 85).

Freud's *On Aphasia* (1891) was written under Jackson's philosophical influence. It is therefore not surprising to find Freud professing a dispositionalist theory of unconscious mental events in it. In the context of a discussion of the neurophysiological modifications corresponding to latent memories, Freud writes that:

> It is highly doubtful whether there is anything psychical that corresponds to this modification either. Our consciousness shows nothing of a sort to justify, from the psychical point of view, the name of a "latent memory image". But whenever the same state of the cortex is provoked again, the psychical aspect *comes into being* once more as a mnemonic image (55; emphasis added).

That Freud continued to entertain the dispositional theory is shown in the following passage from 'The neuro-psychoses of defence' (1894).

> The separation of the sexual idea from its affect and the attachment of the latter to another, suitable but not incompatible idea - these are processes which occur without consciousness. Their existence can only be presumed, but cannot be proved by any clinico-psychological analysis.... Perhaps it would be more correct to say that these processes are not of a psychical nature at all, they are physical processes whose psychical consequences present them-selves as if what is expressed by the terms 'sepa-

ration of the idea from its affect' and 'false connection' of the latter had actually taken place (53).

The dissociative account is presented most clearly in the sections of the 'Studies on hysteria' written by Freud (Freud & Breuer, 1895) and in Freud and Breuer's 'Preliminary communication' of 1893.[51]

> The longer we have been occupied with these [hysterical] phenomena the more we have become convinced that the splitting of consciousness which is so striking in the well-known classical cases under the form of "double conscience"[52] is present to a rudimentary degree in every hysteria, and that a tendency to such a dissociation, and with it the emergence of abnormal states of consciousness...is the basic phenomenon of this neurosis (Freud & Breuer, 1893: 12).

The concept of the dissociation, splitting or 'doubling' of consciousness ('*double conscience*') was a mainstay of nineteenth-century psychology. As James (1890), who rejected the concept of unconscious mental events, put it, 'the total possible consciousness may be split into parts which coexist but mutually ignore each other, and share the objects of knowledge between them' (206). The term '*double conscience*' originated in British psychiatry in the early nineteenth-century, and was apparently introduced into French psychiatry by Azam (1877), who also used such terms as '*doublement de la vie*' '*dédoublement de la vie*' and '*dédoublement de la personnalité*' for the same purpose (Hacking, 1995). The concept of double consciousness became a frequently invoked concept in late nineteenth-century French psychiatry.[53] Apart from Azam, those authors who used this term included the philosophers Taine (1870) and Ribot (1885), and psychologists Janet (1886) and Binet (1889, 1892). It is certain that Breuer was familiar with some of the works of Taine (Macmillan, 1991). Freud owned a copy of Taine's *De l'intellegence* (1870) (Davies & Fichtner, forthcoming). Freud followed the work of Pierre Janet, for a while one of the most prominent advocates of the dissociationist theory of hysteria, whose ideas had an important influence on Freud's thinking after 1892 (Macmillan, 1991). It was James (1890) who, having encountered Janet's work, introduced the term 'dissociation' into the English-language psychological literature. Although James was vehemently opposed to the theory of unconscious mental events, he was hospitable to the dissociationist theory.

> How far this splitting up of the mind into separate consciousnesses may exist in each one of us is a problem. M. Janet holds that it is only possible where there is abnormal weakness, and consequently a defect of unifying co-ordinating power. An hysterical woman abandons part of her consciousness because she is too weak nervously to hold it together. The abandoned part meanwhile may solidify into a secondary or sub-conscious self (1890, Vol. I: 210).

Freud must certainly have encountered this and related terms in his readings on hysteria and hypnosis. In 1885 when Freud obtained a small grant to travel to Paris it was to study with Jean-Martin Charcot, the neuropathologist who understood both hysterical paralyses, and those induced by hypnosis, in terms of the action of 'an idea, or coherent group of associated ideas, which become lodged in the mind in the manner of a parasite, remaining isolated from all the rest' (289, cited in Macmillan 1991).

In the world of philosophy, the concept of *dédoublement* was enthusiastically embraced by many French positivists, who used it as ammunition against the thesis of a unitary substantial soul or self (Hacking, 1995).[54]

The notion of 'double consciousness' was used during most of the nineteenth century to describe the phenomenon of 'split' or, later, 'multiple' personality. For example, Azam 's celebrated case of Félida X, which sparked the French interest in doubling is described as follows:

> When Azam first encountered Félida, she would experience fierce pain in the temples and fall into a state of extreme fatigue, almost like sleep. This lasted ten minutes. She would then appear to wake up and would enter her *condition seconde*. This lasted a few hours, when she would again have a brief trance and return to her ordinary state. This happened every five or six days. In her second state she greeted people around her, smiled, exuded gaiety; she would say a few words and continue, for example, with her sewing, humming as she did so. She would do household chores, go shopping, pay visits, and she had the good cheer of a healthy young woman of her age. After her second brief trance, she woke up in her normal state and had no memory of what had happened or of anything she had learned in her second state (Hacking, 167.).

This use of the concept of was nonetheless a psychological or even a metaphysical construction upon clinical observation. This became clear in debates about whether or not the doubling of consciousness occurred in certain psychopathological states (e.g., debates about whether doubling occurs in individuals suffering from fugue states - see Hacking, 1995). Freud and Breuer (1895) took the concept of dissociation further by claiming that in it lay the root of the hysterical disposition, and that it can be inferred in cases displaying none of the florid manifestations of 'split' personalities. For Freud and Breuer, the chronic associative inaccessibility of traumatic ideas in the minds of their hysterical patients, considered in conjunction with the Cartesian identification of mentality with consciousness, was taken to underwrite the thesis of inevitable split consciousness in hysteria. If mentality is coextensive with consciousness, and hysteria is characterized by dissociated, associatively inaccessible mental contents, it follows that hysteria is a disorder involving the splitting or dissociation of consciousness itself.

TRANSITION TO THE TOPOGRAPHICAL CONCEPTION (1895)

Prior to 1895 Freud explained pathological defence mainly in terms of a 'splitting of consciousness' rather than in terms of unconscious mental representations.[55] His advocacy on a dissociationist theory of hysteria reflected his advocacy of the French approach to neuropathology[56], an approach with which Breuer concurred. Breuer's theoretical chapter in the 'Studies on hysteria' contained a section entitled 'Unconscious ideas and ideas inadmissible to consciousness - splitting of the mind'[57], and used a 'double consciousness' approach to the explanation of hysteria.[58]

Freud finished work on the 'Studies' in the spring of 1895. The mental unconscious makes its first published appearance in his work in 'Further remarks on the neuropsychoses of defence' (1896a), a paper which was composed in January 1896.[59]

It is evident that Freud made a major change in his theory of the mind at some point during the nine months separating the composition of the 'Studies on hysteria' and 'Further remarks on the neuropsychoses of defence'. The term 'psychoanalysis' was introduced simultaneously[60] with the concept of a mental unconscious (in 'Heredity and the neuroses' [1896b] written at the same time as 'Further remarks on the neuropsychoses of defence'). This conjunction is not coincidental. The theory of a mental unconscious which made possible the development of psychoanalysis was itself based on a philosophical shift to the identity theory of the mind/brain relation.

FREUD'S CLINICAL THEORY

Freud's clinical theory underwent a gradual shift during the period of his collaboration with Breuer from 1886 until 1895. Freud believed that hysterics and other psychoneurotics suffered from pathogenic mental conflicts of which they were not aware. He therefore needed to find some way to accommodate what would later be called 'unconscious mental conflict' (mental conflict involving at least one unconscious idea) within his dualistic model of the mind. The commitment to dualism placed strong constraints on his theorizing in this connection. One way forward would have been to understand such cases in terms of a conflict between conscious ideas and neurophysiological events. This option is vulnerable to standard objections to dualism. How can something that is just physical come into conflict with something that is just mental? Freud's second option would have been to discard the concept of unconscious conflict on purely philosophical grounds: to claim that, given the purported truth of dualism, unconscious conflict just could not exist. Freud initially adopted the tactic of claiming that consciousness was splittable, asserting that painful conscious conflicts may be dealt with by splitting consciousness itself. The segregation of the two sides of a conflict eliminates the conflict as such. However, the notion of split consciousness did not match the clinical data all that well. Freud's clinical work led him to hypotheses about occurrent mental conflicts which sustain neurotic symptoms, whereas the splitting of consciousness theory, if true, would *eliminate* any occurrent conflict. In addition to this problem, there was the simple fact that most of Freud's patients did not display anything like multiple personalities and were not conscious of the (hypothesized) split-off portions of consciousness. How is it possible to be unconscious of one's consciousness?[61] Finally, by 1895 Freud had come to emphasize the continuity of mental processes. The logical gaps between the elements of mental sequences could only be explained in a manner consistent with the principle of mental continuity by postulating the existence of intrinsically unconscious mental processes. Freud's gradual adoption of the clinical technique of free association during the early 1890s must have made the problems raised by the principle of mental continuity particularly salient. His intellectual struggle is evident in a passage appearing towards the end of the 'Studies on hysteria'.

> Even when.... the patients themselves accept the thought that they thought this or that, they often add: "But I can't remember having thought it". It is easy to come to terms with them by telling them that the thoughts were unconscious. But how is this state of affairs to be fitted into our psychological views? Are we to disregard this withholding of recognition on the part of patients, when, now that the work is finished, there is no longer any motive for their doing so? Or are we to suppose that we are really dealing with thoughts which never came about, which merely had a possibility of existing... It is clearly impossible to say anything about this - that is, about the state which the pathogenic material was in before the analysis - until we have arrived at a thorough clarification of our basic psychological views, especially on the nature of consciousness It remains, I think, a fact deserving serious consideration that in our analyses we can follow a train of thought from the conscious into the unconscious...that we can trace it from there for some distance through consciousness once more and that we can see it terminate in the unconscious again, without this alternation of "psychical illumination" making any change in the train of thought itself, in its logical consistency and in the interconnection between its various parts (300).

This passage merits close scrutiny. Freud's remarks about following trains of thought certainly prefigure his later use of the what I call the Continuity argument. In light of this it would appear that it may have been Freud's concern with the principle of mental continuity that propelled him, by way of the Continuity argument, to abandon his dualism in favor of physicalism. I will describe Freud's formulation and use of the Continuity argument in Chapter Six.

According to Strachey's editorial notes to the 'Studies', this passage was written in March 1895. Scarcely a month later the promised 'thorough clarification of our basic psychological views' was begun in the form of the 'Project'. Kris (1950, 1954), Stewart (1969) and others have suggested that Freud's 'Project' was written in response to Breuer's theoretical chapter in the 'Studies on hysteria', which makes use of the idea of unconscious mental events. The 'Project' both introduces the concept of radically unconscious mental states and links this idea with the identity theory. Consciousness is described as a function of one system of neurons, which he calls the 'ω neurones'. It is worthwhile at this point reproducing again the passage in which Freud first advanced his physicalist interpretation of consciousness.

> A word on the relation of this theory of consciousness to others. According to an advanced mechanical theory, consciousness is a mere appendage to physiologico-psychical processes and its omission would make no alteration is the psychical passage [of events]. According to another theory, consciousness is the subjective side of all psychical events and is thus inseparable from the physiological mental process. The theory developed here lies between these two. Here consciousness is the subjective side of one part of the physical processes in the nervous system, namely of the ω processes and the omission of consciousness does not leave psychical events unaltered but involves the omission of the contribution from (1950: 311)

Freud explicitly differentiated his view from epiphenominalism on the one hand, and a version of the identity theory identifying consciousness as coextensive with the mental on the other, driving a conceptual wedge between consciousness and content. Consciousness is understood as a property of some mental events, and the relationship between conscious mental events and the body becomes a special case of the relationship between mental events and the body. Freud's transition to materialism in the 'Project' had important epistemological implications that were to influence his approach to theory building (particularly with respect to the problem of validation) and to clinical practice. He could now abandon the introspectionistic approach he had inherited from the dominant Cartesian tradition. As he put it in the 'Project':

> We at once become clear about a postulate which has been guiding us up to now [in the present work]. We have been treating psychical processes as something that could dispense with this awareness through consciousness, as something that exists independently of such awareness. We are prepared to find that some of our assumptions are not confirmed through consciousness. If we do not let ourselves be confused on that account, it follows, from the postulate of consciousness providing neither complete nor trustworthy knowledge of the neuronal processes, that these are in the first instance to be regarded to their whole extent as unconscious and are to be inferred like other natural things (1950:308).[62]

This contrasts sharply with remarks in 'Gehirn' that mental states are 'immaterial' and only accessible by means of introspection.

> The psychical, whatever its nature may be, is in itself unconscious and probably similar in kind to all other natural processes of which we have obtained knowledge (284).

This passage remains obscure unless we realize that Freud uses the term 'unconscious' in a special way. If all mental processes are identical to physical processes, all mental processes can in principle be given true objective neuroscientific descriptions. However, the notion of consciousness has no role to play on the level of fundamental physiological description. There is thus a sense in which all mental processes are in themselves - in their essential nature - unconscious. An item that is 'similar in kind to all other processes' is a physical item. The mental properties of these events supervene upon their physical properties. Some neurophysiological events possessing mental properties also possess the property of being conscious or (as we shall see), more correctly, may cause episodes of content-laden consciousness. That he held this general view explains Freud's approval of Lipps' dictum that 'the whole of what is psychical exists unconsciously and ...a part of it also exists consciously' (Freud, 1900:614).

Chessick (1980) condescendingly accuses Freud of philosophical naiveté,[63] claiming that:

> Freud was not a professional philosopher. He seems unaware that by redefining the mental as psychical events which may or may not - usually not - possess the quality of consciousness, he is not eliminating the mind-brain problem. By insisting that mental events at their base have an organic or materialist nature, he runs into the same problem faced by Hobbes: how one moves from this obscure material base to the conscious phenomena of perception (298).

VI

JUSTIFICATION: THE CONTINUITY ARGUMENT

I have already suggested that the impetus for Freud's adoption of the concept of unconscious mental events was provided by his clinical work. It was difficult for Freud to accommodate his clinical observations and inferences within a psychology of consciousness. However, such a transition could not be philosophically innocent. Even as an essentially explanatory concept, the idea of 'the unconscious' might have been formulated along the lines of the dissociative or dispositional models within the framework of dualism. Freud chose the more radical philosophical path of nesting his theory within a materialist conception of mind-brain identity, a conception that contravened intuitions that were widely shared during his lifetime.

Freud addressed the issue of the philosophical justification for his views at various points in his writings. These attempts at justification are to a great extent directed at establishing the merits of the thesis of radically unconscious mental events, conceived within a materialistic framework, relative to the dualistic alternatives. In the present chapter I will examine Freud's use of what I call the Continuity argument primarily to counter the dispositional theory of unconscious events.

THE CONTINUITY ARGUMENT

Freud proposed that explanations of mental events should conform to a pre-theoretical principle of mental (semantic) continuity. I will refer to Freud's argument invoking the principle of mental continuity on behalf of his theory of unconscious mental events as the 'Continuity argument'.

The Continuity argument did not originate with Freud. The argument can be traced at least as far back as Hamilton (1853) who may have been Freud's source.[64] Although it is possible that Freud initially encountered Hamilton's work through his contact with Brentano, we know that Freud purchased a copy of Mill's *Examination of the Philosophy of Sir William Hamilton* (1865) in 1889 for use as philosophical source material for his book *On Aphasia* (1891), which mentions the work in a footnote. Mill's Chapter Fifteen is entitled 'Sir William Hamilton's Doctrine of Unconscious Mental Modifications'. Mill cites Hamilton's (1853) remark that:

> It sometimes happens, that we find one thought rising immediately after another in consciousness, but whose consecution we can reduce to no law of association. Now in these cases we can generally discover by an attentive observation, that these two thoughts, though not themselves associated, are each associated with certain other thoughts, so that the whole consecution would have been regular, had these intermediate thoughts come into consciousness, between the two which are not immediately associated (352-353).

Mill attempts to refute Hamilton, first by claiming that conscious links between the associations have simply been forgotten and then by invoking a version of the dispositional argument.

> It may well be believed that the apparently suppressed links in a chain of association, those which Sir W. Hamilton considers as latent, really are so; the chain of causation being continued only physically, by one organic state of the nerves succeeding another so rapidly that the state of mental consciousness appropriate to each is not produced (282-283).

Another allusion to the principle of mental continuity occurs in a paper by Ewald Hering with which Freud was familiar.[65] Hering was a distinguished physiologist who was Josef Breuer's scientific mentor. While still a medical student, Breuer had collaborated with Hering in research eventuating in the discovery of the role of the vagus nerve in the self-regulating mechanism of respiration, now known as the Hering-Breuer reflex (Sulloway, 1979). Hering is best known for his work on vision.

Hering spoke of unconscious mental events in a lecture, delivered before the Viennese Royal Academy of Sciences in 1870, which was entitled 'On memory as a general function of organised matter' (Hering, 1870) and published in English translation in Butler (1880).

We know of Freud's views on Hering from two sources. The earliest of these is an entry in the *Minutes of the Vienna Psychoanalytic Society* for 14 November 1906 in which Freud refers approvingly to the 1870 lecture. The second source is his comments on a book by the British philosopher Israel Levine.[66] Levine's book entitled *The Unconscious: A Introduction to Freudian Psychology* (1923), summarized fundamental Freudian concepts, placed some of these in the context of the history of ideas and endorsed psychoanalytic views. Levine sent Freud a copy of the book, dedicating it 'To the Master, from a very grateful pupil'. Freud remarked to Jones that: 'I was never so much pleased by a book on ψα matter as by his Unconscious. A rare bird if he is a philosopher' (519). The book was evidently based on his doctoral thesis, as were lectures that he gave on Freud at London University (520). Freud had Levine's book translated into German by his daughter Anna (Levine, 1926). Freud himself translated the section of the book dealing with Samuel Butler and appended a footnote to the text (Strachey, 1957). The footnote reads as follows:

> German readers, familiar with this lecture of Hering's and regarding it as a masterpiece, would not, of course, be inclined to bring into the foreground the considerations based on it by Butler.[67] Moreover, some pertinent remarks are to be found in Hering which allow psychology the right to assume the existence of unconscious mental activity: "Who could hope to disentangle the fabric of our inner life with its thousandfold complexities, if we were willing to pursue its threads only so far as they traverse consciousness? ...Chains such as these of unconscious material nerve-processes, which end in a link accompanied by a conscious perception, have been described as 'unconscious trains of ideas' and 'unconscious inferences'[68] ; and from the standpoint of psychology this can be justified. For the mind would often slip through the fingers of psychology, if psychology refused to keep a hold on the mind's unconscious states" (Freud, in Levine, 1926; cited and translated by Strachey, 1957).

In Butler's translation, the concluding sentence of the paragraph by Hering (omitted by Freud), states that:

> As far, however, as the investigations of the pure physicist are concerned, the unconscious and matter are one and the same thing, and the physiology of the unconscious is no "philosophy of the unconscious"[69] (Hering, in Butler, 1880:113).

Hering explains that he uses the appellation 'physicist' - 'in its widest signification' (99) - to mean what we now call 'physicalist'. Within the context of his arguments, Hering seems to mean that the unconscious is to be understood neurophysiologically.

> Neither sensation, nor idea, nor yet conscious will, can form a link in this chain of material occurrences which make up the physical life of an organism. If I am asked a question and reply to it, the material process which the nerve fibre conveys from the organ of hearing to the brain must travel through my brain as an actual and material process before it can reach the nerves which will act upon my organs of speech. It cannot, on reaching a given place in the brain, change there and then into an immaterial something, and then turn up again some time afterwards in another part of the brain as a material process (100).

Hering's remarks so resemble a passage from Freud's *On Aphasia* (1891) that the hypothesis of some direct influence is at least plausible. Freud (1891) rhetorically inquires:

> Is it justified to immerse a nerve fibre, which over the whole length of its course has been only a purely physiological structure subject to physiological modifications, with its end in the psyche and to furnish this end with an idea or a memory (55)?

Hering advanced a conception of psychophysical covariation, stating that:

> Thus regarded, the phenomena of consciousness becomes functions of the material changes of organised substance, and inversely - though this is involved in the use of the word "function" - the material processes of brain substance become functions of the phenomena of consciousness. For when two variables are so dependent upon one another in the changes they undergo in accordance with fixed laws that a change in either involves simultaneous and corresponding change in the other, the one is called a function of the other (102-103).

Like Jackson however, Hering avoided grasping the ontological nettle.

> The materialist regards consciousness as a product or result of matter, while the idealist holds matter to be a result of consciousness, and a third maintains that matter and spirit are identical; with all this the physiologist, as such, has nothing whatever to do (103).

So, for Hering consciousness and neurophysiology covary, and that continuity-supplying neurophysiological states which do not correspond to conscious states can, in some sense, be treated as mental. The relationship between these neurophysiological states and their corresponding states of consciousness is understood along dispositionalist lines.

> I was conscious of this or that yesterday, and am again conscious of it today. Where has it been meanwhile? It does not remain continuously within my consciousness,

nevertheless it returns after having quitted it. Our ideas tread but for a moment upon the stage of consciousness[70], and then go back again behind the scenes, to make way for others in their place. As the player is only a king when he is on the stage, so they too exist as ideas so long only as they are recognised. How do they live when they are off the stage? For we know that they are living somewhere; give them their cue and they reappear immediately. They do not exist continuously as ideas; what is continuous is the special disposition of nerve substance in virtue of which this substance gives out today the same sound which it gave yesterday if it is rightly struck (109-110).

Neurophysiological dispositions are held to supply the semantic continuity of mental life, and these dispositions are treated as unconscious mental states by virtue of their causal power to produce conscious mental states.

The bond of union, therefore, which connects the individual phenomena of our consciousness lies in our unconscious world; and as we know nothing of this but what investigation into the laws of matter tells us - as, in fact, for purely experimental purposes, "matter" and the "unconscious" must be one and the same thing - so the physiologist has a full right to denote memory as, in the wider sense of the word, a function of brain substance (111).

Given that Hering was a close associate of Breuer and that Hering invited Freud, while still a student, to become his assistant in Prague (Sulloway, 1979), it seems plausible that Freud would have been acquainted with these ideas considerably earlier than 1895.

Finally, Herbart proposed a concept of mental continuity. This was described in Lipps' book *Grundtatsachen des Seelenlebens* (1883) as follows:

Unconscious mental excitations (*seelische Erregungen*), of whose nature we are ignorant, are interposed between our conscious ideas; every conscious idea arises out of, and dies away into, such an unconscious excitation (125, cited in Baldwin [Ed.], 1902: 724).

Freud owned a copy of Lipps' *Grundtatsachen.* Herbart's views on mental continuity are also described in Lipps' 'Der Begriff des Unbewussten in der Psychologie' (1897) which Freud cites in 'The interpretation of dreams' (1900) and 'Jokes and their relation to the unconscious' (1901).

Freud's version of the Continuity argument is expressed most fully in 'The unconscious' (1915a), the text upon which I will rely below (but see also Freud, 1912, 1913, 1926a, 1926b, 1940a, 1940b). The principle of mental (semantic) continuity states that in any sequence of thoughts $t_1, t_2, t_3 \ldots t_n$ when any two non-contiguous thoughts are such that the latter is cognitively derived from the former, some continuity-supplying thoughts must be assumed to have occurred during the interval between them; (this is explained more fully below).

> The data of consciousness have a very large number of gaps in them; both in healthy and in sick people psychical acts often occur which can be explained only by presupposing other acts, of which, nevertheless, consciousness affords no evidence. These not only include parapraxes and dreams in healthy people, and everything described as a psychical symptom or an obsession in the sick; our most personal daily experience acquaints us with ideas that come into our head, we do not know from where, and with intellectual conclusions arrived at we do not know how [71] (166-67).

Such experiences remain causally inexplicable so long as one retains the assumption that all mental processes possess the property of being conscious. If mental contents can be unconscious it becomes possible to interpolate unconscious mental contents in order to fill in the gaps in conscious mental life.

Freud next points out that at any given time, one is conscious of only a tiny subset of all of the mental contents potentially available to consciousness. In the case of memories, it is clear that most of our memories exist in a latent, descriptively unconscious state. It is at this point that Freud introduces the objection that the dispositional model is able to explain these phenomena without recourse to hypothetical unconscious mental events.[72]

> But here we encounter the objection that these latent recollections can no longer be described as psychical, but that they correspond to residues of somatic processes from which what is psychical can once more arise (1915a:167).

The point was made slightly more explicitly in 1912, when Freud noted that:

> At this very point we may be prepared to meet with the philosophical objection that the latent conception did not exist as an object of psychology, but as a physical disposition for the recurrence of the same psychical phenomenon (1912a:260).

The argument to which Freud objects was indeed advanced by his contemporaries. Here is an example from the work of Wundt's pupil Titchener.

> The nervous system does not cause, but it does explain mind.... In a word, reference to the nervous system introduces into psychology just that unity and coherence which a strictly descriptive psychology cannot achieve.
>
> Mind lapses every night, and reforms every morning; but the bodily processes go on, in sleep and in waking. An idea drops out of memory, to recur, quite unexpectedly, many years later; but the bodily processes have been going on without interruption. Reference to the body does not add one iota to the data of psychology, to the sum of introspections. It does furnish us with an explanatory principle for psychology; it does enable us to systematize our introspective data. Indeed, if we refuse to explain mind by body, we must accept the one or the other of two, equally unsatisfactory alternatives: we must either rest content with a simple description of mental experience, or must invent an unconscious mind to give coherence and continuity to the conscious. Both courses have been tried. But if we take the first we never arrive at a science of psychology and if we take the second, we voluntarily leave the sphere of fact for the sphere of fiction (1917: 39-40, cited in Klein, 1977).

Titchener's ontological dualism foreclosed the possibility of envisaging that the central nervous system itself possesses those unconscious cognitive properties which alone are suitable for supplying the mental continuity to which he refers.

I have already discussed Freud's ambiguous passage in the 'Outline' in which I have taken him to be using the Continuity argument on behalf of a physicalist conception of mind. Macmillan (1992) interprets this passage differently, commenting that:

> The only alternative Freud ever saw to assuming that psychological processes were not unbroken sequences, complete in themselves, was to assume that the concomitant "physical or somatic processes" were "more complete" than the psychological (118-119).

Macmillan is driven to this interpretation by taking at face value Freud's remark about 'supposedly somatic concomitant phenomena'. Apart from its inconsistency with Freud's repeated emphasis on the physical nature of mental events, and hence their physical continuity, there are other reasons for regarding Macmillan's interpretation as implausible. Note, for example, that in Freud's remarks the 'psychical sequences' are taken to be conscious mental episodes.

Freud presented an argument of the following form: If all mental events are just conscious events and if we grant that there are gaps in the sequences of conscious mental events, then we must conclude that these gaps can be accounted for by the neurophysiological processes underpinning conscious mental sequences. But if the underlying and continuous neurophysiological processes can explain the gaps between items in mental sequences (sequences of events under mental descriptions), and if the resulting explanation is framed in terms of semantic continuity, we must regard these neurophysiological processes as somehow instantiating mental contents. If we grant that the continuity-supplying neurophysiological processes are also mental, then it follows that truly mental processes can be unconscious.

Freud grants that the relevant neurophysiological processes are 'more complete' than conscious mental episodes and uses this to argue in favor of the identity theory and against epiphenominalism.

THE LINGUISTIC CRITICISM

Freud points out that the dispositionalist objection takes for granted an axiomatic equation of the mental with the conscious. As early as 1905 Freud had realized that the equation of the mental with the conscious can be understood as pertaining either to fact or to language. If it is the latter - 'a trifling matter of definition' (1940a: 158) - it is not open to empirical investigation (see also Freud, 1912a, 1913, 1916-17, 1923b, 1925b, 1940a).[73] If the objection is taken as merely begging the question it is uninteresting. In 'Jokes and their relation to the unconscious' (1905), Freud referred scathingly to the linguistic argument as follows:

> I am aware that anyone who is under the spell of a good academic philosophical education, or who takes his opinions long range from some so-called system of philosophy, will be opposed to the assumption of an "unconscious psychical"...and will prefer to prove its impossibility on the basis of a definition of the psychical. But definitions are a matter of convention and can be altered (162).

Freud did not believe that scientific psychology should be constrained by the conventions of ordinary language. He was concerned with the scientific ramifications of linguistic constraints.

OBJECTIONS TO THE MIND-CONSCIOUSNESS EQUATION

Freud (1915a) advances four objections to the axiomatic equation of mind with consciousness. He argues that equating mind with consciousness is inconsistent with the principle of the semantic continuity of the mental, that equating mind with consciousness encounters the Cartesian problem of how the interaction between mind and brain is to be understood, that equating mind with consciousness exaggerates the psychologically explanatory value of conscious mental states and that equating mind with consciousness inappropriately delimits the domain to which psychological explanation can be legitimately applied.

The equation of the psychical with the conscious is inconsistent with the notion of mental continuity. Consider the situation, mentioned by Freud, of being preoccupied with some seemingly intractable intellectual problem (at time T_1) only to find that at some later moment (time T_2) when one is consciously occupied with something else entirely, the solution seems to drop out of the blue. The view that latent mental processes are actually physical (and non-mental) dispositions for (conscious) mental states would have us believe that during the interval between the conscious preoccupation with the problem and the emergence of the solution there was no mental processing of the event, i.e., that a sequence of neural events occurring at times T_1 and T_2 and giving rise to the solution to the problem consciously abandoned at T_1 was not a sequence of neural events satisfying functions instantiating mental events. According to this view the neural events in question were not mental under any description and yet, in some mysterious fashion, cognitive work was performed by them. The hypothesis of unconscious mental activity, on the other hand, allows us to retain the continuity of the mental by asserting that the specified sequence of neural events occurring between T_1 and T_2 realize mental processes without displaying the property of being conscious and can legitimately be described using mental predicates.

Storr (1989) gives several examples of the sort of unconscious problem-solving that Freud apparently had in mind. He provides the example of the German mathematician Gauss' own account of discovering the solution to a difficult mathematical problem:

> Finally, two days ago I succeeded, not on account of my painful efforts, but by the grace of God. Like a sudden flash of lightning, the riddle happened to be solved. I myself cannot say what was the conducting thread which connected what I previously knew with what made my success possible (Gauss, in Hadamard, 1949:15).

In this instance there was no interval between the preoccupation with the problem and the discovery of the solution, but there remains a cognitive gap unless one accepts the hypothesis of unconscious mental activity. The example of Poincaré's discovery of Fuchsian functions, also given by Storr, is even better for Freud's case.

> For fifteen days I strove to prove that there could not be any functions like those I have since called Fuchsian functions. I was then very ignorant; every day I seated myself at my work table, stayed for an hour or two, tried a great number of combinations and reached no results. One evening, contrary to my custom, I drank black coffee and could not sleep. Ideas arose in crowds. I felt them collide until pairs interlocked, so to speak, making a stable combination. By the next morning I had established the existence of a class of Fuchsian functions, those which come from the hypergeometric series; I had only to write out the results, which took but a few hours (Poincaré, 1913: 383-394).

After this, Poincaré decided to go on holiday in order to forget about his mathematical concerns. However:

> Having reached Coustances, we entered an omnibus to go some place or other. At the moment I put my foot on the step the idea came to me, without anything in my former thoughts seeming to have paved the way for it, that the transformations I had used to define the Fuchsian functions were identical to those of non- Euclidian geometry. I did not verify the idea; I should not have had time, as, upon taking my seat in the omnibus, I went on with a conversation already commenced, but I felt a perfect certainty. On my return to Caen, for conscience's sake I verified the result at my leisure (Ibid.).

Either a process of unconscious cognition occurred during the time between the moment Poincaré discovered Fuchsian functions and the moment of his discovery that their defining transformations are identical to those of non-Euclidian geometry or, very implausibly, the thought about non-Euclidian geometry was not causally related to Poincaré's prior preoccupation with the problem of Fuchsian functions. As Freud (1940a) puts it, if we confine ourselves to the conscious dimension we find 'broken sequences' which are 'obviously dependent on something else' (158).

The equation of the mental with the conscious brings back the insoluble difficulties of psychophysical parallelism. By 'psychophysical parallelism' Freud appears to mean 'dualism' (see Freud, 1940a). This view is a consequence of the equation of the mental with the conscious insofar as it presupposes the existence of non-mental physical dispositions for non-physical conscious mental events, giving rise to the notorious philosophical problem of how physical events could possibly cause non-physical events or be miraculously synchronized with them.[74]

The equation of the mental with the conscious over-estimates the role played by conscious events in cognitive processes. There is no obvious reason why one should insist that the mental is coextensive with the conscious, whilst there are good reasons to deny it.

The equation of the mental with the conscious forecloses the possibility of psychological research into nonconscious states without providing an alternative approach, implying that the gaps in conscious mental life cannot possibly be explained by means of hypothetical mental events. A line of demarcation is thus drawn between psychology and physiology, securing comparatively little territory for the former. Yet, there are no competing hypotheses of a purely physiological kind offered to explain just what goes on during nonconscious episodes and how these unknown processes might bring about conscious mental events. In other words, the equation of the mental with the conscious forecloses important avenues for psychological research.[75] Freud addressed this general issue in a response to the linguistic critique in 'The claims of psycho-analysis to scientific interest' (1913).

> If anyone possessing that knowledge [of psycho-analytic data] nevertheless holds to the conviction which equates the conscious and the psychical and consequently denies the unconscious the attribute of being psychical, no objection can, of course, be made except that such a distinction turns out to be highly unpractical. For it is easy to describe the unconscious and to follow its developments if it is approached from the direction of its relation to the conscious, with which it has so much in common.

On the other hand, there still seems no possibility of approaching it from the direction of physical events (178-179).

VII

FREUD AND JACKSON: DUALISM AND ANTI-LOCALIZATIONISM

It is widely recognized that Freud was strongly influenced by the work of John Hughlings Jackson. Freud's intellectual encounter with Jackson occurred in the context of aphasiology. In his book *On Aphasia* (1891), Freud unequivocally endorsed Jackson's views, enlisting his support against the views of German-speaking authorities such as Meynert, Wernicke and Lichtheim.[76] If Freud's debt to Jackson had been confined to his work on the neurophysiology of language disorders, concern with the Jackson-Freud connection would be nothing more that a footnote to the early history of neuroscience. However, aphasiology in the late nineteenth century was an exciting cross-disciplinary field.[77] It was a meeting-point for philosophy, neuroscience and psychology analogous to the status of blindsight studies in contemporary cognitive science.[78] Freud encountered and responded to Jackson's views on the mind-body relationship, the regimentation of neuroscientific and psychological language, anti-localizationism as well as specific neuroscientific propositions. In the present chapter I will examine Freud's response to Jackson's philosophy of mind as well as his eventual rejection of aspects of the Jacksonian position, and then contrast Freud's mature position with that of Jackson.

LOCALIZATIONISM

It was apparently the Roman physician Galen who first suggested that the brain is in some sense the seat of mental events. Little progress in understanding until Vesalius, working in the sixteenth century, proposed that there are no less than three human souls, the chief of which resides in the brain and influences the body by means of the manufacture and transmission of animal spirits. As we have seen, Descartes also regarded the brain as the interface between body and mind, but was more specific than his predecessors in his ascription of the 'seat of the soul' to the pineal gland. By the middle of the eighteenth century, Haller had rejected Descartes' hypothesis and instead proposed that the central mass of both cerebrum and cerebellum is the seat of the soul, additionally claiming that specific mental functions are localized in specific regions of the brain.

It was Haller's work that laid the foundation for Gall's biological 'faculty psychology', which claimed that mental faculties were in some way localized in the brain. Gall's work was a decisive advance over earlier substance-dualist concepts of the powers of the soul. Gall made important contributions to comparative neuroanatomy, but imbedded these contributions within his new discipline of phrenology. Phrenological theory claimed that psychological characteristics could be identified on the basis of the protuberances on an individual's skull, an idea that was based on a theory of cerebral localization: the view that the brain is anatomically specialized to subserve distinct psychological 'faculties'. The twenty-seven faculties discharged by these cerebral 'organs' were individuated along folk-psychological lines. The 'organ of amativeness', for example, was lodged in the base of the skull, while the 'organ of acquisitiveness' was said to lie just above and in front of the ears.

Phrenology was wildly popular until well into the nineteenth century. Phrenological societies were established, as were phrenological journals. A chair of phrenology was founded at Glasgow University. Phrenological marriage guides and child-rearing manuals were published (Altschule, 1965). Benjamin Brodie, one of the fiercest critics of the new 'science', described how:

> The organ of philoprogenitiveness, by which parents are impelled to love their offspring is...placed in the back of the head.... Dr Gall found a protuberance in this part of the heads of women, and for five years he meditated on the subject, but could advance no further. At last he found a similar protuberance in the heads of monkeys. The question then arose, what is there in common between women and monkeys? At this point he obtained the assistance of a clergyman, who observed that monkeys are very fond of their offspring and thus solved the difficulty: The conclusion at which he arrived being afterwards confirmed by the following circumstance: A woman in whom this part of the head was unusually prominent, being ill of a fever,

and (we may suppose) delirious, believed herself to be pregnant with five children (Brodie, cited in Altschule, 1965: 91).

Apart from the then novel concept of neuroanatomical localization, the phrenological movement failed to attract serious interest from most scientists. Flourens tested Gall's thesis using experimental neurosurgery on animals. The ablation of portions of animals' brains did not produce the specific consequences deduced from Gall's theory. Flourens believed that distinct functions could be assigned to the cerebrum and the cerebellum, but held that these functions were distributed throughout these structures. Flourens' reasoning was typically metaphysical. A confirmed Cartesian, Flourens believed that a unitary soul could only interact with the brain as a whole (Leahy, 1987).

As the century progressed, clinical studies of the sequelae to brain damage led many neuroscientists to retain confidence in certain aspects of Gall's scheme. Gall had claimed that the organ of 'verbal memory' lay in a region of the frontal lobe of the cerebrum. Observations by Bouillaud, Aubertin and others seemed to confirm the presence of a 'language center' localized in the left frontal lobe. In 1880 Broca confirmed the existence of a language area located very to the position of Gall's hypothetical organ of verbal memory, and subsequently spent years gathering more confirming instances. This region of the brain became known as 'Broca's area', and the psychological consequences of damage to Broca's area was given the (Platonic) name of 'aphasia'.

Inspired by Broca, other neuroscientists were able to establish the existence of other localizations: Fritsch and Hitzig discovered the motor area of the cerebral cortex and Ferrier established the location of visual and auditory areas. In 1874 Wernicke distinguished between 'Broca's aphasia' (motor aphasia) and what became known as 'Wernicke's aphasia' (sensory aphasia). Wernicke showed that sensory aphasia is associated with damage to a region of the brain situated near the auditory area where, he reasoned, memories of words should be stored ('Wernicke's area'). He further demonstrated that damage to Broca's area results in speech production disorder with unimpaired speech comprehension, while damage to Wernicke's area results in retention of the capacity for speech combined with loss of speech comprehension. As one might imagine, the speech of persons suffering from sensory aphasia is largely incoherent. The flavor of Wernicke's and Broca's clinical data can be appreciated by means of the following excerpt from a dialogue with a motor aphasic patient (Kinsbourne and Warrington, 1963, cited in Dennett, 1991).

> How are you today?
> "Gossiping O.K. and Lords and cricket and England and Scotland battles. I don't know. Hypertension and two won cricket, bowling, batting and catch, poor old things, cancellations maybe gossiping, cancellations arm and argument, finishing bowling".
> What is the meaning of "safety first"?
> "To look and see and the Richmond Road particularly, and look traffic and hesitation right and strolling, very good cause, maybe, zebras maybe these, motor-car and the traffic light".

Wernicke used such observations to deduce that the motor and sensory speech areas must normally be linked by association fibres in order to allow normal speech and predicted the existence of a previously unidentified form of aphasia caused by damage to these association fibres leaving the two speech areas intact. Wernicke successfully predicted that this 'conduction aphasia' would be characterized by 'paraphrasias' (confusions of speech) with unimpaired comprehension.

According to Decker (1977) the localisationist theory had important philosophical ramifications: although the theory of psychophysical parallelism had made the localisationist program possible by suggesting a correspondence between mental and neural phenomena, the development of a neuroscience which demonstrated the dependence of mental processes upon neurophysiological processes made this position increasingly difficult to entertain coherently.

ANTI-LOCALIZATIONISM

The genuine successes of the localizationist program led to excessive and unwarranted claims.

> Large amounts of specific information were gathered about the localization of color vision, sound, taste, smell, heat, cold, touch, pain, sense of motion and sense of balance, and visceral sensations. These successful accomplishments of sensory physiology and psychology, which determined the physiological correlates of sensation, encouraged the search for specific centres of "higher" psychic experiences. The

> parts of the brain were supposed to have their separate functions and their specific energies to which isolated elements of consciousness were supposed to correspond....The psychologists tried to find separate areas of the brain for various images, feelings, and acts of thought and will. Even single ideas were ascribed to their own cells, in which they were supposed to be "deposited". Many psychologists computed from the number of existent brain cells the possible number of ideas that a normal person could form (Decker, 1977: 204).

John Hughlings Jackson took issue with the orthodox doctrines of cerebral localization. Jackson's approach involved considerations of a neuroscientific, methodological and ontological character which are not always easy to disentangle. Freud unreservedly endorsed all these aspects of Jackson's thought in *On Aphasia*, and it was several years before he was able to differentiate Jackson's ontological dualism from his methodological dualism and anti-localizationism, rejecting the former and retaining adherence to the latter two positions.

Jackson argued that the fact that impairments of speech are associated with damage to specific areas of the brain does not necessarily imply that specific elements of language use and comprehension are located in specific areas in the brain. He used neuroscientific evidence to argue that language use and comprehension are underpinned by complex dynamic neural systems. According to this view, damage to Wernicke's area for example, has the effect that it does because the lesion has disrupted the functioning of the speech system. Analogously, if I damage an electronic component within my computer and this causes a document to disappear from the screen of the monitor, this should not automatically be taken to imply that the document was located in the damaged component - that the component is the 'document area' of the computer.

DUALISM

In addition to rejecting localizationism on neuroscientific grounds, as described above, Jackson also rejected it on philosophical grounds.

Jackson objected to the notion that neural anatomy is individuated so as to correspond one-to-one with psychological categories. He therefore held that psychological discourse should be sharply demarcated from neuroscientific discourse. Jackson then extended this purely methodological dualism into overt ontological dualism which he called the 'doctrine of concomitance'.[79]

> The doctrine I hold is this: first, that states of consciousness (or, synonymously, states of mind) are utterly different from nervous states; second, that the two things occur together - that for every mental state there is a correlative nervous state; third, that, although the two things occur in parallelism, there is no interference of one from the other. This may be called the doctrine of Concomitance. Thus, in the case of visual perception, there is an unbroken physical circuit....The visual image, a purely mental state, occurs in parallelism with - arises during (not from) - the activities of the two highest links of this purely physical chain: so to speak it 'stands outside' those links (Jackson, 1884:72).

Jackson seems to have had little interest in the ontological issue per se. He was mainly concerned with the methodological ramifications of his approach for the study of neuropathology.

> A critic of my Croonian Lectures...says that I state this doctrine [of concomitance] in order to evade the charge of materialism...The critic referred to says that the doctrine of concomitance is Leibniz's "two clock theory".[80] It may be; it matters nothing for medical purposes whether it is or is not.

He explained that:

> To put the matter in another way, let it be granted for the sake of argument that the separation into states of the highest centres [of the brain], and what we called the utterly different and yet concomitant states of consciousness, is known to be erroneous and that the...[identity theory] is ascertained to be the true one. I then ask that the doctrine of concomitance be provisionally accepted as an artifice, in order that we may study the most complex diseases of the nervous system more easily (Jackson, 1887:84-85).

As a methodological strategy, the doctrine of concomitance constrained neuroscientific discourse to the use of neuroscientific predicates. Neuroscience could only speak of events subsumed under neuroanatomical and neurophysiological descriptions. Psychological predicates could not be invoked either as *explanans* or *explananda*. Anticipating the views of Thomas Szasz (1972), Jackson went so far as to reject the concept of mental illness as incoherent.

Jackson's anti-localizationism was closely bound up with his dualism, for if mental items are intrinsically different from neural states, the former cannot be regarded as coextensive with the latter. In some passages it seems that Jackson's main concern is the identification of mental and neural kinds, and that in opposing materialism he is really opposing type identity theory.

> Those who accept the doctrine of concomitance do not believe that sensations, volitions, ideas and emotions produce movements or any other physical states....They would not say that an hysterical woman did not do this or that because she lacked will; that an aphasic did not speak because he had lost the memory of words; and that a comatose patient did not move because he was unconscious....They would not in scientific exposition make piebald classifications of symptoms, e.g., *sensory*, *motor*, emotional and intellectual. The two words italicized are names of physical states; the other two of psychical states. Such classifications, perhaps allowable clinically, are, for scientific purposes, as unjustifiable as a classification of plants into endogens, graminacae, kitchen herbs, ornamental shrubs and potatoes, would be (1887: 86-87).[81]

Notwithstanding his radical distinction between mental and physical items, there are many passages in Jackson's works which imply that mental states are what Freud called 'dependent concomitants' of neural states.[82] Perhaps Jackson was groping towards some form of token identity theory, such as Davidson's anomalous monism (the view, implicit in the passage reproduced above, that only physical kinds are natural kinds, might be used to support a theory of token identity). However, Jackson remained a psychophysical parallelist and never dealt with the philosophical defects of such a position. Chief amongst these, of course, is the lack of any explanation for the concomitance between mental and neural events. When Mercier (1888) wrote that, having grasped the doctrine of concomitance, 'the student will enter upon the study of psychology with half his difficulties surmounted', James (1890) responded: 'Half his difficulties ignored, I should prefer to say. For this "Concomitance" in the midst of "absolute separateness" is an utterly irrational notion' (136, cited in Marx, 1967).[83]

FREUD AND JACKSON

It is possible that Freud was under the influence of Jackson's work as early as 1888 (Andersson, 1961; Solms & Saling, 1990).[84] Freud made the Jacksonian distinction between irritative and disruptive cerebral lesions without citing Jackson in his book on infantile cerebral hemiplegias co-authored with Oskar Rie (Freud & Rie, 1891)[85] There is passing reference to Jackson's work on epilepsy in his book on *Infantile Cerebral Paralysis* (Freud, 1897). Sustained consideration of Jackson's work is confined to *On Aphasia* (1891).[86] In the present section I will review those aspects of the intellectual impact of Jackson upon Freud that are directly relevant to the subject of this book. Other aspects - such as Freud's adoption of Jackson's concept of functional dissolution, derived from Herbert Spencer and elaborated by Freud into the concept of psychological regression - will not be discussed.

Freud endorsed Jackson's anti-localizationism[87] and dualism in *On Aphasia*. Freud noted that, in rejecting the strong localizationist claims of faculty psychology, Wernicke had proposed that only the simplest, atomic elements of mental states (in Wernicke's view visual perceptions) can be localized in the cerebral cortex. Freud held that even Wernicke's modest version of localizationism was vulnerable to Jackson's philosophical critique of mixing the psychological and neuroscientific vocabularies.

> But does one not in principle make the same mistake irrespective of whether one tries a localize a complicated concept, a whole mental faculty or a psychic element? Is it justified to immerse a nerve fibre, which over the whole length of its course has been only a physiological structure subject to physiological modifications, with its end in the psyche and to furnish this end with an idea or a memory? Now that "will" and "intelligence", etc. have been recognized as psychological technical terms referring to very complicated physiological states, can one be quite sure that the "simple sensory impression" be anything but another such technical term? (55).[88]

Freud took this principle forward in his account of the connectionist architecture underpinning the topographical model presented in 'The interpretation of dreams'.

> Nevertheless, I consider it expedient and justifiable to continue to make use of the figurative image of the two systems. We can avoid any possible abuse of this method of representation by recollecting that ideas, thoughts and psychical structures in general must never be regarded as localised in organic elements of the nervous system but rather, as one might say, *between* them, where resistances and facilitations [*Bahnungen*] provide the corresponding correlates. Everything that can be an object of our internal perception is *virtual* (Freud, 1900: 611).

Freud makes it quite clear in subsequent passages that his critique of localizationism rests on philosophical rather than neuroscientific grounds.

> I am well aware that the writers whose views I am opposing here cannot have been guilty of thoughtless mistakes in their scientific approach. They obviously mean only that the physiological modification of the nerve fibre through sensory stimuli produces another modification in the central nerve cells which then becomes the physiological correlate of the "concept" or "idea". As they know a lot more about ideas than of the physiological modifications, which are still undefined and unknown, they use the elliptic phrase: an idea is localized in the nerve cell. Yet this substitution at once leads to a confusion of the two processes which need have nothing in common with each other. In psychology the simple idea is to us something elementary which we can clearly differentiate from its connection with other ideas. This is why we are tempted to assume that its physiological correlate, i.e., the modification of the nerve cells which originates from the stimulation of the nerve fibres, be also something simple and localizable (55-56).[89]

Both Freud and Jackson commit a philosophical error, which makes their sophisticated anti-localizationism seem to entail a form of dualism. Rather than consistently differentiating between psychological and neuroscientific descriptions of events, as Davidson would do many decades later,[90] Freud and Jackson take psychological and neuroscientific descriptions to refer to correspondingly separate items. Intensional distinctions are confused with extensional distinctions. Because neuroscientific and psychological descriptions are, plausibly, regarded as irreducibly distinct and hence parts of distinct typologies, Freud and Jackson take them to refer to two ontologically distinct types of event.

> The relationship between the chain of physiological events in the nervous system and the mental processes is probably not one of cause and effect. The former do not cease when the latter set in; they tend to continue, but, from a certain moment, a mental phenomenon corresponds to each part of the chain, or to several parts. The psychic is, therefore, a process parallel to the physiological, "a dependent concomitant" (55).

As Macmillan (1991) has noted, this frequently quoted passage displays greater unease with classical dualism than comparable passages in Jackson's own works. Rather than being prepared to endorse a neo-Leibnizian 'two clock' theory, Freud emphasizes the dependence of mental upon neural processes. This view, taken in conjunction with his denial of any causal relation between brain and mind, caused him considerably difficulty.[91]

> What then is the physiological correlate of the simple idea emerging or re-emerging? Obviously nothing static, but something in the nature of a process. This process is not incompatible with localization. It starts at a specific point in the cortex and along certain pathways. When this event has taken place it leaves behind a modification, with the possibility of a memory, in the part of the cortex affected. It is very doubtful whether this physiological event is in any way associated with something psychic. Our consciousness contains nothing that would, from the psychological point of view, justify the term "latent memory image". Yet whenever the same cortical state is elicited again, the previous psychic event emerges as a memory.[92]

The neural state corresponding, somehow, to a memory is claimed to evoke that memory without causing it. The neural state is not in itself mental: it is just a disposition for a memory. Nevertheless, the memory cannot be described as being realized by means of the neural state, as neural and mental items are regarded as entirely distinct from one another. Freud must have been aware of his failure to provide a coherent description of the mind-brain relationship, and his notion of dependent concomitance seems incompatible both with notions of causal dependence and with concepts of the neural instantiation of mental items.

It has been claimed that Freud retained a Jacksonian orientation throughout the remainder of his career (Solms & Saling, 1986). The fact that Freud shifted from ontological dualism to materialism, and that this involved the attribution of mental properties to neural states (in the context of the Continuity argument) shows this claim to be false if understood philosophically. On the neuroscientific dimension, Sacks (1998) holds that Freud's dynamic neuroscience:

> Goes beyond Jackson when he implies that there are no autonomous, isolable centers in the brain, but, rather systems for achieving cognitive goals – systems which have many components, and which can be created or greatly modified by the experiences of the individual (15).

Notwithstanding these caveats, it seems that Jackson's methodological dualism, his neuroscientifically grounded anti-localizationism and his sensitivity to the problems attendant upon the mixing of neuroscientific with psychological vocabularies all had a lasting influence on Freud's work.

VIII

FREUD'S THEORY OF CONSCIOUSNESS

Freud wrote comparatively little about consciousness explicitly and seems to have been dissatisfied with his thoughts on the topic.[93] Furthermore, his most sustained discussion on the topic of consciousness dates from early in his career, leading to uncertainty about how faithful he remained to these ideas during his more mature years. These difficulties are compounded by the fact that two of the early sources - the 'Project' and the letters to Fliess - were never intended for publication.

In 1915 Freud wrote an essay entirely devoted to the subject of consciousness. The paper was one of six metapsychological essays which were never published, and it is presumed to have been destroyed. Silverstein (1986) writes that:

> We know that Freud was not happy with the consciousness essay from the start. When on 1 August, 1915 he told Abraham that he had completed all twelve essays, and called them "war-time atrocities," he also told him "Several, including that on consciousness, still require thorough revision." In "The unconscious" (1915a) Freud repeatedly recognized the need to answer questions about the nature of consciousness and the mode of functioning of the system *Cs.*, but always postponed the discussion for a later time, probably intending to deal with the issues in the "Consciousness" essay (181).

Silverstein goes on to speculate that:

> We can never know for certain why Freud decided not to publish any of the remaining essays of the metapsychology series. Based on their titles,[94] however, we can offer an educated guess concerning some of them. Several of the essays forced Freud to wrestle with the enigma of consciousness and the problem of mind-body interaction, issues that had perplexed him throughout his career. He probably pursued some ideas related to the mind-body dilemma as far as he could in trying to clarify obscure theoretical issues, but found no solution that satisfied him (181).[95]

As we shall see, Freud understood consciousness as similar to an internal sense organ taking mental processes as its objects.[96] This general concept of consciousness was described in Locke's Essay Concerning

Human Understanding (which Freud possessed) and was particularly emphasized by Brentano, who may have been Freud's proximate source (1874).

CONSCIOUSNESS IN THE 'PROJECT FOR A SCIENTIFIC PSYCHOLOGY'

In the preceding chapter I have described how Freud's research into aphasiology led to his adopting a basically Jacksonian philosophical position. In the years following *On Aphasia*, Freud's interests moved to the study of hysteria. There was considerable continuity between this development and his earlier neuroscientific work. Freud's neuroscientific reputation rested largely on his work on the hemiplegias, which formed a natural bridge to the study of hysterical paralyses. Concerns about the mind-body relationship that were so salient in Jackson's work were even more so in the study of hysteria. Finally, the dynamic, functional and physiological approach to the brain which Freud advocated was clearly suited for the study and explanation of hysteria, a disorder which could not be understood in terms of neuroanatomical lesions.

I have already described how Freud's writing of his chapter on psychotherapy for 'Studies on hysteria' impelled him to re-assess his psychological views and how this re-assessment resulted in the composition of the 'Project for a scientific psychology' or, as Freud himself called it, 'Psychology for neurologists'.

THE PURPOSE OF THE 'PROJECT'

The 'Project' was Freud's first and most elaborate physicalist model of the mind; (his account of the 'speech apparatus' in *On Aphasia* is scarcely comprehensive enough to merit this designation). He hoped to use the model to explain both features of normal psychology (e.g., memory) as well as those features of abnormal psychology with which he was concerned. In addition to this, Freud specified three explanatory constraints that he believed any such model must satisfy. An adequate model of the mind must (1) give an account of the neural processes responsible for mental events, (2) give a naturalistic account of our capacity for conscious thought and experience and (3) explain why it is that consciousness is not directly aware of its own physical basis.

It is apparent from the way that Freud formulated his three criteria that his philosophical horizons had considerably altered. It is immediately clear that distinguished between intentionality and consciousness (the explanation of mental events as such is distinguished from the explanation of conscious mental events), began to problematize consciousness rather than simply take it for granted and, in light of this, called into question the validity of introspective research. That neural processes as such are beyond the reach of any possible introspection shows that mental events under neural descriptions are intrinsically unconscious.

> We at once become clear about a postulate that has been guiding us up to now. We have been treating psychical processes as something that could dispense with this awareness through consciousness, as something that exists independently of such awareness. We are prepared to find that some of our assumptions are not confirmed through consciousness. If we do not let ourselves be confused on that account, it follows, from the postulate of consciousness providing neither complete nor trustworthy knowledge of the neuronal processes, that these are in the first instance to be regarded to their whole extent as unconscious and are to be inferred like other natural things (308).[97]

Although Freud's project is couched in neurophysiological language, it is unlikely that he regarded it as a reductive psychophysiological account. Rather - as was the case with his later metapsychology - Freud seems to have been attempting to describe a functional psychological model, drawing as much as possible upon neuroscientific language with a view to effecting such a reduction at some future date. The inconsistencies between the principles invoked by Freud in the 'Project' and the neuroscientific knowledge of the time (in which Freud was steeped) have been pointed out by Mancia (1983) and Solms and Saling (1986). In this respect, Freud's blatant and extreme localizationism in the 'Project' - his identification of mental representations with individual neurons, which flies in the face of the sophisticated anti-localizationist position that he had advanced four years previously in the aphasia book - does not amount to a retreat into neuroanatomical localizationism. Rather, the neurons of the 'Project' should probably be understood as functional entities that might have been represented as neural assemblies with no loss of meaning.

THE ARCHITECTURE OF MIND IN THE 'PROJECT'

What does Freud mean by 'consciousness'? In the main, he identifies consciousness with 'psychical qualities' (qualia). In Block's (1995) terminology, Freud is talking about phenomenal consciousness.

Freud holds that qualities are 'different' from one another. By 'different' Freud apparently means something like incommensurable - of a different order. The quality 'green' is incommensurable with, say, the quality 'pain'. The distinction between such qualities cannot on the face of it be explained by invoking some purely quantitative distinction; 'green' is neither more nor less than 'pain'). As Freud says, 'Within this difference there are series, similarities and so on but there are in fact no quantities in it' (308). He further asserts that qualities are individuated on the basis of their relationship with the external world, and that qualities inhere to sensations.

Consciousness - the experience of quality - is caused by the activation of a special system within the central nervous system which Freud calls ω which 'consists of contrivances for transforming external quantity into quality'. Consciousness is just the activation of ω. Thus 'consciousness is the subjective side of one part of the psychical processes in the nervous system' (1950: 311).[98] I will adopt Natsoulas' (1984) term 'intrinsic consciousness' for Freud's conception of consciousness as just the experience of sensory qualities.

The ω system abuts two other neural systems: ϕ and ψ. The sensory input system, which conveys to the mind stimulation from the external world, is called ϕ. The ϕ neurons must be easily permeable to psychical energy; that is, the passage of excitement or, to use more contemporary language, 'information' must leave no permanent modifications in them. The content-bearing processing and memory system is called ψ.[99] Passage of information through this system must leave behind modifications in the (synaptic) connections between neurons in order for memory traces to be laid down, a process now known as Hebbian learning (Sacks, 1998). Freud conceived of the flow of information within the brain as a moving electrical quantity, as the phenomenon of local polarization/depolarization was not yet understood by neurophysiologists (Guttman, 1998; Linke, 1998). The activation of ω by ϕ results in raw sensation (intrinsic consciousness), whereas its activation by ψ produces consciousness of a mental content.[100] Natsoulas calls the latter 'derived consciousness' for reasons that will shortly become clear.

Only sensations are intrinsically conscious. Sensations may arise from items in the world or from the body itself; (affect is a case of the latter). Freud assumes that it is the frequency ('period') of neural excitations that gives rise to qualities.[101] The sense organs are described as transducers that are selectively sensitive to particular input frequencies. These must then produce specific neural frequencies that co-vary with the received frequencies. This information passes through the input system, and the cognitive processing/memory system until it finally reaches the consciousness-producing system. Freud admits that he is unable to explain the mechanism by means of which the arousal of the ω neurons gives rise to consciousness.

In addition to the sensory qualities described above, intrinsic consciousness also exhibits a second set of qualities: 'the series of sensations of pleasure and unpleasure' (312). Freud suggests that the sensations of unpleasure and pleasure correspond respectively to the increase and decrease of arousal in the ω system. Sensory discriminations are eroded by the extremes of unpleasure or pleasure.

Although ω is clearly demarcated from ϕ, consciousness has a special role to play in the process of perception. As we have already seen, sensory information passes through transducers into the input system and excites the consciousness-producing system (producing perceived sensory qualities). According to Freud, each excitation produces a discharge from the consciousness-producing system which serves as an 'indication of reality' (an indication that the source of the stimulus is a perception rather than a thought). Indications of reality are also termed 'indications of quality' because the experience of sensory qualities is the normal subjective index for distinguishing reality from recollection. Why is it that input enervations from the external world produce indications of quality while enervations (transmitted by the cognitive processing system) from the interior of the body do not? Freud's answer is quantitative: input pathways can carry great quantities of excitation, while processing pathways are subject to inhibitions imposed by a functional unit of this system, which Freud calls the 'ego' ('*das Ich*').

The main function of the ego is to ensure adaptation to the environment. Accordingly, it strives to ensure that endogenous stimuli such as the pressure of biological drives do not impinge upon the consciousness-producing system in such large quantities that they produce indications of quality (i.e., that they do not give rise to hallucinations).

> It is accordingly inhibition by the ego which makes possible a criterion for distinguishing between perception and memory. Biological experience will then teach that discharge is not to be initiated till the indication of reality has arrived, and that with this in view the cathexis of the desired memories is not to be carried beyond a certain amount (326).

As well as inhibiting discharge from ψ, which would overwhelm ω with hallucinations, the ego deploys the function of attention. Freud defines the 'hypercathexis' of attention as the deployment of heightened (unconscious) activity towards significant content signaled by its expression as a corresponding qualitative event in ω. Consciousness thus serves to focus the cognitive capacities in ψ.

According to the 1895 model consciousness is essentially passive.[102] Thinking is a function of ψ and as such is intrinsically unconscious. But how do such mental items become conscious? For Freud, mental representations do not themselves become conscious. Rather, they terminate in conscious events (bring about the stimulation of ω).

LANGUAGE AND CONSCIOUSNESS

If a mental item can only enter consciousness by evoking some sensory quality with which it corresponds or co-varies in some rule-governed manner, how can an abstract mental item possessing no intrinsically sensory qualities ever enter consciousness? Freud finds an answer in mental representations of phonemes.

> This purpose is fulfilled by speech association. This consists in the linking of ψ neurones with neurones which serve sound-presentations and themselves have the closest association with motor speech-images.... In any case, from the sound-image the excitation reaches the word-image and from it reaches discharge (365).[103]

The 'indications of speech-discharge':

> Put thought-processes on a level with perceptual processes, lend them reality and make memory of them possible [i.e., make it possible to recollect thought-processes] (366).

'Word-presentations' are activated representations of the words of a natural language, which have been acquired by means of learning ('verbal residues').[104] Certainly, mental items are normally associated with the physical process of speaking (including writing, sign-language and so on), but how is it that verbal memories can lend consciousness to thoughts? To put it differently, how can the representation of a linguistic item - stored in ψ - become conscious? Freud bases his answer on a special connection between mental representation of words and the act of speaking.

Freud states that the predecessor of verbalization initially functions as a mode of discharge. The unhappy infant cries and screams. Crying and screaming are typical modes of discharge during the period before the infant has developed the cognitive and motor capacities enabling it to perform intentional actions ('specific action') to secure satisfaction. This mode of discharge also has the function of drawing the attention of the caretaker (who, as Freud notes, is usually the wished-for object itself). The discharge process therefore takes on a communicative function: the originally automatic, unintentional process of discharge becomes an intentional ('specific') action. Freud believed that the mind has a natural tendency to turn away from those representations of experiences that give rise to pain. The association of painful memories with the intense enervations of screaming and crying assists in making painful memories conscious: 'the information of one's own scream serves to characterize the object' (367). On other occasions we are spoken to by others. Freud believes that infants have an innate disposition to imitate others, and that the representations of sounds heard, which are associated with particular experiences, readily flow over into attempts to imitate these sounds: 'it is possible to find the information of movement attaching to this sound image' (367).

Although thoughts become conscious by means of association with motor impulses to produce words and sentences, this theory also proposes something like a 'language of thought' hypothesis to explain events occurring earlier in the cognitive sequence.

> The perceptual complex...can be dissected into a component portion, neurone a, which on the whole remains the same...and a second component portion, neurone b, which for the most part varies. Language will later apply the term judgement to this dissection and will call neurone a the thing and neurone b...its predicate (328).

In performing a judgement concerning another person, the object term is understood by means of recognizing the similarity between one's own person and the other person (identification). The predicate term, on the other hand, is reached through a process of imitation. It is only by imitating the behavior of one's parents and then assimilating these imitations to memories of one's own experiences that one can come to understand their attributes.[105] It is the process of imitation in judgement which leads to the laying-down of the first motor speech patterns that give thinking access to consciousness. The 'indications of speech' are, by virtue of being motor impulses, able to affect the ω-system and yield muted indications of quality. Thinking does not always give rise to indications of quality - this normally occurs only at certain points in a cognitive sequence.

> This process of thought is in fact the far more frequent, without being abnormal; it is our ordinary thought, unconscious with occasional intrusions ["*Einfalle*"] into consciousness - what is known as conscious thought with unconscious intermediate links, though these can be made conscious (373).[106]

The indications of speech are also called the 'indications of thought-reality'. These provide the 'securest form of cognitive thought-process' (p. 374). However, this is not the only way that thoughts can become conscious (375). Representations of objects can become conscious as quasi-pictorial analog representations, but such modes of representation cannot capture the logical operations required for cognition.

NATSOULAS' 'MEANINGLESS WORDS' PROBLEM

Natsoulas (1985) has identified a problem with the 1895 theory of consciousness that seems to have been entirely ignored by other writers. Natsoulas writes that:

> If the contents of consciousness are cognitive and not purely sensory or qualitative, would they not require an underlying cognitive structure, where they are located, a structure that is susceptible to modification by previous occurrences of conscious psychical processes? That is, the cognitive requires more than a patterning of qualities, more than the experience of a sensory gestalt (202).

How does the verbal indexing of unconscious thinking result in meaningful conscious thought? How is meaning carried over from unconscious to conscious thought? Why is it that the process of becoming conscious does not strip a mental item of its cognitive content?

Natsoulas approaches this problem by inquiring in the first instance into the difference between hearing meaningful speech and hearing meaningless speech-sounds. Following Freud, he states that in the latter case there must be some link between items in ω and corresponding items in ψ. It is only when links between ω and ψ are in some sense severed that the meaningless-sound phenomenon could occur.[107]

> What can we call on, out of Freud's theory, to render conscious psychical processes meaningful? We need to give a less restrictive interpretation to the thesis that consciousness gives only qualities. Moreover, we need to conceive of the psychical processes of the perception-consciousness system in such a way that the "conscious representative" of an unconscious psychical process can immediately seem to the person who has it to be an assertion of a kind (205).

Apart from these rather general remarks, Natsoulas does not appear to provide a solution to the meaningless words problem.

Natsoulas may have experienced difficulty resolving the meaningless words problem because the problem itself is misconceived. As a first step towards understanding how preconscious word-presentations can possess meaning, one should address the more fundamental question of how it is that unconscious mental representations can possess meaning. Natsoulas seems to regard the answer to this problem as self-evident but, of course, the question of how we can naturalistically account for the intentionality of any mental item is a major philosophical problem. The problem as it applies to word-presentations is no more mysterious than it is in connection with unconscious representations.

Natsoulas' central question is 'How can a mere patterning of sensations, caused by some meaningful unconscious item, inherit its meaning?' Let us assume for the sake of argument that the explanation of how an unconscious item can possess meaning is unproblematic or irrelevant. Further, let us follow Freud in assuming that the conscious state inherits its intentionality from the unconscious item that has brought it about. We are still free to claim that the conscious state acquires its meaning by virtue of inheriting the causal role proper to its corresponding unconscious item. This general approach is not limited to causal role semantics. Any naturalistic semantics must explain meaning by adverting to objective features of cognitive systems. If intentionality is an objectively explicable feature of unconscious mental items, there is no obvious objection to claiming that this objective property is transmitted to patterns of sensation caused by the unconscious item in question. Meaning is thus causally transmitted.

THEORETICAL REVISIONS IN THE FLIESS CORRESPONDENCE

In a letter to Wilhelm Fliess dated 1 January 1896 Freud (1887-1904) revises the scheme presented in the 'Project'. In this version, the input system transmits only quality to the processing system (without affecting its quantitative level of excitation), whereas the segments of the processing system terminating at the interior of the organism transmit quantity only. The consciousness-producing system is a modified part of the input system capable of receiving little quantitative cathexis. The consciousness-producing system is no longer seen as discharging quantity into the processing system. Instead, the ω neurons, when aroused, indicate the pathways to be taken by the processing system.

These thoughts lead Freud to the following consolidation of his model of the mind:

> According to this view the perceptual processes would *eo ipso* involve consciousness and would only produce their further psychic effects after becoming conscious. The ψ processes themselves would be unconscious and would only subsequently acquire a secondary, artificial consciousness through being linked with processes of discharge and perception (speech association) (160).

In a letter of 6 December Freud returned to his model, this time substituting psychological for neurological terms. The ϕ neurons of the 'Project' are re-christened '*Wahrnehmung*en' ('perceptions') - perceptual neurons which are not modified by the passage of information through them. The information passing through the perceptual system towards consciousness is then analyzed by three more systems. The first of these, '*Wahrnehmung*zeichen' (indications of perception), arranges information in terms of associations by simultaneity. The next one, '*Unbewusstsein*' (unconsciousness), arranges information in terms of causal and conceptual relations. The information stored in each of these systems has no direct access to consciousness. Finally, '*Vorbewusstsein*' (preconsciousness):

> Is the third transcription, attached to word presentation and corresponding to our official ego. The cathexes proceeding from this Vb [*Vorbewusstsein*] become conscious according to certain rules, and this secondary thought consciousness is subsequent in time and is probably linked to the hallucinatory activation of word presentations, so that neurones of consciousness would once again be perceptual neurones and in themselves without memory (208).

In the 6 December 1896 model, unconscious mental processing is both preceded and followed by episodes of consciousness. Freud states explicitly that consciousness 'attaches' to '*Wahrnehmung*'. Presumably he understood this to consist of uninterpreted raw sensations which are then subjected to cognitive processing before emerging into '*Bewusstsein*' as interpreted sensory experience. This would explain why '*Bewusstsein*' is described as 'secondary thought consciousness'.

CONSCIOUSNESS IN THE INTERPRETATION OF DREAMS

Freud represents the mind in 'The interpretation of dreams' (1900 as 'a compound instrument, to the components of which we will give the name of "agencies" ["*Instanzen*"], or..."systems" (537). Information enters the apparatus through a perceptual terminal (the ϕ neurons in the earlier model) which remains unmodified by the passage of information. The cognitive function of the perceptual system is to transmit information to an array of memory systems (ψ neurons in the earlier model). Memory systems are by definition modified by the passage of information through them. The first of these '*Wahrnemungzeichen*' in the letter of 6 December) 'will naturally contain the record of association in respect to simultaneity in time' (539). In the subsequent systems, 'the same perceptual material will be arranged...in respect to other kinds of coincidence' (Ibid.).

In accord with earlier formulations, it is the perceptual system which provides consciousness 'with the whole multiplicity of sensory qualities' (Ibid.). Information stored in the memory systems is in itself unconscious. Memories can become conscious, but this makes no difference to their causal role within the apparatus. When memories become conscious, they exhibit little sensory quality in comparison with the qualities delivered by perception.

Normally, information propagates through the apparatus from the perceptual terminal and then the memory systems towards discharge through the motor terminal. However, information must pass through a filtering system called 'the unconscious' before motor discharge. Freud does not describe this system as a memory system, as he does in the Fliess correspondence, although this possibility is not ruled out. The system unconscious rather submits information to criticism. After passing through the unconscious, information enters the system preconscious, which 'holds the key to voluntary movement' (541) and hence, extrapolating from the 'Project', consciousness. Although the emphasis is rather different, the censoring function of the system unconscious as described in the dream book clearly presupposes the cognitive attributes of system '*Unbewusst*' described in the letter to Fliess, as the capacity for censorship is dependent upon the capacity to bring mental items under concepts.

According to the schematic diagrams presented in 'The interpretation of dreams' the perceptual system abuts the memory systems rather than feeding directly into *Cs*. However, this is misleading and does not cohere with Freud's discussion of his model of the mind included in the same text. Freud apparently did not recognize this for many years, as it is not until the 1919 edition that we find the following footnote.

> If we attempt to proceed further with this schematic picture, in which the systems are set out in linear succession, we should have to reckon with the fact that the system next beyond the *Pcs.* is the one to which consciousness must be ascribed - in other words *Pcpt.* = *Cs.* (541).

So it is clear that Freud meant to retain his thesis that perceptual information always passes through consciousness in an uninterpreted form prior to cognitive processing and to its emergence into consciousness in an interpreted form. This is why he described hallucination as caused by a reverse flow of excitement from the memory systems to the perceptual system. Freud's condensation of the perceptual and consciousness-producing systems is explicable with reference to the view, introduced in the 1 January 1896 letter, that the consciousness-producing system is a functional unit of the perceptual system.

Freud emphasizes that we should not imagine that the preconscious and unconscious systems are identical to anatomical structures within the central nervous system: they are best understood as functional units or systems. Furthermore, mental representations do not pass from one system to the other. Instead we must imagine a mental content standing in some relation to one or the other of these functional units. To take a leaf from Fodor, an idea can be in the unconscious 'box' or the preconscious 'box'.

The unconscious system is more comprehensive than the preconscious system and the conscious system, for all preconscious and conscious items were once unconscious.

> The unconscious is the larger sphere, which includes within it the smaller sphere of the conscious. Everything conscious has an unconscious preliminary stage; whereas what is unconscious may remain at that stage (612 - 613).

The 'unconscious preliminary stage' must, in the case of perceptions, be taken as the stage of unconscious processing prior to the emergence into consciousness of the processed information.

Consciousness is defined as a sense organ for the perception of qualities and is a function of a unit of the mind which Freud now terms the conscious system (*Cs.*). *Cs.* is affected by the passage of information which yields qualities without suffering permanent modification by it; (it has no memory). In this respect the *Cs.* resembles the perceptual system. Also, whereas the perceptual system receives information impinging on the sense-receptors, *Cs.* receives output from the cognitive processing units. *Cs.* receives information, via both the processing units from the 'interior of the apparatus' and the perceptual system.

A descriptively unconscious item becomes conscious by acquiring quality. This is effected by the formation of links with verbal memories.

A CONCEPT OF UNCONSCIOUS PERCEPTION (1910-1915)

There is little documentary evidence concerning Freud's view of consciousness between publication of 'The interpretation of dreams' (1900) and his paper on 'The unconscious' (1915a). One such document is Freud's brief paper on 'The psycho-analytic view of psychogenic disturbance of vision' (1910b). In this paper Freud discusses the phenomena of hysterical and hypnotically induced blindness. He states that:

> Appropriate experiments have shown that people who are hysterically blind do nevertheless see in some sense....Thus hysterically blind people are only blind as far as consciousness is concerned; in their unconscious they see (212).

This sounds like a new departure implying that perceptual information does not have to cross consciousness. Freud may be asserting that it is only after cognitive processing has taken place that a mental content becomes conscious.

In 'Formulations on the two principles of mental functioning' (1911), Freud once again describes consciousness as 'attached' to the sense organs. He retains the view that thought, as distinct from perception, is essentially unconscious and only becomes conscious through connection with 'verbal residues'. A year later in 'A note on the unconscious in psycho-analysis' (1912a), he states that:

> The...most probable theory which can be formulated at this stage of our knowledge is the following. Unconsciousness is a regular and inevitable phase in the processes constituting our psychical activity; every psychical act begins as an unconscious one, and it may either remain so or continue developing into consciousness (264).

If perception is construed as a 'psychical activity', which surely it must be, then Freud is continuing with the innovation apparently first mooted in 1910, i.e., that perceptual information is transmitted to the unconscious cognitive processors without first passing through consciousness.

Finally, in 'The unconscious' (1915a), Freud describes the relationship between unconscious and conscious mentation in terms reminiscent of the passage from 1912 reproduced above.

> Proceeding now to an account of the positive findings of psycho-analysis, we may say that in general a psychical act goes through two phases as regards its state...In the first phase the psychical act is unconscious and belongs to the system *Ucs.* (173).[108]

The 'psychical act' must pass through a filter - in Freud's terminology, 'censorship' or 'testing' - before becoming part of system *Cs.*, an abbreviation that Freud uses here for the preconscious part of the mind. It seems confusing to designate the preconscious sector of the mind as *Cs.* An examination of the context reveals that Freud himself was uncertain or confused.

> If, however, it [a mental item] passes this testing it enters the second phase and thenceforth belongs to the second system, which we will call the system *Cs.* But the fact that it belongs to that system does not yet unequivocally determine its relation to consciousness. It is not yet conscious but it is certainly capable of becoming conscious (to use Breuer's expression) - that is, it can now, given certain conditions, become an object of consciousness without any special resistance. In consideration of this capacity for becoming conscious we also call the system *Cs.* the 'preconscious'. If it should turn out that a certain censorship also plays a part in determining whether the preconscious becomes conscious, we shall discriminate more sharply between the systems *Pcs.* and *Cs.* For the present let it suffice us to bear in mind that the system *Pcs.* shares the characteristics of the system *Cs.* and that the rigorous censorship exercises its office at the point of transition from the *Ucs.* to the *Pcs.* (or *Cs.*) (173).

Why the equivocation over the 'two (or three) psychical systems' (Ibid.)? Freud seems to want to reserve the term 'system' to designate cognitive systems. The old consciousness-producing (ω) system had no strictly cognitive function. Freud continues, in the same paper, to fudge the distinction between *Cs.* and *Pcs.* He refers, for example, to 'the system *Cs.* (*Pcs.*)' (179, 194).

RETURN TO THE FIRST THEORY (1917-1921)

In 'A metapsychological supplement to the theory of dreams', which was written shortly after 'The unconscious' but not published until 1917, Freud returns to the issue of demarcating system *Cs.* from system *Pcs.*

> The answer can be given if we now proceed to define more precisely the third of our psychical systems, the system *Cs.*, which hitherto we have not sharply distinguished

> from the *Pcs*. In 'The interpretation of dreams' we were already led to a decision to regard conscious perception as the function of a special system, to which we ascribed certain curious properties, and to which we shall now have good grounds for attributing other characteristics as well. We may regard this system, which is there called *Pcpt.*, as coinciding with the system *Cs.*, on whose activity becoming conscious usually depends (1917b:232).

With respect, then, to the relationship between consciousness and perception Freud has now returned to his earlier position. As we read on, however, we discover differences between this position and its antecedents. The conscious system is not a passive 'read-out' device. Like the *Cs.*(*Pcs.*) system of earlier papers, the conscious system of 1917 controls motility. It 'must have at its disposal a motor enervation which determines whether the perception can be made to disappear or whether it proves resistant [i.e., the mechanism of reality-testing]' (233). Freud then says that reality testing is 'among the major institutions of the ego' (Ibid.). This shows that Freud is treating the ego very differently than he had in the 'Project', where it was seen as a descriptively unconscious functional unit of the cognitive processing (ψ) system. However, inconsistently, he states in the next paragraph that in cases of amentia 'the ego...withdraws the cathexis from the system of perceptions, Cs.' (Ibid.), once again differentiating the ego from the conscious system. In 'A difficulty in the path of psycho-analysis' (1917a), Freud describes introspective consciousness as a form of 'inner perception' (141) and talks of the consciousness-producing system as a component of the ego.

Freud returns to these and related matters in section four of 'Beyond the pleasure principle' (1920). Here he describes consciousness as a function of system *Cs.* Because consciousness registers information from within the body and from the external world, *Cs.* must be located at the borderline between inner and outer and, anatomically speaking, is probably identical to some portion of the cerebral cortex. Information ('excitatory processes') impinging upon consciousness leave no permanent traces in *Cs.*, as consciousness must always be fresh for the receipt of new information. The sensory receptors, which convey information to *Cs.* from the external world, are devices which both take samples[109] of external stimuli for cognitive processing, and provide a barrier against the extremely intense stimuli impinging upon the organism from the external world. Freud also advances the thesis - which he states in a rather diffident and sketchy manner - that Kant's notion of temporality is not applicable to unconscious mental contents:

> As a result of certain psycho-analytic discoveries, we are today in a position to embark on a discussion of the Kantian theorem that time and space are "necessary forms of thought". We have learned that unconscious mental processes are in themselves "timeless"...On the other hand our abstract idea of time seems to be wholly derived from the method of working of the system *Pcpt.-Cs.* and to correspond to a perception on its own part of that method of working (28).

The admission of sensory information into consciousness provides the basis for the conscious intuition of temporality.

The mind has no such direct stimulus barrier operating against endogenous stimuli, because these are normally of far less intensity than exogenous stimuli. In order to protect itself against excessive quantities of internal stimulation ('unpleasure'), the mind has a tendency to treat endogenous stimulation as though it were exogenous, and in that way bring the stimulus barrier to bear upon it, (e.g., the psychological defence mechanism of 'projection').

In 'Psycho-analysis and telepathy' (1941) (written in 1921 but not published until 1941) and 'Dreams and telepathy' (1922), Freud is once again inclined towards the view that information may be unconsciously processed before becoming conscious. He suggests that the telepathic reception of thoughts may come about unconsciously, and that both preconscious and unconscious mental contents can be transmitted in this manner.

FURTHER REFLECTIONS ON LANGUAGE AND CONSCIOUSNESS (1923)

After the vacillation and uncertainty of the preceding years, Freud once again tackles the problem of consciousness in a focal and sustained fashion in 'The ego and the id' (1923b). Freud begins his discussion with a consideration of the question 'What do we mean when we say that a mental item becomes conscious?' Consciousness is described as laying at the 'surface' of the mental apparatus. Freud says explicitly that he means this in both a functional and an anatomical sense. Consciousness is a property of 'a system which is spatially the first one reached from the external world....' (1923:19), and 'All perceptions which are received from without (sense-perceptions) and from within - what we call sensations and feelings - are *Cs.* from the start' (ibid.). In other words, Freud once again returns to his earliest account of the relationship between consciousness and perception. What about what we 'roughly and inexactly' (Ibid.) call thought processes? Thinking is in the first instance unconscious. How does it become conscious? Does consciousness somehow extend itself to the unconscious thoughts, or do the unconscious thoughts somehow make their way into consciousness? 'Both of these possibilities,' writes Freud, 'are equally unimaginable; there must be a third alternative' (Ibid.).

Freud goes on to reiterate the view that the essential distinction between *Ucs.* and *Pcs.* items is that the latter are brought into connection with mental representations of words. Given this, we might ask the question 'How does an unconscious item become preconscious?' as a precursor of, if not a substitute for, our original question. The answer suggested is that unconscious items become preconscious by becoming linguistically indexed.

> These word-presentations are residues of memories; they were at one time perceptions, and like all mnemic residues they can become conscious again. Before we concern ourselves further with their nature, it dawns upon us like a new discovery that only something that has been a *Cs.* perception can become conscious, and that anything arising from within (apart from feelings) that seeks to become conscious must try to transform itself into a perception: this becomes possible through memory-traces (20).

Items recorded in memory are stored in systems adjacent to consciousness-perception. Memories therefore readily assume a measure of sensory intensity, sometimes so intensely that they take on hallucinatory vividness. Memories of auditory phenomena (sentences) for the basis of conscious thinking, because (as Freud pointed out in the 'Project') language is specifically suited to express the syntactic properties of (unconscious) information processing. Of course, one can 'think in pictures', but this sort of thinking is limited to the representation of concrete objects and is unable to capture abstractions and relations. The psychoanalytic process, then, which seeks to make unconscious items conscious, must do so by supplying appropriate verbal links.

What about (by definition, conscious) feelings of pleasure and unpleasure? Freud repeats the view expressed in the 'Project' that pleasure and unpleasure are identical to the diminution and increase of excitement respectively. Sensations of pleasure and unpleasure seem to possess special properties for although they do not originate from outside the organism, they are not dependent upon any linkage with memory residues in order to become conscious: they seem somehow to be intrinsically conscious. This suggests the following question:

> Let us call what becomes conscious as pleasure and unpleasure a quantitative and qualitative "something" in the course of mental events; the question then is whether this 'something' can become conscious in the place where it is, or whether it must first be transmitted to the system *Pcpt.* (22).

Freud chooses the latter alternative. The neural state with which unpleasure is identical - that of tension beyond some unspecified threshold - only becomes a conscious experience of unpleasure to the extent that this state physically impinges upon the perceptual system. Freud thus goes on to remark that:

> We then come to speak, in a condensed and not entirely correct manner, of "unconscious feelings", keeping up an analogy with unconscious ideas which is not altogether justifiable. Actually the difference is that, whereas with *Ucs.* ideas connecting links must be created before they can be brought into the *Cs.*, with feelings, which are themselves transmitted directly, this does not occur. In other words: the distinction between *Cs.* and *Pcs.* has no meaning where feelings are concerned; the *Pcs.* here drops out - and feelings are either conscious or unconscious. Even when they are attached to word-presentations, their becoming conscious is not due to that circumstance, but they become so directly (22-23).

Implicitly, thoughts are representational items, whereas feelings are not. As representational items, thoughts must come into connection - must be 'mapped onto' - a sufficiently rich representational system that is also capable of evoking conscious experiences of qualities, (the precondition for an item entering consciousness). For Freud, as we have seen, linguistic representations fulfil these criteria. As feeling-states are not representations, at least in this sense of the word, they do not require a mediating representational system in order to impinge upon consciousness: their raw physiological impact is sufficient for this purpose. Freud thus regards thinking as intrinsically unconscious and only capable of becoming conscious in a derived manner, whereas feeling can enter consciousness without the benefit of mediation. As he had early on described repression as a failure of 'transcription' from the unconscious to the preconscious representational codes, it follows that unconscious ideas can be repressed, but affects - which do not require transcription - cannot be repressed. It is probably because of these considerations that Freud cautions the reader against too strict an analogy between unconscious feelings and unconscious thoughts. In both cases, though, mental items become conscious by producing sensory effects. These sensory effects are then processed by the perceptual system just as though they were inputs from the 'external' world.

> The part played by word-presentations now becomes perfectly clear. By their interposition internal thought-processes are made into perceptions. It is like a demonstration of the theorem that all knowledge has its origin in external perception. When a hypercathexis of the process of thinking takes place, thoughts are actually perceived - as if they came from without - and are consequently held to be true (23).

Freud does not seem to have modified his view of the nature of consciousness from 1923 until his death in 1939. Discussions of the subject in these later works merely reiterate aspects of the position given in 'The ego and the id'.

To summarize in broad outline the development of Freud's view of consciousness, we can say that Freud proposed two general concepts of the relationship between the perceptual system, cognitive system and consciousness-producing system. In one account perceptual information enters consciousness directly, and is thus intrinsically conscious. These 'raw feels' are then unconsciously processed to return to consciousness as interpreted percepts. In the other, incoming information is unconsciously analyzed before reaching consciousness. In both accounts Freud proposes a modular conception of consciousness. In addition, in both models consciousness is identified with sensation, and a sensory, propositionally ordered symbol system is required to enable thought to become conscious. This function is fulfilled by natural language. Thoughts are indexed to the motor representations of speech, which then cause afferent feedback along input channels to impinge upon the consciousness module in much the same way as perceptions. In Freud's view, consciousness is therefore distinct from intentionality.

Strictly speaking, mental contents never become conscious: they just produce conscious effects that express them. In contrast to thought, affect and sensation have no representational character and are intrinsically conscious.

IX

ANIMISM, REALISM AND ANTI-REALISM

The contemporary debate about the status of folk-psychology is a continuation and extension of criticisms of introspection offered by philosophers and psychologists earlier in the century. These efforts grew out of the failure of introspectionism to provide a basis for a scientific psychology. Boring (1933) and others advanced the view that far from yielding a pure and incorrigible account of mental states introspection delivers an 'interpreted' (theorized) picture.

The contemporary debate originated in Sellars' 'Empiricism and the philosophy of mind' (1956). Sellars, who offered his view in criticism of Ryle's dispositionalism, contended that folk-psychological items are theoretical because they explain behavior in the context of an implicit network of causal laws. The idea that folk-psychology is theoretical in nature made it easier to call the validity folk-psychological concepts into question. Quine's work on the indeterminacy of translation provided a powerful incentive for rejecting the view that folk-psychology could provide a basis for a science of psychology, for if it is true that the attribution of intentional states is holistic and normative, then there is little hope of situating intentional items within a network of strict laws.[110] Meanwhile Putnam (1975) launched his celebrated 'Twin Earth' thought experiment, which purported to show that atom-for-atom physical twins in identical brain states may, nonetheless, be in different intentional states, thus giving impetus to an externalist account of intentional states. Putnam's work suggested that a science of psychology could not advert to intentional states (see Schiffer, 1981), and that a science of psychology must confine itself to the consideration of those properties of mental states which cause other mental states (their 'formal' or 'syntactical' properties). Many philosophers have been unhappy with this highly constrained domain for psychology, and have attempted to legitimize a scientific niche for semantics.

Davidson (1970, 1973, 1974) decisively advanced the debate in the context of his ingenious argument on behalf of anomalous monism. For Davidson, intentional and neuroscientific accounts of mental phenomena are just alternative descriptions of the same events. Because mental and physicalisistic vocabularies are structured on the basis of divergent and irreconcilable constitutive principles, it is *a priori* impossible to frame strict causal laws linking mental events under physical descriptions with mental events under psychological descriptions. Furthermore, the holistic and normative character of mental description, their intrinsically rational structure, renders the framing of strictly psychological laws impossible. According to Davidson, mental events psychologically conceived are nonetheless token-identical to the neural events instantiating them.

Freud's view of the significance of folk-psychological concepts and terminology is aptly illustrated by means of a passage from 'The unconscious' (1915a).

> In psycho-analysis there is no choice for us but to assert that mental processes are in themselves unconscious, and to liken the perception of them by means of consciousness to the perception of the external world by means of the sense organs. We can even hope to gain fresh knowledge from the comparison. The psycho-analytic assumption of unconscious mental activity appears to us on the one hand, as a further expansion of the primitive animism which caused us to see copies of our own consciousness all around us, and on the other hand, as an extension of the corrections undertaken by Kant of our views on external perception. Just as Kant warned us not to overlook the fact that our perceptions are subjectively conditioned and must not be regarded as identical with what is perceived though unknowable, so psycho-analysis warns us not to equate perceptions by means of consciousness with the unconscious mental processes which are their object. Like the physical,[111] the psychical is not necessarily in reality what it appears to us to be (171).

Freud wrote in a similar spirit in 'The interpretation of dreams' (1900) that:

> The unconscious is the true psychical reality; in its innermost nature it is as much unknown to us as the reality of the external world, and it is as incompletely presented by the data of consciousness as is the external world by the communications of our sense organs (613).[112]

Freud draws on a Kantian theme in his discussion of the nature of the mind in order to make the point that the essence of the mental is something other than we naively take it to be. Freud neither makes use of nor endorses Kantian metaphysics. For instance, he rejects the Kantian claim that psychology cannot be a natural science (Kant, 1786). Instead, he employs a Kantian idiom to express the view that, despite appearances, mental items are constituted by neurophysiological states. The mental is 'in itself' physical. Freud often uses the locution 'in itself' ('*an sich*') when alluding to this idea. An example occurs in the 'Outline of psycho-analysis' (1940a).

> Whereas the psychology of consciousness never went beyond the broken sequences which were obviously dependent upon something else, the other view, which held that the psychical is unconscious in itself, enabled psychology to take its place as a natural science like any other. The processes with which it is concerned are in themselves just as unknowable as those dealt with by other sciences, by chemistry or physics, for example; but it is possible to establish the laws which they obey and to follow their mutual relations and dependences unbroken over long stretches - in short, to arrive at an "understanding" of the field of natural phenomena in question (158).

Here is another example, this time from 'A short account of psycho-analysis' (1924).

> From a philosophical standpoint this theory [psycho-analysis] was bound to adopt the view that the mental does not coincide with the conscious, that mental processes are in themselves unconscious and are only made conscious by the functioning of special organs (agencies or systems) (198).

Freud implicitly treats conscious and unconscious items as though they were Kantian phenomena and noumena.[113] Mental contents possess a neurophysiological ontology, and it is only by dint of the physical organization of our brains that these processes issue in conscious experiences. It is by virtue of its neurophysiological ontology that the sphere of the mental conforms to laws and a science of psychology is possible.

I take Freud to be asserting (1) that conscious mental events are causally dependent upon unconscious mental events,[114] (2) that we are directly conscious only of the effects of unconscious mental processes upon a particular neuropsychological system, (3) that we have no direct, non-inferential knowledge of the unconscious processes themselves, (4) that unconscious mental items are theoretical entities, (5) that causal relations between unconscious mental events instantiate laws, (6) that unconscious mental events issue in conscious mental events by dint of special neuropsychological processes, and that (7) only by virtue of an explanatory strategy adverting to unconscious mental events occurring within a nomologically-governed causal nexus, that scientific psychology is possible.

Although Freud does not discuss the issues of the nomologicity of the causal relations between conscious events and their unconscious causes, his claim that unconscious events are inferred from conscious events implies the existence of such nomologicity. Therefore (8) the causation of conscious mental events by unconscious mental events instantiates causal laws.

Freud's remarks about animism in 'The unconscious' (1915a) invite the question 'In what sense does the attribution of unconscious mental states resemble primitive animism?' Freud answers 'in seeing copies of our consciousness all around us' (171). Freud seems to be arguing that human beings possess an innate propensity for psychological attribution, a propensity expressed both in our false attributions of mentalistic properties to non-mental items and in our interpretations of human beings. Freud appears to describe this process in 'The unconscious' as projective: the attribution to others of those features of mentality that we perceive in ourselves, although elsewhere in the context of his discussions of the relationship between language and consciousness he implicitly appears to endorse a normative account. The normative thesis, which has been more recently advanced by Davidson and others, explains our propensity for psychological attribution in terms of our conceiving of both ourselves and others within the framework of a single conceptual scheme. In other words, when we attribute an unconscious mental state to a person, we (inappropriately, on the analogy with animism) conceive of the unconscious mental state as though it were a conscious mental state.[115]

According to Freud (1950), as folk-psychological explanations make no reference to neurophysiology and mental states possess a neurophysiological ontology, folk-psychology must be wrong. But why is it that folk-psychology seems to be true? Indeed, why is it so difficult to recognize the theoretical status of folk-psychology? Why is it that folk-psychological understandings appear to be the incorrigible results of direct access to our own mental states? Freud implicitly rather than explicitly answers these questions. I will attempt to unpack his explanation.

Recall that Freud believes that. in order for a thought to become conscious, it must get mapped on to sensory representations of sentences. In becoming conscious of our thoughts, we inevitably cast them in the mould of the ontological categories of our natural language. Our mental processes therefore seem to conform perfectly to folk-psychology. Folk-psychology just seems to describe how it is inside of us for the simple reason that its acceptance, through our acquisition of language, is the condition for becoming aware of inner processes. Of course, the falsity of folk-psychology is quite compatible with its usefulness. Freud (1950) routinely invoked Darwinian ('biological') explanations of mental phenomena in the 'Project'.[116] The idea that folk-psychological theory has proliferated because of its adaptive advantages - because it 'works' in ways that matter for survival and reproductive success - would be perfectly compatible with his thinking. One can (and Freud did) employ the folk-psychological idiom to take advantage of its amazing utility while maintaining an anti-realist line on folk-psychological items.

In the pages preceding his comment about animism, Freud was concerned with establishing the legitimacy of his theory of unconscious mental processes through an argument about 'other minds'. Although each of us has direct acquaintance only with our own mental states,[117] we 'infer' that other people also experience mental states by drawing 'an analogy from their observable utterances and actions, in order to make this behavior of theirs intelligible to us' and this capacity to project ourselves into the minds of others 'is a sine qua non of our understanding [of them]' (169).

> This inference...was formerly extended by the ego to other human beings, to animals, plants, inanimate objects and to the world at large.... Today, our critical judgement is already in doubt on the question of consciousness in animals; we refuse to admit it in plants and we regard the assumption of its existence in inanimate matter as mysticism (169).

We attribute mental states by analogy. I will assume that the projective approach outlined by Freud is underpinned by normative considerations; i.e., that, by virtue of one's (relative) rationality, one can derive content-ascriptions by means of imaginatively filling another person's shoes.

> If we do this, we must say: all the acts and manifestations which I notice in myself and do not know how to link up with the rest of my mental life must be judged as if they belonged to someone else: they are to be explained by a mental life ascribed to this other person (169).

This is Freud's justification for what I will call his 'methodological homunculism'. If, in our rationality-maximizing interpretations of our own mental processes, certain events do not fit the pattern, we have license to apply principles of charity to these 'leftovers' and thereby posit and attribute propositional attitudes to intrapsychic homunculi. My choice of the term 'methodological homunculism' turns on Freud's cautious wording. It is clear that he understands all of this as an interpretive activity: the number of 'minds' at work in oneself at any given moment is partially a function of one's skill at discovering rational patterns. The idea that such sub-personalities only exist relative to some interpretive strategy, and that two interpreters with different interpretive competencies or priorities might cut the pie in different ways, is therefore consistent with Freud's anti-realism with respect to folk-psychology[118].

Let us pause to contrast the homuncular functionalism that informed Freud's model making with his methodological homunculism. Freud views homuncular functionalism as a legitimate explanatory strategy for scientific psychology. The conjectured homunculi are hypothetical entities supervening upon neurophysiological processes, realistically interpreted and in principle open to falsification. The homunculi generated by methodological homunculism are folk-psychological artifacts of a particular interpretive strategy. As such they are not hypothetical entities and must be interpreted anti-realistically. Although these methodological homunculi do not correspond one-to-one to neural kinds, they are nonetheless token-identical to neurophysiological states and are informative with respect to psychology: they provide a guide to the functional structure of the mind.

If the anti-realist interpretation of Freud seems strange and strained, it will perhaps seem less so if we examine other examples from Freud's writings where he considers the ontological status of folk-psychological entities. The earliest hints of intentional instrumentalism in Freud's writings are embedded in the dualist metaphysics that Freud embraced during the early years of his career. If epiphenominalism is true, and neurophysiological events provide only the causal basis for mental events, then those neurophysiological events which fail to cause their corresponding (by definition, conscious) mental events, can be described figuratively as unconscious mental events 'as if what is expressed by the terms "separation of the idea from its affect" and "false connection" of the latter had really taken place' (1894:53).[119]

In 'Further remarks on the neuro-psychoses of defence', the first paper written after his shift to the identity theory, Freud (1896) wrote that:

> In order to describe clearly and with probable accuracy the processes of repression, the return of the repressed and the formation of pathological compromise-ideas, one would have to make up one's mind to some quite definite assumptions about the substratum of psychical events and of consciousness. So long as one seeks to avoid this, one must be content with...remarks which are intended more or less figuratively (170).

The 'substratum of psychical events and of consciousness' is, of course, the brain. Freud is therefore saying that, until we understand the neurophysiological basis of unconscious mental processes, we have no option but to characterize them by means of the figurative (but unclear and inaccurate) language of folk-psychology.

A few years later, in 'The interpretation of dreams', he wrote 'Whether we are to attribute reality to unconscious wishes I cannot say' (620). Given that the notion of unconscious wish is perhaps the single most important causal component specified in Freud's theory of dreaming, I take him to be referring to the folk-psychological entity rather than the neurophysiological state which it models in a rough and ready way.

In the 'Introductory lectures on psycho-analysis' Freud (1916-17) could write of his psychological theories, expressed in the language of the folk, that:

> They are preliminary working hypotheses, like Ampère's manikin swimming in the electric current, and they are not to be despised in so far as they are of service in making our observations intelligible (296).

Freud is here referring to the electrodynamic theory of André-Marie Ampère. Ampère was not only an accomplished mathematician, chemist and physicist, but he also sustained a deep interest in metaphysics and philosophy of science. He rejected the extreme positivism of the *Idéologues* in favor of his own interpretation of Kant's metaphysics. Ampère equated Kant's unknowable noumena with theoretical entities the existence of which are deduced from scientific experimentation (Williams, 1989). Like Ampère, then, Freud attempted to deduce the existence of theoretical entities within the mind on the basis of psychoanalytic observation. Also like Ampère, his scientific strategy ran counter to the phenomenalist epistemology of Viennese positivism (Quinton, 1972). According to Williams:

> Ampère noted that there are often relations – *rapports,* to use his word – between phenomena. These *rapports*, he believed, must be analogous to *rapports* between the noumena underlying those phenomena. Hence it should be possible to learn about the interactions between unobservable noumena by studying phenomenal *rapports* (75).

Ampère's epistemological stance, as described by Williams, is uncannily reminiscent of Freud's (1940a) statement that:

> The processes with which it [psychoanalysis] is concerned are in themselves just as unknowable as those dealt with by other sciences, by chemistry or physics, for example; but it is possible to establish the laws which they obey and to follow their mutual relations and interdependencies...in short, to arrive at what is described as an 'understanding' of the field of natural phenomena in question (158)

Ampère's 'manikin' was presumably an explanatory construction preliminary to an exhaustively electrodynamic account. Freud's hypotheses are 'preliminary' in just this sense: the sense alluded to by the passage from 'Further remarks on the neuro-psychoses of defence' (1896): they are preliminary to an exhaustively neuroscientific account, an interpretation corroborated by his reductionist (or possibly eliminativist) remark that:

> The deficiencies in our description [of the mind] would probably vanish if we were already in a position to replace the psychological terms by physiological or chemical ones' (Freud, 1920:60).[120]

In the 'Outline of psycho-analysis' (1940a) Freud compares the problem of overcoming folk-psychological concepts in psychoanalytic theory with the problem of overcoming folk physical concepts in scientific physics.

> We have to discover something else which is more independent of the particular receptive capacity of our sense organs and which approximates more closely to what may be supposed to be the real state of affairs. We have no hope of being able to reach the latter itself, since it is evident that everything new that we have inferred must nevertheless be translated back into the language of our perceptions, from which it is simply impossible for us to free ourselves. But herein lies the very nature and limitation of our science (196).

In other words, the folk-psychological accounts of mental processes are provisionally useful for psychology even though they do not type-correspond to neurophysiological items. Folk-psychology is inevitable because of the linguistic constraints on the process of becoming conscious. The analogy with 'the language of our perceptions' (in physics) turns on Freud's long-standing model of the ω system as an 'internal sense organ'. The damage incurred by the use of terms derived from a folk-psychological ontology can be limited by our awareness that the use of such language is pragmatic and figurative, pointing to functional features of the brain.

Freud's remarks in the 'New introductory lectures on psycho-analysis'' (1933) provide a gloss on the passage quoted above.

> I have tried to translate into the language of our normal thinking what must in fact be a process that is neither conscious nor preconscious, taking place between quotas of energy in some unimaginable substratum (90).

Freud's use of the term 'unimaginable substratum' is at first sight puzzling and might be taken to betray a lingering commitment to Kantian metaphysics. For Freud, the brain is the substratum of mental events, but the brain is certainly not 'unimaginable'. It seems that Freud expresses himself somewhat imprecisely here. I take him to mean that we are unable, at present, to understand how it is that neurophysiological events instantiate mental items. The processes cannot be characterized as conscious or preconscious because they cannot be accurately expressed in the language of our normal thinking.

Finally, in the 'Outline of psycho-analysis Freud (1940a) Freud wrote that:

> We have discovered technical methods of filling up the gaps in the phenomena of our consciousness, and we make use of those methods just as a physicist makes use of experiment. In this manner we infer a number of processes which are in themselves "unknowable" and interpolate them in those that are conscious to us. And if, for instance we say "At this point an unconscious memory intervened", what that means is: "At this point something occurred of which we are totally unable to form a conception, but which, if it had entered our consciousness, could only have been described in such and such a way" (197).

Freud was adamant that it is only through embracing a physicalistic ontology that any psychology can lay claim to being scientific. As physicalism entails the notion of true unconscious (neurophysiological) descriptions of all mental processes, it follows that from Freud's perspective any scientific psychology must accept the idea of unconscious mental processes. Any psychology that rejects the existence of an unconscious domain (so conceived) must embrace some form of dualism that removes the mental from the natural order. An understanding of Freud's physicalism, and the logical role of the concept of the unconscious within his philosophy of mind, is required in order to understand passages like the following one from 'The ego and the id' (1923b).

> The division of the psychical into what is conscious and what is unconscious is the fundamental premise of psycho-analysis; and it alone makes it possible for psycho-analysis to understand the pathological processes in mental life...and to find a place for them in the framework of science (13).

Freud was anxious to make it clear that although he interpreted folk-psychological characterizations of mental events in an instrumentalist manner, the unconscious processes to which they correspond are perfectly real.

> We can challenge anyone in the world to give a more correct scientific account of this state of affairs [obsessional neurotic symptoms], and if he does we will gladly renounce our hypothesis of unconscious mental processes. Till that happens, however, we will hold fast to the hypothesis; and if someone objects that here the unconscious is nothing real in a scientific sense, is a makeshift, *une façon de parler*[121] we can only shrug our shoulders resignedly and dismiss what he says as unintelligible. Something not real, which produces effects of such tangible reality as an obsessional action! (1916-17: 278).

X

FREUDIAN FUNCTIONALISM

In this chapter I will explore some of the implications of homuncular functionalism and causal role functionalism for Freud's conception of the mind. I understand causal role functionalism as the doctrine that mental items are type-individuated on the basis of their causal role. I take homuncular functionalism to be the view that psychological processes are rightly understood as brought about by interconnecting components 'homunculi'), each of which is functionally individuated, and each of which can be broken down into simpler sub-components, until the simplest neuroanatomical level is reached (Lycan, 1990).

FREUD'S HOMUNCULAR FUNCTIONALISM

Freud wrote in 'The question of lay analysis' (1926b), in response to an imaginary interlocutor that:

> It will soon be clear what the mental apparatus is; but I must beg you not to ask what material it is constructed of. That is not a subject of psychological interest. Psychology can be as indifferent to it as, for instance, optics can be to the question of whether the walls of a telescope are made of metal or cardboard. We shall leave entirely on one side the material line of approach, but not so the spatial one. For we picture the unknown apparatus which serves the activities of the mind as being really like an instrument constructed of several parts...each of which performs a particular function and have a fixed spatial relation to one another: it being understood that by spatial...we really mean in the first instance a representation of the regular succession of the functions (194).[122]

Freud's model is an example of homuncular functionalism. He points out that a characterization of the mind in terms of what it does entail no commitment to specific neuroanatomical hypotheses: we need only identify what would now be called the 'information processing' competencies and their sequence of operation. After this account the psychical apparatus, the 'impartial person' reproaches Freud for introducing an 'anatomy of the soul ['*die Seele*'[123]] - a thing which, after all, no longer exists at all for the scientists.' Freud replies that the topographical model:

> Is a hypothesis like so many others in the sciences: the very earliest ones have always been rather rough. "Open to revision" we can say in such cases. It seems to me unnecessary to appeal to the "as if" which has become so popular. The value of a "fiction" of this kind (as the philosopher Vaihinger would call it) depends on how much one can achieve with its help (194).

Vaihinger was the author of *The Philosophy of 'As If'* (1911) which was immensely popular in German-speaking countries between the world wars. Described as a European pragmatist he was a neo-Kantian and an advocate of conventionalism in the philosophy of science (Passmore, 1966).

Vaihinger made a distinction between 'fictions' and 'hypotheses'. Fictions are unverifiable and unfalsifiable notions which guide human activity and are evaluated on a purely pragmatic basis, whereas hypotheses are judged based on their correspondence to reality. In choosing his words as he did, Freud evidently wished to emphasize that the functional units of his model must correspond to real functional divisions in the central nervous system if the topographical hypothesis is to be retained. Until we are able to determine whether or not this is the case, we retain the model for its heuristic virtues. This form of realism is entirely compatible with homuncular functionalism (Dennett, 1978).

A final detail of Freud's attitude towards the items included in functional models of mental activity must not be overlooked. That the homunculi included in such models are to be understood realistically does not mean that every feature of the model can bear a realistic interpretation. Freud addressed this issue in a debate with Adler over the ontological status of the concept of libido (psychical energy) (Nunberg & Federn, 1967). Adler claimed that the notion of libido should be rejected on the grounds that it does not exist, to which Freud replied:

> One has to judge [the concept of] the libido according to its consequences...If one says of the libido, that it is not real, that is correct; but to say that it is false is totally arbitrary and an unscientific conception (148-149).

Freud evidently gave an anti-realist interpretation to his core theoretical concept of the libido.[124]

FREUD'S REJECTION OF CAUSAL ROLE FUNCTIONALISM

Having clarified Freud's relationship to homuncular functionalism, I will move on to consider causal role functionalism. Rubenstein (1965) attributes a position of causal role functionalism to Freud.

Rubenstein claims that those psychoanalytic theoretical statements that mention specific unconscious mental events can, in principle, be replaced by neuroscientific statements. This is made possible by the fact that these statements refer to neurophysiological events. In what sense, then, can psychoanalytic theoretical statements be taken to refer to mental events? How, within the purview of psychoanalytic theory can we regard neurophysiological events as mental events? Rubenstein cites a passage from 'The unconscious' (1915a). Freud wrote with reference to unconscious mental events that:

> As far as their physical characteristics are concerned, they are totally inaccessible to us: no physiological concept or chemical process can give us any notion of their nature. On the other hand, we know for certain that they have abundant points of contact with conscious mental processes; with the help of a certain amount of work they can be transformed into, or replaced by, conscious mental processes, and all of the categories which we employ to describe conscious mental acts, such as ideas, purposes, resolutions and so on, can be applied to them. Indeed, we are obliged to say of some of these latent states that the only respect in which they differ from conscious ones is precisely in the absence of consciousness. Thus we shall not hesitate to treat them as objects of psychological research, and to deal with them in the most intimate connection with conscious mental acts (168).

Freud's assertion that we cannot understand unconscious mental events with reference to their neurophysiology bears on his comments on the brain as an 'unimaginable substratum' quoted earlier. Freud seems to be saying that we are unable to understand what features of our neurophysiology enable the brain to instantiate mental functions.

As I will have occasion to return to this argument, I will call it the 'Similarity argument' for ease of reference. The Similarity argument, a corollary of the Continuity argument, is deployed against the claim that so-called unconscious mental events are identical to neurophysiological dispositions for conscious mental events. If we use the principle of the continuity of the mental to assert that the gaps found in coherent sequences of conscious mental events imply the existence of continuity-supplying unconscious mental events, we implicitly claim that these unconscious items possess an appropriate causal and/or logical character. This in turn seems to imply that we individuate unconscious mental events based on their functional roles.

Considerations of continuity therefore license inferences invoking unconscious mental states. These unconscious items resemble conscious items in every respect except that they do not possess the quality of being conscious. Items that resemble conscious mental items in every respect except that of being conscious are mental items. Therefore, those unconscious items interpolated between discontinuous conscious mental items are genuinely mental.

Rubenstein remarks that the Similarity argument:

> Clearly amounts to a functional definition of unconscious mental events: They can be transformed into conscious events, and they have similar behavioral effects. Hence, regardless of their actual nature, they may be spoken about in the same language and referred to by the same words as the corresponding conscious events. To make this point unmistakably clear Freud added in the same paragraph that "...the only respect in which they [i.e., the unconscious events] differ from conscious ones is precisely in the absence of consciousness." (42)

According to Rubenstein, those unconscious neurophysiological events functionally resembling conscious mental events are dispositions to experience functionally identical conscious experiences, and 'part-dispositions' for derivative dream contents, neurotic symptoms, character traits and so on.

There is no doubt that causal role functionalism possesses a special appeal for Freudian apologists. This special appeal lies in the fact that it allows one to individuate mental items without reference to their qualia, which are, of course, absent in the case of unconscious mental items. Prior to the emergence of the theory of causal role functionalism, psychoanalysis could be criticized on the grounds that, because unconscious mental items are said to possess no qualia and given the (false) premise that mental items must be individuated on the basis of their qualia, it follows that there can be no such thing as unconscious mental items.

This argument was raised, to give but one example, by Field in his contribution to a symposium in the 1920s on the question 'Is the conception of the unconscious of value in psychology?'(Klein, 1977). Field suggested that the concept of the unconscious was merely a theoretical placeholder for unknown causes of conscious phenomena. He then went on to state that:

> This, of course, would not be admitted by the advocates of the claims of the Unconscious. And we find them, accordingly, continually speaking of the activities of the unconscious mind in exactly the same terms as the activities of the conscious mind, so that we hear of unconscious desires, emotions,[125] wishes, fears, or of unconscious thoughts or memories. These unconscious mental processes as Dr Ernest Jones tells us "present all the attributes of mental ones, except that the subject is not aware of them." And consciousness thus becomes, he says, "merely one attribute of mentality, and not an indispensable one." I have searched in vain for a clear statement for what the other attributes of mentality are which these processes do possess. And when I reflect on what I mean by a wish or an emotion or a feeling, I can only find that I know and think of them simply as different forms of consciousness...And to ask us to think of something which has all the characteristics of a wish or a feeling except that it is not conscious seems to me like asking us to think of something that has all the attributes of red or green except that it is not a colour (Field, 1922).

We have seen that Rubenstein uses a passage from 'The unconscious' to justify the claim that mental kinds are individuated by means of their causal roles. In doing this he makes a patently inaccurate extrapolation from Freud. The extracted passage tendentiously omits a section of the text which is incompatible with the position Rubenstein wishes to attribute to Freud.

> Indeed, we are obliged to say of some of these latent states that the only respect in which they differ from conscious ones is precisely in the absence of consciousness (1915a: 168).

The word 'some' informs us that we are dealing with a subset of the class of unconscious states. The subclass of (descriptively) unconscious states consisting of those states that resemble conscious states in every respect save for their not being conscious are, of course, preconscious states.[126] As I have shown, Freud held preconscious states to be quite unlike systematically unconscious states. Preconscious states have been poured into the template of the subject's language and have thus taken on the structure that will enable them to become conscious. The philosophical point of the Similarity argument is to drive a wedge between consciousness and intentionality by showing that unconscious items can plausibly be described as mental. It relies on the principle that preconscious items share their causal roles with intentionally corresponding conscious items.

There are compelling reasons why the Similarity argument cannot be successfully used to justify the mental character of systematically unconscious states. To deal with this fully involves a detailed discussion of Freud's views on the causal powers of systematically unconscious items and the special characteristics of the unconscious mental system, subjects which will be presented in Chapter Eleven. I will therefore confine myself to a relatively schematic account at this point.

Consider some mental content *c* in relation two mental state types *U* (unconscious) and *C* (conscious), such that *Uc* and *Cc* instantiate tokens of the same intentional type. If *Uc* were to be transformed into *Cc* it would not follow that the effects of *Cc* would remain the same as the effects of *Uc*. In fact, Freudian theory states that the effects of *Cc* cannot be the same as the effects of its corresponding *Uc* because the transformation of the item from an unconscious to a conscious state is accompanied by a change in their respective effects. This is easily illustrated by the example of a neurotic symptom. Psychoneurotic symptoms are believed by Freudians to be effects of unconscious mental causes. According to this view, the making conscious of a repressed pathogenic idea necessitates the disappearance of the symptom which it causally supports (Grünbaum, 1984, 1993). Whereas while in its unconscious state the idea caused a neurotic symptom, in its conscious state the idea brings about a state of conflict and a disposition to perform certain conflict-laden actions. Similarly, if this transformation of effect does not occur, psychoanalytic theory claims that the targeted unconscious idea has not become conscious. If *Uc* does not retain its output after having been transformed into *Cc*, it follows that causal role specifications are insufficient for individuating unconscious contents.

Strictly speaking, Freudian theory claims that unconscious ideas cause conscious ideas, and it is this causal process that we loosely and misleadingly describe as 'becoming conscious'. The unadorned causal-role thesis is compatible only with those instances of *U* activating some *C* expressing the same content *c*. To say that *Uc* becomes *Cc* means that *Uc* causes *Cc*: *Uc* activates speech residues that express ideas corresponding to *c*. A more rigorous Freudian account therefore specifies an asymmetry between the causal role of *Uc* and *Cc* as follows: the causal role of *Uc* is, at least in part, to bring about *Cc*, whereas *Cc* does not possess the role of causing *Uc*. This asymmetry can be reconciled with causal-role functionalism in that both *Uc* and *Cc* possess the causal role of bringing about some action congruent with *c*. So, for example, if *c* tokens some desire type *d*, the causal role of both *Uc* and *Cc* is to bring about the satisfaction of *d*. Indeed, *Uc* brings about the satisfaction of *d* by virtue of causing *Cc*.

In the situation mentioned above, which is hostile to the causal role account, we encounter the notorious problem of normativity. Let us take the hypothetical example of someone who harbors an unconscious sexual wish (U) which, because of the guilt it would induce if made conscious, evokes the substitutive derivative idea of wishing to eat (©). Intuitively, one wants to claim (and Freud does claim) that in such instances the content of © is a disguised expression of the content of (U), but this seems ruled out by a descriptive causal role semantics.

The problem of disguised expressions of unconscious ideas can be handled by recourse to Millikan's normative teleofunctionalism. In Millikan's (1984, 1992) view, the claim that some item is supposed to bring about another item is to say that the proper function of the first is to bring about the second. 'Proper function' is defined as that function which, when discharged, historically accounts for an item's existence. As such, claims about an item's proper function have historical implications: an item's proper function is such because of its history. Proper function claims are not claims about an item's actual functioning, as an item may never fulfil its proper function. Millikan (1984) illustrates this with the example of a spermatozoon. The proper function of sperm cells - the reason that they exist - is to fertilize ova. The likelihood that any given spermatozoon will actually fertilize an ovum is, however, vanishingly small.

Let us assume, in a manner consistent with Freudian theory, that the proper function of unconscious wishes is to ensure the gratification of such wishes by means of activating conscious ideas (verbal residues) expressing the same content and, conversely, that the proper function of such conscious ideas is to enable the discharge of the unconscious wishes that have evoked them. Consider an individual who compulsively overeats because the conscious wish to eat has come to function as a derivative of an unconscious erotic idea; (in psychoanalytic jargon, eating has become 'sexualized'), the evocation of a conscious desire to eat instead of the conscious wish to perform a sexual act is the failure of conscious and unconscious ideas to fulfil their proper functions. Within this framework the claim that the desire to eat is a disguised representation of the desire for sex is just the claim that the unconscious desire for sex has failed to fulfil its proper function - evoking a conscious idea bearing the same content - and instead has evoked a conscious idea of which a proper function is to be caused by an unconscious desire to eat.[127]

In conclusion, we see that Freud's Similarity argument is a causal role functionalist argument designed to show how mental items can be individuated on the basis of their causal powers rather than on the basis of their conscious properties. However, the Similarity argument is not applicable for the individuation of unconscious mental contents: it is a weak or restricted causal role functionalist thesis. So, although Freud is able to deploy a causal role functionalist argument for a specific philosophical purpose, he cannot be regarded as advancing a causal role functionalist theory of mind. More strongly, his view of unconscious mental contents seems incompatible with such a theory of mind.

XI

CHARACTERISTICS OF UNCONSCIOUS THINKING

It will be clear from the discussion so far that Freud uses the term 'unconscious' in several ways. Sometimes the term is used to designate a functional system of the mind containing mental representations that are unconscious but not preconscious. (and possessing special irrational characteristics, described below). Following Freud, I will refer to this as 'System *Ucs.*' or just '*Ucs.*' I will also refer to this sense of 'unconscious' as 'unconscious$_{irr}$'. At other times Freud uses 'unconscious' to denote all of those mental items that are not consciously represented. This includes the contents of System *Ucs.* as well as the contents of system *Pcs.* Freud refers to these items as 'descriptively' unconscious. I will refer to this as 'unconscious$_{desc}$' Finally, Freud sometimes describes as 'unconscious' all mental items under neuroscientific descriptions ('unconscious$_{neu}$').

Freud does not always make it clear just how he is using the term 'unconscious', and one must often rely on contextual clues to reach a satisfactory conclusion. An appreciation of this ambiguity is crucial for the evaluation of Freud's claims, for an argument that is sound with respect to 'unconscious$_{desc}$', for example, is not necessarily adequate for the justification of claims about 'unconscious$_{neu}$'.

CHARACTERISTICS OF SYSTEM UCS.

In 'The unconscious' (1915a), Freud underscores the point that *Ucs.* processes are intrinsically dissimilar to conscious (and therefore preconscious) processes. Earlier in the same paper, Freud had used the Continuity, Similarity and Other Minds arguments to show that attributions of unconscious mental states are philosophically legitimate and that unconscious$_{desc}$ contents should be regarded as true mental contents and not just as physical dispositions for conscious mental states. Aware that the

Other Minds arguments can be taken to imply the existence of an 'unconscious consciousness' - a consciousness of which the subject is not aware - and thus license a return to a dualistic dissociationist theory of the type advanced prior to the writing of the 'Project', he devotes some space to arguing that this alternative is implausible. His arguments are (1) that the idea of an unconscious consciousness is incoherent; (2) given that unconscious$_{irr}$ contents are not ordered in such a way as to cohere tightly with one another, the use of charity to attribute an unconscious consciousness must lead to the 'assumption of a third, fourth, perhaps of an unlimited number of states of consciousness, all unknown to us and to one another' thus leading to a *reductio ad absurdum*[128] (170) and (3) that unconscious$_{irr}$ has 'characteristics and peculiarities which...run directly counter to the attributes of consciousness with which we are familiar'(170).

Freud emphasized the peculiar characteristics of unconscious mentation at several points in his writings.[129]

> The logical laws of thought do not apply in the id,[130] and this is true above all of the law of contradiction. Contrary impulses exist side-by-side, without canceling each other out or diminishing each other: at the most they may converge to form compromises.... There is nothing in the id that could be compared with negation.... There is nothing in the id that corresponds to the idea of time (73-74).

In 'The unconscious' Freud listed six basic characteristics of unconscious$_{irr}$ mental processes: exemption from mutual contradiction, exemption from negation, displacement, condensation, timelessness and disregard for reality.[131]

The first two characteristics listed imply that unconscious$_{irr}$ processes do not conform to or represent logical relations. That this is what Freud had in mind is clear from the following account of the role of unconscious activity in the formation of dreams:

> What representation do dreams provide for "if", "because", "just as", "although", "either-or", and all the other conjunctions without which we cannot understand sentences or speeches? In the first resort our answer must be that dreams have no means at their disposal for representing these logical relations.... For the most part dreams disregard all these conjunctions, and it is only the substantive content of the dream thoughts that they take over and manipulate (1900:312).

As Levine (1923) puts it, 'we might say that the unconscious system has no logic' (127).

Freud's fourth characteristic, the replacement of one content for another, is determined by associative rather than logical relations.

Freud's fifth characteristic should be interpreted strongly. Not only are unconscious$_{irr}$ items unaffected by the passage of time, they 'are not ordered temporally...they have no reference to time at all' (Freud, 1915a:187).

Freud's sixth characteristic must be understood in connection with his claim that unconscious$_{irr}$ processes are highly responsive to the activation of those biological motivational states which he calls 'drives'.[132] System *Ucs.* represents only the (biological) satisfaction-conditions of the drives and is unable to represent the world in anything other than these terms.

THE CONTINUITY ARGUMENT REVISITED

Let us consider the scope of the Other Minds argument, the Similarity argument and the Continuity argument in light of the various ways that Freud used the term 'unconscious'.

As I have shown, Freud used the Similarity argument to break the back of the Cartesian assertion that intentionality must involve consciousness. Turning as it does on the organization common to conscious states and some latent states, the Similarity argument justifies the attribution of preconscious states.

Insofar as the Other Minds argument depends upon the principle of charity, it is constrained by the norms of rationality and therefore appears to justify only the attribution of preconscious states.

The Continuity argument attempts to justify the attribution of unconscious mental states by highlighting the need to account for semantic and syntactic gaps in the continuity of conscious mental processes. The strongest case for the Continuity argument is made with Poincaré-type examples that demand that the transitions between consecutive unconscious mental states be constrained by logical norms. The Continuity argument therefore justifies the attribution of preconscious states, and the continuity-securing unconscious$_{neu}$ states with which they are identical, but seems once again impotent to justify the attribution of unconscious$_{irr}$ states because of the independence of the latter from logical norms.

Before proceeding further along these lines, it will be necessary to examine briefly some of Freud's ideas about mental causation. Causal relations hold by virtue of certain properties possessed by the causally interacting objects; e.g., it is the mass of an apple that causes its falling rather than its color, flavor or shape, (all of which may enter into other causal relations). It seems clear from evidence presented above that Freud believed that causal relations hold between mental events by virtue of physical properties of the neurophysiological states constituting them. Freud's physicalism allowed him to understand the mind as part of the natural order, subject to causal law, and as something to be investigated in accord with the canons of natural science.[133]

> As a specialist science...[psycho-analysis] is quite unfit to construct a weltanschauung of its own; it must accept the scientific one...the uniformity of the explanation of the universe...the intellect and the mind are objects for scientific research in exactly the way of any non-human things (1933a: 158-159).

Freud used the terms 'psychical determinism' and 'the determination of mental life' to refer to the principle that mental events are subject to causal laws. He writes, for example, in 'Five lectures on psycho-analysis' (1910a) that:

> Psycho-analysts are marked by a particularly strict belief in the determination of mental life. For them there is nothing trivial, nothing arbitrary or haphazard. They expect in every case to find sufficient motives where, as a rule, no such expectation is raised (38).

We have seen above that Freud also seems to uphold the thesis of the nomological character of mental causation.

Of course, if determinism in this sense holds for all physical events and if mental events are identical to physical events, then it is trivially true that determinism holds for all mental events. It does not follow that mental events are thus determined by virtue of their mental properties.

Let us examine how Freud makes use of the principle of psychical determinism. His preferred illustration is the process of free association (e.g., Freud, 1905; 1916-17). 'Free association' is a translation of the German '*freier Einfall*'.[134] '*Freier*' of course, means 'free'. '*Einfall*' signifies the incursion of a mental content into consciousness 'out of the blue'. Freud argues that ideas that enter consciousness in an apparently random fashion can be shown to be caused by the subject's antecedent preoccupations, and that this can be demonstrated by further free association taking the intrusive mental content as a point of departure. Here is an example from the 'Introductory lectures on psycho-analysis' (1916-17).

> In the course of treating a young man I had occasion to discuss this topic, and mentioned the thesis that, in spite of an apparently arbitrary choice, it is impossible to think of a name at random which does not turn out to be closely determined by the immediate circumstances, the characteristics of the subject of the experiment and his situation at the moment. Since he was skeptical, I suggested that he should make an experiment of the kind himself on the spot. I knew that he carried on particularly numerous relationships of every kind with married women and girls, so I thought he would have especially large choice open to him if it were to be a woman's name that he were asked to choose. He agreed to this. To my astonishment, or rather, perhaps, to his own, no avalanche of women's names broke over me; he remained silent for a moment and then admitted that only a single name had come into his head and none other besides: 'Albine'. ---How curious! But what does that name mean to you? How many 'Albines' do you know? ---Strange to say, he knew no one called 'Albine' and nothing further occurred to him in response to the name. So it might be thought that the analysis had failed. But not at all: it was already complete, and no further associations were needed. The man had an unusually fair complexion and in conversation during the treatment I had often jokingly called him an albino. We were engaged at the time in determining the feminine part of his constitution. So it was he himself who was this 'Albine', the woman who was the most interesting to him at the moment (107 - 108).

Freud was well aware that he was opening himself to the charge of committing the fallacy of 'causal reversal' (Glymour, 1983; Grünbaum, 1984).[135] The charge of causal reversal states that the associations proceeding from an idea are the effects of that idea and cannot, therefore, be construed as their causes. The debates surrounding the charge of causal reversal deal with the justification for making inferences about the presence of specific causes by means of Freud's associative method, an issue which does not directly concern us here and which I will leave to one side. It is important for the purposes of the present work to detach the ontological issue of psychical determinism from the epistemological debate about the causal inferences that can legitimately be drawn from free associations.[136]

In the case of preconscious processes, transitions between content-laden states are mainly governed by causal constraints[137] that function in accord with logical norms. From what Freud says about the peculiarities of unconscious$_{irr}$ states, we should not expect to find logically ordered transitions between them. According to Freud, transitions between unconscious mental states conform to laws of association; (of course, as an associationist, Freud holds that logical transitions between ideas are ultimately just a special case of association). Associations are the causal links between mental representations, or representational states, based on (a) the functional proximity (within the memory systems) of one representation and another, and (b) the ease with which excitation travels along the neural pathways bringing about transitions between neurophysiological states corresponding to proximate representations.[138] Unrepressed unconscious$_{irr}$ representations find their way to linguistic representation in the preconscious system by means of well-facilitated neural pathways. Contents of unconscious$_{irr}$ are prevented from taking a direct pathway to preconsciousness (the relevant neural vectors possess a high degree of resistance to the passage of excitation) and are thus diverted into alternative associative sequences. The operation of the primary processes of displacement and condensation in such instances eventuates in derivatives of the repressed content entering consciousness. Preconscious derivatives of unconscious$_{irr}$ representations neither denote nor are entailed by their unconscious$_{irr}$ instigators: the relationship between the two is purely causal and associative. When Freud refers to the unconscious$_{irr}$ meaning of a derivative, he therefore refers to the unconscious instigator of a derivative.

We can now rejoin the examination of the consequences of Freud's account of System *Ucs.* for the force of his Continuity argument. Freud was well aware that unconscious$_{irr}$ processes cannot fit the explanatory pattern presupposed by the Continuity argument. His earliest remarks pertaining to this problem can be found in 'The interpretation of dreams' (1900).

> Reports of numerous cases as well as the collection of instances made by Chabaneix (1897)[139] seem to put it beyond dispute that dreams can carry on the intellectual work of daytime and bring it to conclusions that had not been reached during the

day, and that they can resolve doubts and problems and be the source of new inspiration for poets and musical composers. But though the fact may be beyond dispute, its implications are open to many doubts, which raise matters of principle (64-65).

Freud elaborates upon these remarks much later in the same work, suggesting that these phenomena may only occur because of the circumstance of preconscious intellectual activity fortuitously serving a derivative function in relation to unconscious$_{irr}$ items. These are called 'dreams from above' (Freud, 1900, 1923c; 1929).

In 'Recommendations to physicians practicing psycho-analysis' (1912b), he wrote about unconscious mental activity in a manner which seems to imply its rationality.

To put it in a formula: he [the analyst] must turn his own unconscious like a receptive organ towards the transmitting unconscious of the patient. He must adjust himself to the patient as a telephone receiver is adjusted to the transmitting microphone. Just as the receiver converts back into sound waves the electric oscillations in the telephone line which were set up by sound waves, so the doctor's unconscious is able, from the derivatives of the unconscious which are transmitted to him, to reconstruct that unconscious, which has determined the patient's free-associations (115-116).

In 'The disposition to obsessional neurosis' (1913a) he wrote that:

I have had good reason for asserting that everyone possesses in his own unconscious an instrument with which he can interpret the utterances of the unconscious in other people (320).

And later the same year in 'Totem and taboo' (1912-13):

Even the most ruthless suppression [of mental impulses] must have room for distorted surrogate impulses and for reactions resulting from them. If so, however, we may safely assume that no generation is able to conceal any of its more important mental processes from its successor. For psycho-analysis has shown us that everyone possesses in his unconscious mental activity an apparatus which enables him to interpret other peoples reactions, that is, to undo the distortions which other people have imposed upon the expression of their feelings (159).

A passage in 'The unconscious' ends more equivocally, presumably because this very paper also explicitly emphasized the non-rational character of System *Ucs.* (1915a).

It is a very remarkable thing that the *Ucs.* of one person can react upon that of another without passing through the *Cs.* This deserves closer investigation, especially

> with a view to finding out whether preconscious activity can be excluded as playing a part in it; but descriptively speaking, the fact is incontestable (194).

By 1923b, however, Freud seems to have decided that these processes are preconscious in nature.

> We have evidence that even subtle and difficult intellectual operations which ordinarily require strenuous reflection can equally be carried out preconsciously and without coming into consciousness. Instances of this are quite incontestable; they may occur, for example, during the state of sleep, as is shown when someone finds, immediately after waking, that he knows the solution to a difficult mathematical problem with which he had been wrestling in vain the day before (26).

THE SECOND TOPOGRAPHY

How could Freud resolve the seeming contradictions between his psychological observations and his theory of System *Ucs.*? He had three options.

The first option, which Freud chose in 'The interpretation of dreams' and 'The ego and the id', was to explain instances of unconscious rationality as instances of preconscious rationality. The second option would have been to abandon his thesis of the special characteristics of unconscious$_{irr}$ processes. This choice would have involved Freud's abandoning of a thesis that he regarded as possessing great explanatory value, and he therefore avoided it. The third option would be to distinguish subsystems within System *Ucs.* In fact, Freud modified his model of the mind in 1923 in such a manner as to accommodate such a division: the so-called 'second topography' (or 'structural model') presented in 'The ego and the id' (1923b). Freud's transition from the first to the second topography seems to have been inspired in large measure by a growing conviction that there are radically unconscious states which do not possess the bizarre characteristics of System *Ucs.*

> We have formed the idea that in each individual there is a coherent organization of mental processes; and we call this his ego. It is to this ego that consciousness is attached; the ego controls the approaches to motility - that is, to the discharge of excitations into the external world; it is the mental agency which supervises all its own constituent processes, and which goes to sleep at night, though even then it exercises the censorship on dreams. From this ego proceed the repressions, too, by means of

which it is sought to exclude certain trends in the mind not merely from consciousness but also from other forms of effectiveness and activity. In analysis these trends which have been shut out stand in opposition to the ego, and the analysis is faced with the task of removing the resistances which the ego displays against concerning itself with the repressed. Now we find during analysis that, when we put certain tasks before the patient, he gets into difficulties; his associations fail when they should be coming near the repressed. We then tell him that he is dominated by a resistance; but he is quite unaware of the fact, and, even if he guesses from his unpleasurable feelings that a resistance is now at work in him, he does not know what it is or how to describe it. Since, however, there can be no question but that this resistance emanates from his ego and belongs to it, we find ourselves in an unforeseen situation. We have come upon something in the ego itself which is also unconscious (17).

So, Freud postulates the existence of unconscious ego functions, to which I will refer as 'unconscious$_{ego}$'. The old System *Ucs.*, with its bizarre and irrational characteristics, is now re-christened 'the id' ('*das Es*'). Freud states that the unconscious$_{ego}$ system possesses the characteristics of (1) coherence; that is, 'a tendency to synthesis in its contents, to a combination and unification in its mental processes which is totally lacking in the id' (1933a: 76); (2) an intimate relation to perception; 'It [the ego] starts out from the system Pcpt. [perception]' (1923b: 23); (3) control of access of mental items to (pre-) consciousness and action (see above); (4) representation of temporal relations; 'the relation to time...is...introduced into the ego by the perceptual system' (1933a: 76); (5) rationality; 'the ego represents what might be called reason and common sense' (1923b: 25); (6) adaptation to external reality; the ego 'seeks to bring the influence of the external world to bear upon the id' (1923b: 25); and (7) computational access to the mind (see above).

Unconscious ego functions are logically ordered although not indexed to linguistic items.

The second topography reinstates conjectures about unconscious ego states and unconscious rationality that had been suggested over twenty-five years previously in the 'Project'. The rational organization of the unconscious$_{ego}$ system allows its invocation in the context of the Continuity argument, thus augmenting the force of that argument. It also permits the functional characterization of at least some unconscious$_{ego}$ contents and supports the Other Minds strategy for understanding some unconscious states.

Although the notion of unconscious$_{ego}$ states satisfies the arguments which would otherwise do no more than establish the case for preconsciousness and physicalism, the problem first encountered in relation to System *Ucs.* has simply been deferred. Freud has not yet supplied any explicit justification for the attribution of mental contents to the id. This is no small matter as Freud's explanations after 1923 are normally framed in terms of the conflict between id-contents and unconscious$_{ego}$ ego functions.

MAKING SENSE OF ATTRIBUTIONS OF UNCONSCIOUS$_{IRR}$ CONTENT

The problem announced in the heading above encompasses two distinct issues for Freud's philosophy of mind: By virtue of what features is the id able to possess mental content and, given its special properties, how it is that one can reasonably attribute determinate mental contents to it?

It is the very incoherence and non-rationality of the id, as described in the present chapter, which ought to alert us to the possibility that in considering this mental system we cannot be dealing with a content-bearing mind - or sub-mind - as ordinarily conceived. The very incoherence of the id is perhaps enough to rob it of any claim to possessing the status of being a mind. As it is not a mind, we cannot reasonably attribute mental contents to it.[140]

If we cannot attribute contents to the id, because it is not a mind, what are we to make of Freud's claim that the id contains mental contents? The following passage from the 'New introductory lectures on psycho-analysis'' (1933a) provides some indications.

> We approach the id with analogies: we call it a chaos, a cauldron full of seething excitations. We picture it as being open at its end to somatic influences, and as there taking up into itself instinctual needs which find their psychical expression in it.... It is filled with energy reaching it from the instincts, but it has no organisation, produces no collective will, but only a striving to bring about the satisfaction of the instinctual needs.... (73).

Before proceeding along the lines suggested from this passage an objection must be raised and met. Laplanche and Pontalis (1980) do not believe that Freud should be taken at his word when he claims that the id possesses no organization. They state that:

> Freud transfers to the id most of the properties which in the first topography had defined the system *Ucs.*, and which constitute a positive and unique form of organisation: operation according to the primary process, structure based on complexes, genetic layering of the instincts, etc. (198-199).

The value of this assertion clearly turns on the sense given to the term 'organization'. Laplanche and Pontalis appear to use the term 'organization' to encompass rather heterogeneous features of the id. Of these, 'operation according to the primary process' denotes a freedom from associative constraint and is therefore a general functional characteristic of the id. 'Complexes', in Freud's system, are groups of relatively stable association-vectors. They thus provide a form of causal organization. The genetic layering of the instincts (i.e., drives) is a form of biological rather than mental organization. In contrast to these views, Freud seems to be claiming that the id is devoid of logical organization. This conclusion is suggested by the fact that Freud's reference to the id lacking organization is glossed by the remarks, already cited, that:

> The logical laws of thought do not apply in the id and this is true above all of the law of contradiction. Contrary impulses exist side-by-side, without cancelling each other out or diminishing each other: at the most they may converge to form compromises.... There is nothing in the id that could be compared with negation....There is nothing in the id that corresponds to the idea of time....(73-74).

It is this very lack of logical organization which is carried over from System *Ucs.* in the first topography to the id in the second topography. Obviously, the lack of logical organization mentioned by Freud does not exclude the causal and biological forms of organization specified by Laplanche and Pontalis.

Freud's concept of the id is that of a functional system receiving inputs from the instinctual drives and manifesting these in the form of primitive intentional structures. According to Freud, these intentional structures are not logically ordered and are confined to the representation of the conditions of satisfaction for the instinctual drives that they express. The absence of logical organization in the id suggests that Freud would deny that the id is constituted holistically.

We have already seen that due to its irrational and incoherent structure, the attribution of mental contents to the id cannot be effected by means of normal (charity-based) interpretative strategies. In the id, anything can mean anything. This, combined with the absence of those functions denoted by the logical operators, insures that it is not possible to make principled inferences about the id's intentional states based on the use of logical norms.[141] However, the comment by Laplanche and Pontalis concerning 'complexes' opens possibility that the id possesses an associative structure that might permit one to make inferences about mental content. Such a view might require the deployment of some superordinate a posteriori methodological principle such as Freud's 'Tally argument' (Grünbaum, 1984) to underwrite attributions of content.[142] Methodologically, of course, such psychoanalytic attributions of content are only inferred on the basis of information gleaned through the process of free association, a process designed to assist the analyst in identifying the associative connections between ideas in the patient's mind, and the cogency of the practice of making inferences on the basis of information derived from the use of free association has been sharply criticized (e.g., Grünbaum, 1993). Unfortunately, a full discussion of the pertinent epistemological issues is beyond the scope of the present work.

XII

WITTGENSTEIN AND MACINTYRE: THE UNCONSCIOUS AS *'FAÇON DE PARLER'*

Wittgenstein was one of the first philosophers to scrutinize psychoanalysis seriously. He apparently began reading Freud around 1919 (McGuiness, 1981; Monk, 1990) and later incorporated remarks on Freud in his teaching. Until very recently, philosophical consideration of Freud's work was, at least within the analytical tradition, dominated by Wittgenstein's thinking[143] .

The *locus classicus* for the neo-Wittgensteinian approach to Freud is Alisdair MacIntyre's *The Unconscious: A Conceptual Study* (1958). In the present chapter, I will briefly outline contributions by Wittgenstein and MacIntyre concerning the concepts of the unconscious, and then move on to a critique of the main planks of the Wittgenstein/MacIntyre platform. I will confine my remarks about Wittgensteinto a few of his specific claims, as a thorough examination of Wittgenstein's arguments with Freud would involve an extended examination of the former's philosophical views exceeding the constraints of this study. The interested reader can consult Bouveresse (1995) and Levy (1996) for a more elaborate treatment.

WITTGENSTEIN

Although critical of a number of Freud's fundamental claims, Wittgenstein described himself as a 'disciple' of Freud. Indeed, Wittgenstein's fundamental criticisms of Freud's approach to the mind were similar to his objections to his own *Tractatus* (and a host of other philosophical works) (Bouveresse, 1995).

Wittgenstein (1982) stated in his lectures of 1932-33 that:

> I wish to examine in what way Freud's theory [of jokes] is a hypothesis and in what way not. The hypothetical part of his theory, the subconscious, is the part that is not

> satisfactory.... When we laugh without knowing why, Freud claims that by psychoanalysis we can find out. I see a muddle here between a cause and a reason. Being clear about why you laught is not being clear about a cause. If it were, than agreement with the analysis given of the joke as explaining why you laugh would not be a means of detecting it. The success of the analysis is supposed to be shown by the person's agreement. There is nothing corresponding to this in physics. Of course we can give causes for our laughter, but whether those are in fact the causes is not shown by the person's agreeing that they are.... The difference between a reason and a cause is brought out as follows: the investigation of a reason entails as an essential part one's agreement with it, whereas the investigation of a cause is carried out experimentally. Of course the person who agrees to the reason was not conscious at the time of its being his reason. But it is a way of speaking to say that the reason was subconscious. It may be expedient to speak in this way, but the subconscious is a hypothetical entity which gets its meaning from the verifications these propositions have (10).

I take Wittgenstein to mean that (1) both causes and reasons bring about events, taking 'events' in a broad sense to include actions; (2) explanations adverting to reasons are verified by avowal by agents whose actions are thereby explained; (3) explanations adverting to causes are verified by experimental procedures (assent is of no probative value when assessing causal claims); (4) psychoanalytic hypotheses are properly verified by appealing to assent by the agents to whom they pertain; therefore (5) psychoanalytic explanations properly advert to reasons and not to causes.

Within this framework, talk of unconscious items is nothing more than a way of describing ones unawareness of reasons for actions. The truth of such hypotheses can be underwritten only by assent to them

MACINTYRE

Alisdair MacIntyre's *The Unconscious* (1958) is in many respects an extension of Wittgenstein's thesis concerning psychoanalytic explanation. Unlike Wittgenstein, MacIntyre does not wish to reject the notion of the unconscious on verificationist grounds:

> Certainly the unconscious and its contents are *ex hypothesi* unobservable, and if philosophy were still at the stage when positivism was waging a war to the death with unobservables no doubt the whole conception of the unconscious would have to be rejected. But the positivism that rejected unobservables in so wholesale a fashion

> was not merely too a priori in its framing of criteria by which concepts were to be judged legitimate or the reverse; it was also profoundly in error as to the character of scientific theorising. For in such theorising concepts which refer to unobservables have a legitimate, important and necessary place (46).

According to MacIntyre, drawing on Passmore (1955), the psychological verb 'intend' can be interpreted in two distinct ways. On one hand, when we say that someone 'intends' something, we mean that they plan to do it, as when one intends to telephone the dentist. On the other hand, when we say that someone intends something, we mean that their behavior tends towards some goal, irrespective of whether or not this has been planned. In the ensuing discussion, MacIntyre replaces this dichotomy with the dichotomy between avowed intentions and intentions implicit in behavior, and goes on to extend this analysis to all psychological verbs. So, with respect to propositional attitude P, the agent may avow P or behave in a way that warrants the attribution of P or both. MacIntyre describes the psychoanalytic process as the analyst's attempt to induce the analysand to avow disavowed intentions (or other types of propositional attitude) implicit in his or her behavior. However, he goes on to repeat Wittgenstein's error of granting the analysand what Grünbaum calls 'privileged epistemic access', stating that 'unless the patient will in the end avow his intention the analyst's interpretation of his behavior is held to be mistaken' (56).[144] Like Wittgenstein, MacIntyre goes on to chide Freud for his confusion of reasons with causes. Disavowed attitudes are intentions, not causes.

MacIntyre is also concerned with the ontological status of the unconscious (in its topographical sense, as distinct from particular unconscious propositional attitudes). The unconscious, he states, is either a real existent or a theoretical entity. In the former case, some evidence for its existence is required which, as the unconscious unobservable, is impossible to produce.[145] In the later case we are owed some account of the logical role of the unconscious within Freudian theory that shows this concept to be non-superfluous. MacIntyre is unable to find any justification for this concept of the unconscious interpreted either realistically or anti-realistically, and he comes around to a weaker version of Wittgenstein's verdict. Talk of the 'the unconscious' is just, as Janet had claimed, *une façon de parler*, and a hazardous one that is 'half-way to reduplicating the Cartesian substantial conscious mind by a substantial unconscious mind. The unconscious is the ghost of the Cartesian consciousness' (73).

'The unconscious' should be properly taken as a metaphor - as a way of representing features of psychological phenomena - rather than as a real or theoretical entity. 'The unconscious' thus has what we might term representational value, but is devoid of explanatory value. Such terms are part of Freud's novel notational system, the Freudian 'language game' (Bouveresse, 1995). The properties which Freud attributes to the unconscious are just properties abstracted from the psychological events which Freud (illicitly) uses the concept of the unconscious to explain. So, for instance, the fact that dreams are to a great extent irrational does not license the inference that dreams are caused by a mental system which does not conform to the norms of rationality. This is the same sort of error as claiming that 'Mr. Nobody is in the room' rather than 'Nobody is in the room' (Bouveresse, 1995).

CRITICISM

In his enthusiasm for diagnosing Freud's 'muddle', Wittgenstein illicitly introduces the premise that psychoanalytic hypotheses are properly verified by appealing to assent by the agents to whom they pertain which, contrary to his claim, does *not* express the Freudian view of the means by which psychoanalytic hypotheses are corroborated.[146]

Freud did not claim that it is the patient's agreement that underwrites the validity of psychoanalytic clinical hypotheses. His strong anti-Cartesian, anti-introspectionist stance would make any such claim sound rather peculiar. As Grünbaum (1984) shows, Freud appealed to the consiliance of inductions and the therapeutic effect of interpretations as suitable forms of validation. Although Freud's classic discussion of the evaluation of psychoanalytic hypotheses was not published until 1937, there was sufficient information available in Freud's writings published before 1932 to allow Wittgenstein to express the Freudian view more accurately. Freud (1937) maintained the view that the judgement of the truth of an interpretation is not sealed by the analysand's assent and insisted throughout his career that the human mind is to be studied like other natural things. If Wittgenstein's premise is illegitimate, the argument is inadequate to support his conclusion. It is not clear why we should say that psychoanalytic explanations advert to reasons rather than to causes. Concerning the demarcation of reasons from causes, given Freud's naturalism and his views on the unity of science, he would (and did) have no patience with this sort of distinction. Freud's naturalism demanded that 'reasons' supervene upon the causal order. His anti-realism with respect to folk-psychological entities such as intentions entailed the view that the language of reasons and intentions is a practical shorthand system for representing complex causal and functional relationships. His appreciation of the theoretical nature of folk-psychology prevented him from claiming that the assent of the subject is sufficient for the verification of propositional attitude attributions.

XIII

JOHN SEARLE: THE DISPOSITIONAL UNCONSCIOUS

John Searle has devoted critical attention to the concept of unconscious mental phenomena as one strand of his well-known program directed against certain features of cognitive science. Searle is concerned to show that all unconscious intentional states are in principle accessible to consciousness, referring to this dictum as the 'connection principle'. According to this view, unconscious states are only 'mental' by virtue of their causal powers to produce (truly mental) conscious states. They are, as it were, derivatively mental.

Searle's arguments for the connection principle are aimed at notions of unconscious mental events deployed in contemporary cognitive science, such as Marr's two-and-a-half dimensional sketch and Chomsky's rules of generative grammar. In the present chapter I will not criticize Searle's concept of the connection principle. Rather, I will argue that his dispositionalist theory of unconscious mental states is vulnerable to Freudian criticism, and therefore that, even if the connection principle happens to be sound, Searle's argument on its behalf fails because the connection principle cannot be adequately underwritten by a dispositionalist theory of unconscious mental events.

SEARLE'S VIEW OF THE MENTAL

Searle claims that we can describe as mental only (a) conscious states and (b) neurophysiological states that possess dispositional powers to cause conscious states. Neurophysiological dispositions for conscious mental states are referred to as 'unconscious mental states'. These states are therefore only indirectly or derivatively mental.

Searle sometimes formulates this relationship between conscious and unconscious mental states differently. Saying that:

> It may seem strange to say that consciousness is the central mental notion when at any given moment most of our mental states...are unconscious. But the crucial connection between consciousness and the unconscious can be stated as follows: There is a logical connection between the notion of consciousness and the notion of the unconscious such that in order for a state to be an unconscious *mental* state it must be the sort of thing that could be conscious in principle. I call the 'Connection Principle' (Searle, 1995: 548).

Searle thus offers us two accounts of the relationship between conscious and unconscious mental states: a causal account and a logical account. The causal account entails the logical account, but not vice versa. That is, it could be the case that those items which are the sort that can become conscious are occurrently rather than just dispositionally mental. The dispositionalist element enters the picture because of Searle's belief that only conscious items are occurrently mental. As a logical claim, the connection principle therefore does not underwrite the dispositionalist thesis.

SEARLE'S POSITION WITH REGARD TO SUPERVENIENCE

As Searle's attitude towards the principle of supervenience is critical in his argument for the connection principle, it will prove helpful to clarify this at an early point in the discussion. Searle (1992) endorses a version of the principle of supervenience, stating:

> On the account I have been proposing, mental states are supervenient on neurophysiological states in the following respect: Type-identical neurophysiological causes would have type-identical mentalistic effects. Thus, to take the famous brain-in-a-vat example, if you had two brains that were type-identical down to the last molecule, then the causal basis of the mental would guarantee that they would have the same mental phenomena. On this characterization of the supervenience relation, the supervenience of the mental on the physical is marked by the fact that physical states are causally sufficient, though not necessarily causally necessary, for the corresponding mental states. That is just another way of saying that as far as this definition of supervenience is concerned, sameness of neurophysiology guarantees sameness of mentality; but sameness of mentality does not guarantee sameness of neurophysiology (124-125).

Of course, there are many variants of the supervenience thesis. One important factor distinguishing these variants is the precise nature of the dependent relation between supervening mental states and their subvenient physical base. After briefly explaining Hare's (1952) constitutive notion of ethical supervenience, Searle presents his own position as follows:

> So there are at least two notions of supervenience: a constitutive notion and a causal notion. I believe that only the causal notion is important for discussions of the mind-body problem. In this respect my account differs from the usual accounts of the supervenience of the mental on the physical. Thus Kim (1979, especially p.45ff) claims that we should not think of the relation of neural events to their supervening mental events as causal, and indeed he claims that supervening mental events have no causal status apart from their supervenience on neurophysiological events (125).

Searle's story about supervenience is confusing in two respects. First, in discussing constitutive dependence, he speaks as though the kind of supervenience invoked by Hare is the only sort of constitutive supervenience. This is not the case. The principle of ethical supervenience is constitutive in the sense of being conceptually constitutive: it asserts the existence of some universal property that provides all tokenings of a type with their particular ethical status (Hare, 1984). In contrast to this, most writers on psychophysical supervenience invoke the relation of instantiation as the relevant form of constitutive dependence.

Second, it is noteworthy that Searle speaks in the passage quoted above of supervenient and subvenient events rather than descriptions or properties. Elsewhere in the same text, Searle describes the same relation in terms of the supervenience of mental properties on neural properties. Of course, the latter formulation is the formally correct one. Supervenience holds between properties or, if one prefers, predicates.

What sort of causation is Searle talking about? He states that:

> It seems to me obvious from everything we know about the brain that macro mental phenomena are all caused by lower-level micro phenomena. There is nothing mysterious about such bottom-up causation; it is quite common in the physical world. Furthermore, the fact that the mental features are supervenient on neuronal features in no way diminishes their causal efficacy. The solidity of the piston is causally supervenient on its molecular structure, but this does not make solidity epiphenominal (125-126).

Searle's causal dependency is, in the end, just what philosophers normally call instantiation. Instantiation is usually treated as a relation of identity rather than as a causal relation. The molecular structure of the piston does not cause its solidity, it is its solidity. Putting this in a different way, it is the causal relation between the molecules of which the piston is composed that constitutes its solidity, and it is by virtue of this molecular structure that the piston possesses its specific casual powers (Cf., Heil, 1992).

Searle concludes his brief discussion of supervenience as follows:

> My conclusion is that once you recognize the existence of bottom-up, micro to macro forms of causation, the notion of supervenience no longer does any work in philosophy. The formal features of the relation are already present in the causal sufficiency of the micro-macro forms of causation (126).

Searle thus disposes of supervenience by stretching the concept of causation to encompass instantiation. Why render the term 'causation' ambiguous in this fashion? Perhaps Searle's philosophical motive is to block the Davidsonian move of regarding psychoneural supervenience as rooted in event identity. In any case, given that causal relations hold between events, Searle's commitment to a causal account of the dependent relation between mental and physical seems to force the event thesis. However, as Searle usually really means 'instantiation' when he uses 'causation', he is naturally impelled to revert to talk of properties.

Searle (1992:115) describes his theory as causally reductive, but not ontologically property reductive. By this he means that although mind is caused by brain, mental properties cannot be reduced to neural properties. The irreducibility of mental properties lies in their subjectivity. Searle (1995) believes that the ontological subjectivity of mental properties is most clearly displayed in their possession of 'aspectual shape'.

> Every intentional state has what I call an 'aspectual shape'. This just means that it presents its conditions of satisfaction under some aspects and not others. Thus, for example, the desire for water is a different desire from the desire for H_2O, even though water and H_2O are identical. If I represent what I desire under the aspect 'water', that is a different aspectual shape from representing the same substance under the aspect 'H_2O'. What is true of this example is true generally. All intentional states represent their conditions of satisfaction under some aspects and not others; and this has the consequence that every intentional state, conscious or unconscious, has an aspectual shape (548).

'Aspectual shape' includes perceptual perspectivity as well.

> Aspectual shape is most obvious in the case of conscious perceptions: think of seeing a car, for example. When you see a car, it is not simply a matter of an object being registered by your perceptual apparatus; rather, you actually have a conscious experience of the object from a certain point of view and with certain features. You see the car as having a certain shape, as having a certain color, etc. (Searle, 1992:157).

Searle rests his irreducibility thesis on the claim that aspectual shape 'cannot be exhaustively or completely characterized solely in third-person, behavioral or even neurophysiological predicates' (157-158).

SEARLE'S THEORY OF THE UNCONSCIOUS

Searle (1992) depicts unconscious mental states as 'corresponding to an objective neurophysiological ontology' and describes them in terms of their 'capacity to cause conscious subjective mental phenomena' (168). That is, he believes that unconscious states are neural states that are mental only in so far as they are capable of bringing about conscious states. Searle thus advances a dispositionalist account of unconscious mental contents, which are legitimately described as 'mental' only by virtue of their causal power to bring about conscious - and therefore intrinsically mental - intentional states. Searle supports this position by arguing that (1) intentional realism is a true thesis, (2) unconscious mental states are intrinsically intentional, (3) mental contents always appear under some aspectual shape, (4) unconscious mental states possess a purely neurophysiological ontology, (5) neurophysiological predicates cannot exhaustively characterize aspectual shape and (6) therefore we must conclude that unconscious intentional phenomena are just possible conscious contents.

As Searle (172) sums up: 'The ontology of the unconscious is strictly the ontology of a neurophysiology capable of generating the conscious', just as Hering had claimed in 1870.

Searle's concept of intentional realism is connected to his theory of intrinsic and as-if intentionality. True intrinsic intentional ascriptions correspond to a person's real intentional states. As-if intentionality is merely metaphorical intentionality, the 'intentionality' of a computer or thermostat. Searle thus contends, in the second premise that true attributions of unconscious intentionality tally with real intentional states in their objects. We have already seen that 'aspectual shape' is a property that Searle attributes to all mental states.

Searle's third claim, that unconscious intentional states possess a purely neurophysiological ontology, is supported in the following manner:

> Imagine that a man is in a sound dreamless sleep. Now, while he is in such a state it is true to say of him that he has a number of unconscious mental states.... But *what fact about him makes it the case that he has these unconscious beliefs?* Well, the only facts that could exist while he is completely unconscious are neurophysiological facts. The only things going on in his unconscious brain are sequences of neurophysiological events occurring in neuronal architectures. At the time when the states are totally unconscious, there is simply nothing there except neurophysiological states and processes (159).

Given that unconscious mental states are nothing but neurophysiological states, one is confronted with what Searle takes to be the fact that the neurophysiological states corresponding somehow to unconscious mental states do not possess aspectual shape. This idea drives Searle's argument that unconscious mental states are not occurrent mental states at all because, if so, 'they must *in some sense*' possess aspectual shape; (159, italics added). Rather, he suggests that they are just neurophysiological dispositions for (conscious) mental states.[147] Searle thus believes that unconscious 'mental' states are only mental by virtue of their dispositional causal powers, and that when we speak of unconscious mental states we predicate intentionality in a looser, more indirect or extrinsic sense when we speak of conscious mental states.

IS SEARLE'S CONCLUSION UNDERWRITTEN BY HIS PREMISES?

In the example of the sleeping man, used as evidence on behalf of the non-mental character of unconscious states, Searle simply asserts that because the man is unconscious, there is nothing with aspectual shape going on inside his head. Searle provides no justification for this claim. It is not clear why we should not say that the neurophysiological processes occurring within the man instantiate supervenient mental functions possessing aspectual shape. Of course, these functions cannot be exhaustively characterized using neuroscientific language, but this is equally true of conscious mental states! The issue of the unsuitability of neuroscientific language for fully characterizing intentional states has no bearing on the issue of the token-identity of mental items, complete with aspectual shape, with subvenient neurophysiological items.

It is now obvious that Searle's ambiguous use of the concept of causation gives him the conceptual slack that he needs to reach his conclusion. If we say that mental events are caused by neural events, while forgetting that Searle treats instantiation as a form of causation, it is easy to conclude that the neural states of the sleeping man are simply failing to realize their dispositional powers. However, if we bear in mind that 'causation' includes instantiation unconsciousness need not be an obstacle to the instantiation of mental functions, and Searle fails to justify his conclusion that one possesses only dispositions toward mentality while unconscious.

FREUD'S ANTI-DISPOSITIONALIST ARGUMENT APPLIED TO SEARLE

As we have seen, Searle's analysis leads him to a dispositional notion of unconscious mental states. The reader will recollect that Freud identified such dispositional accounts as rivals to his own thesis about the nature of unconscious mental events. I will therefore deploy Freud's two main objections against the dispositionalist strategy to criticize Searle.

Freud's first criticism flows from his Continuity argument. Consider the following situation. An astronomer puzzles over the relationship between the Morning Star and the Evening Star. Exactly two days later he realizes that, unexpectedly, the Morning Star is identical to the Evening Star. As Freud points out, it is difficult to escape the conclusion that unconscious cognitive work has occurred between the two events described in the vignette.[148]

In order to preserve his dispositional account in the face of this objection, Searle has two obvious options: he can deny, pace Freud, that the intervening events were content-bearing and/or he can assert that dispositions enter into occurrent mental processes. Putting it baldly, the first option would amount to saying that, although the astronomer's thoughts at time T_1 were about the Morning Star and the Evening Star so conceived, and his thoughts at time T_2 were about the Morning Star/Evening Star so conceived, there were no thoughts occurring during the intervening period about these celestial bodies. In fact, they were not thoughts about anything at all: they were merely neurophysiological states capable of producing thoughts about celestial bodies.

This conclusion is implausible. In order to protect his thesis, Searle might attempt to argue that the content of such 'mental' items is only fixed at the time they become conscious. Indeed, this approach seems inescapable for Searle in light of his insistence that content cannot be characterized in purely neuroscientific terms. However, Searle is simultaneously committed to the seemingly contradictory thesis that there must be some sense in which the aspectual shape of a mental content is latent in its corresponding neurophysiological disposition. Indeed, it is unclear to me how a neurophysiological state can possess the causal power to produce some specific conscious state, replete with aspectual shape, without bearing some properties which covary in a principled way with the aspectual shapes of conscious mental events. Unless one makes this assumption, it follows that the specific content of a conscious state is underdetermined by its non-conscious neurophysiological counterpart, a thesis which would contravene Searle's claim that neurophysiology suffices to explain mental events[149] But, if neurophysiological states covary in a principled way with the features of conscious mental states which constitute their aspectual shape, the claim that these neurophysiological states do not possess aspectual shape is true only in a trivial sense, if at all. Surely, the neural states constituting the dispositions for mental states must in some sense have aspectual shape latent within them or else the resultant aspectual shape of conscious mental items remains inexplicable. Alternatively, one might say in defense of Searle that these neural states cause other neural states that serve as dispositions for conscious mental states with aspectual shape, but this does nothing except relocate the problem while introducing an unnecessary complexity.

Returning to our example, it is clear that some sort of mental process occurred between T_1 and T_2. Is it conceivable that this process performed operations on dispositional capacities? Searle writes:

> This sort of dispositional ascription of causal capacities is quite familiar to us from common sense. When, for example, we say of a substance that it is bleach or poison,

> we are ascribing to a chemical ontology a dispositional causal capacity to produce certain effects (161).

Effects on what? In the examples given by Searle, the causal agent and its object are segregated. However, in his account of mental dispositions, this is not the case: neurophysiological dispositions are not said to act on anything to produce conscious states, a claim that would imply some form of dualism. The bleach\bleached, poison\poisoned relations are examples of what Searle calls 'horizontal causation', a term that he uses for what are normally termed causal relations (in contrast to relations of instantiation). However, by his own account, the relationship between neurology and consciousness holds by virtue of 'vertical causation' (instantiation). So, there exists significant disanalogy between the examples of dispositionality and the mental phenomena that they are supposed to illuminate. In both forms of 'causation', environmental factors play a crucial role. A poison can only realize its venomous disposition if it comes into contact with a living organism possessing the right kind of physiology. Substances like bleach and poison require certain causal circumstances to release their dispositional powers. In these examples, the dispositional properties are inert in the absence of such causal circumstances. The disposition to be poisonous, for example, has no effect in the absence of an organism to poison. The reason for this, of course, is that the relevant dispositions of poison and bleach are relational dispositions; that is, they are dispositions only realizable through 'horizontal' forms of causation.

But if we turn to examples of 'vertical causation', such as the relationship between the molecular structure of water and its liquidity, the relationship between microscopic and macroscopic properties is internal to the object or substance under consideration. Talk of vertical causation is talk of non-relational properties. Furthermore, those features of an item which instantiate non-relational properties are never simply inert, although their effects co-vary with the causal circumstances. It is their constitutive significance which insures that they are never causally inert: it is the very molecular structure of water which, at suitable temperatures, instantiates liquidity that in other circumstances instantiates solidity. It makes no sense to say, assuming an unvarying causal environment, that the microscopic features by means of which a macroscopic feature is instantiated provide a mere disposition for the macroscopic feature to be realized (Cf. Papineau, 1993). Given appropriate and constant environmental circumstances, there is no way that the molecular structure of water could not be realized as liquidity. Of course, the liquidity of water involves its possessing certain dispositional powers, but this is distinct from the claim that the relation between its micro- and macro-properties is dispositional.

AN ADDITIONAL IMPLICATION OF FREUD'S CRITIQUE OF DISPOSITIONALISM.

In Searle's own example, the dispositional capacity of a poison supervenes upon its chemical ontology. A poison is some substance with the causal power to poison, irrespective of whether or not this power is exercised. An appropriate modification of the chemical structure of a poisonous substance may eliminate the dispositional capacity. By the same token, a modification in the neurophysiological state disposing one to the conscious thought that the Morning and Evening Star are distinct celestial bodies might result in a neurophysiological state disposing one to think that the Morning and Evening Star are after all one and the same. This approach to the problem raises a second issue that has hitherto remained latent. If we grant the possibility of this sort of dispositional transformation, we are left with the intuition that the operations brought to bear on the initial neurophysiological state are themselves mental. The transformation of the neurophysiological disposition to think that the Morning Star and the Evening Star are distinct into the disposition to think that the Morning Star and the Evening Star are identical seems inescapably mental. It seems intuitively wrong to describe this transformation as anything other than an example of cognition.[150]

Searle's general strategy can be brought to bear upon this problem by suggesting that the operations in question are mental only by virtue of the fact that they involve states which have dispositional capacities to produce conscious mental events. However, Searle's argument about dispositional powers is rooted in his thesis about aspectual shape: it is just because aspectual shape cannot be exhaustively characterized neurophysiologically that he concludes that a dispositional relationship holds between neurophysiological states and their corresponding conscious mental states. What of the principled, logically ordered transformation of one disposition into another? Surely, inferential algorithms do not possess aspectual shape! Equally surely, we must regard such processes as mental. The process by means of which I come to think of the Morning and Evening Stars as identical is a mental process devoid of aspectual shape. If such operations inherit their mental quality from the dispositional powers of the states over which they range; this is not warranted by Searle's argument as it stands.

FREUD'S ARGUMENT FROM UNCONSCIOUS CONFLICT

Searle makes the following claim about Freud's attributions of unconscious mental states:

> The evidence that Freud gives us for the existence of the unconscious is invariably that the patient engages in behavior that is as if he had a certain mental state, but because we know independently that the patient does not have any such conscious mental state, Freud postulates an unconscious mental state as the cause of the behavior (170).

Although there is some truth in this account of Freudian reasoning, Searle also leaves out critical features of the Freudian story, and fails to address the implications of these omissions that are deeply incompatible with his dispositionalist thesis. Of course, the failure of Searle's theory to encompass fully the explanatory details of Freudian theory has no clear bearing on the validity of his ideas. It might be argued that this instead calls Freud's theses into question. However, these difficulties clearly damage the plausibility of Searle's claim to provide a viable alternative philosophical underpinning for Freud's theory of occurrent unconscious mental events.

Searle is correct in claiming that Freud attributed unconscious mental contents to persons insofar as they behaved in conformity with those hypothetical states, whilst truthfully denying any first-person awareness of them. Searle's account nonetheless fails to capture Freudian reasoning in the following way. The unconscious states of interest to Freud in his clinical writings almost always involve repressed mental contents. The process of repression is bound up with unconscious conflict: items are repressed because of the conflicts to which they give rise. Repressed items are expressed indirectly by means of what Freud calls 'derivatives' - proxy ideas having some associative link with the repressed mental content. The repressed ideas corresponding to derivatives can only be accurately inferred by using the method of free-association in conjunction with specifically psychoanalytic auxiliary hypotheses (theory of symbolization, primary process, etc.). Freud's patients typically behave as if they have an (unconscious) idea only in light of specifically Freudian auxiliary hypotheses used to draw inferences from their speech behavior.[151]

Given Freud's notion of unconscious conflict, Searle must consider whether or not dispositions can enter into conflictual relations with occurrent ideas if he is to square his own account with Freud's observations. Searle provides the illustration of a boy who is driven by unconscious hatred of his father. As a Freudian example, which is what Searle intends, we must assume that this boy is unconscious of his hatred for his father because his hatred conflicts with a contrary attitude, say his love of his father. Let us assume that the boy is (pre)conscious of his love of his father. According to Searle's thesis, if his hatred is unconscious he just has a disposition to experience conscious hatred towards his father. It is only in such a conscious experience that the latent disposition would become actual.

Two objections arise at this point. First, if the boy just has a disposition to hate his father, and if this disposition is prevented from becoming manifest (i.e., if it is repressed) is it reasonable to say that he harbors an unconscious hatred towards his father? Searle might say that under these circumstances the boy's disposition to hate his father remains a disposition to hate his father even if it is permanently unrealized, just as a jar of poison remains a jar of poison even if it is never used to poison anyone. This analogy turns upon the concept of 'horizontal' causation, which as I have already shown, is not the sort of causation Searle has in mind with respect to unconscious neurophysiological states. The use of a concept of 'horizontal' dispositionality in this context opens the way for the following objection. Imagine that, by virtue of a genetic mutation, Hobart's body secretes a hormone that neutralizes the otherwise toxic properties of this particular poison when it is administered to him. The poison would kill anyone else, but not Hobart to whom the substance is not poisonous. By the same token, the disposition to hate one's father results for most individuals in conscious manifestations of such hatred; but in the case of the boy described by Searle, there is a countervailing factor, the process of repression, that prevents this from occurring. If we continue to regard unconscious attitudes as merely dispositional, in the 'horizontal' sense, it seems unwarranted to attribute unconscious hatred to the boy in Searle's example.

Searle's use of 'horizontal' causal analogy invites us to picture a scenario in which neurophysiological states act upon a subject from which they are ontologically segregated in a quasi-Cartesian scenario that conflicts with his commitment to naturalism. How, then, does the concept of 'vertical' dispositions fare in the context of this argument?

Using the example of water, the molecular structure of which disposes it to liquidity or solidity depending upon the temperature of its environment, it is clear that in this case the notion of conflicting dispositions makes no sense, because states of matter are not the right sort of entities to come into logical conflict with one another. Although a sample of water at certain temperature ranges may temporarily be in two states of matter, (e.g., melting ice,) this in no way involves a state of conflict. On a strong analogy with water, it might be argued that neurophysiological states disposing one to conscious mental states may be so constituted as to instantiate logically incompatible mental states as a function of the environment activating them. So, for example, some neurophysiological state *N* might be understood as instantiating the exclusive disjunction 'loving father or hating father', and might be realized as 'loving father' in causal circumstance *A* and as 'hating father' in causal circumstance *C*. Now imagine some causal circumstance *B*, lying mid-way between *A* and *C* which realize the neurophysiological disposition in the form 'loving and hating father'. Let us further assume that each of these three attitudes apply globally to father (or, alternatively, always apply to father in an identical respect). The intermediate state 'loving and hating father' possesses intentional content and so, unlike the intermediate states of water, gives rise to mental conflict. However, the conflict is produced only when the dispositions are realized in consciousness. The dispositions themselves do not enter into logical relations. In this account, the idea of 'unconscious mental conflict' would be metaphorical in precisely the same sense as Searle's concept of 'unconscious mental contents': unconscious neurophysiological states enter into conflict only by virtue of their causal powers. The same holds true if we imagine conflict to stem from demarcated neurophysiological dispositions.

The problem lies in Searle's foreclosure of the possibility that his neurophysiological states can possess real intentional content. If the boy in Searle's example does in fact possess a repressed disposition to hate his father, and given the thesis that this attitude is repressed because it conflicts with his love for his father, we must, within the purview of Searle's philosophical framework, regard this either as an instance of conflicting dispositions or as a case of a disposition entering into conflict with an occurrent conscious mental state. In the case of conflicting dispositions, Freudian theory claims that it is a necessary but not a sufficient condition for instances of unconscious conflict that the contrary attitudes are directed towards the same object or towards several objects having amongst them a relationship which secures the existence of mental conflict. For Freud, impulses conflict by virtue of the objects towards which they are directed. In both cases it is the objects of unconscious attitudes which determine whether or not the two attitudes come into conflict with one another.[152] Now, as (according to Searle) dispositional states are not in themselves intentional but consist in dispositions toward intentional states, and as (according to Freud) unconscious conflict exists only by virtue of mental representation of objects, it follows that Searle's dispositional theory of unconscious mental states is inconsistent with Freud's theory of unconscious conflict. The same argument holds in cases of conflict between unconscious dispositions and occurrent conscious states. If psychoneurotic symptoms are sustained by unconscious conflicts, then these conflicts must be occurrent and intentional rather than merely dispositional.

XIV

FREUD VERSUS SEARLE

Searle's (1992) discussion of Freud underestimates the complexity and subtlety of Freud's position.[153] Searle believes that, in contrast to his own concepts, Freud's view of the ontology of unconscious mental states is incoherent, and summarizes Freud's position as claiming that (1) unconscious mental states are occurrent rather than dispositional, (2) unconscious mental states possess a mental ontology, (3) all mental states are unconscious in themselves and (4) becoming conscious of a mental content is like perceiving an object. Searle argues that this position is inconsistent with present-day neuroscientific understanding of the brain, and that the analogy between episodes of consciousness of intentional content and episodes of perception does not make sense.

With respect to the first criticism, Searle claims that in the case of a totally unconscious person (say, a person in deep dreamless sleep) the mental contents which they may be assumed to have can only be understood as somehow lodged in their neural states. But a person's neural states cannot possibly possess aspectual shape or subjectivity, which are evidently taken to be irreducible properties of consciousness.[154] If, then, unconscious mental states are occurrent, Searle (1992) contends that Freud:

> Has not made intelligible what events could be going on in the brain in addition to the neurophysiological events to constitute unconscious subjectivity and intentionality (170).

Whenever Freud attributes unconscious mental states, he 'thinks that there is something there...that is not just neurophysiological, but is not conscious either'. This implies dualism because 'Freud is postulating a class of non-neurophysiological mental phenomena' (Ibid.).

With respect to the second criticism, Searle argues that Freud's view that mental contents are in themselves unconscious implies that consciousness is itself an extrinsic, inessential feature of mental states. This leads naturally to the conclusion that consciousness is a species of perception.

This theory of consciousness is untenable for three reasons. First, in the case of perception, subject and object can be distinguished from one another.

> Suppose I see a bicycle. In such a perceptual situation there is a distinction between the object perceived and the act of perception. If I take away the perception, I am left with a bike; if I take away the bike, I am left with a perception which has no object, for example, a hallucination. But it is precisely these distinctions that we cannot make for the conscious thought. If I try to take away the conscious thinking of this token thought, say, that Bush is president, I have nothing left. If I try to take away the token thinking of the thought away from the conscious thinking of it, I don't succeed in taking anything away. The distinction between the act of perceiving and the object perceived does not apply to conscious thoughts (171).

Second, if Freud is right that all mental phenomena are unconscious as such, it would follow that acts of perception are in themselves unconscious. In order for acts of perception to become conscious, higher-level acts of perception would be required leading, it seems, to an infinite regress.

Third, perception is based on the causal relationship between objects and nervous systems. If the 'object' of perception is an unconscious mental content, how does this square with the causal account of perception?

RESPONSE TO SEARLE'S CRITICISMS OF FREUD

Of the four points given in Searle's summary of what he takes to be Freud's position on the ontology of unconscious mental states, only the second is inaccurate. As we have seen in preceding chapters, Freud took a physicalistic stance toward the mental: he believed that mental events are identical to physical events and that intentionality is to be understood naturalistically as a (physical) property of nervous systems.

Searle's first criticism is driven by the contradiction that emerges if we accept his six premises. Searle attempts to resolve the contradiction by interpreting the second premise as stating that the intentionality of unconscious mental items lies in their causal powers and not their ontology.

The price that Searle pays for this option has been briefly alluded to above: it seems that the neurophysiological items disposing one to have conscious intentional states do not themselves possess intentional content. It is difficult to understand how it is that a non-intentional neurophysiological state can be understood as a disposition to think about *x*, if the values for *x* are not somehow built into the neurophysiological state itself. Freud's continuity argument also creates problems for Searle's solution: given an inferential process beginning with a conscious premise (at time T_1) and terminating in a conscious conclusion (at time T_2) how is it that the continuity of intentional content is secured between T_1 and T_2. Indeed, why does a man emerging from dreamless sleep *still* believe that the Eiffel Tower is in France if this content is not somehow inscribed in his neurophysiology? How is it that his neurophysiology disposes him precisely to this belief?

Searle might have attempted to resolve his contradiction by modifying the fifth premise rather than the second. He might have argued that if neurophysiological states are causally sufficient to generate conscious mental contents, then these contents must in some way be inscribed within these very neurophysiological states, an approach that would require him to abandon or significantly modify the fifth premise, leaving him with a doctrine far closer to the conventional forms of materialism from which he is anxious to distance himself.

With respect to Searle's first criticism, his dualistic language somewhat obscures the issues. Freud has no problem attributing occurrent mental states to a totally unconscious person because he believes that mental content is a property of the central nervous system. These states are not merely neurophysiological, because not all neurophysiological states are also intentional. Far from propounding a dualistic doctrine of non-neurophysiological mental states, Freud advances a radically monistic view of content-bearing neurophysiological states.

With respect to Searle's second criticism, Searle does not appreciate that Freud treats becoming-conscious as a form of perception as the latter is neuroscientifically theorized in the context of the topographical model.[155] It is important to consider Freud's theory of perception before going on to evaluate the thesis that the process of becoming-conscious is similar to the process of perception. The reader will recall that Freud postulated the existence of a special unit of the nervous system, which he called the 'ω neurones' or 'System *Cs.*' that clothes mental contents in consciousness. It is a necessary condition for any item becoming conscious that (a) it is either intrinsically perceptual or gets indexed to representations of perceptual information and (b) that it impinges upon the ω neurons. Acts of perception have a direct, non-stop route to the ω neurons. Short of some malfunction, transduced information automatically goes through ω and becomes conscious there and then. The becoming-conscious of non-perceptual intentional content must ride piggyback on perceptual representations, such as sentences or images, in order to pass through ω. It is in this sense that the becoming conscious of an unconscious item is analogous to a process of perception. A version of Searle's bicycle story can be embraced by the parameters of Freud's model. For Freud, the act of seeing a bicycle involves the transducing of visual information and its impingement upon ω. Becoming conscious of a thought about a bicycle similarly involves impingement of a physical representation of a bicycle upon ω. The requisite duality exists not primarily between person and object, but between ω and information impinging upon ω. This information is caused by either a perceptual object or a mental representation both of which, for Freud, possess a physical ontology. The causal character of perception is preserved in the causal impact of the neurophysiological state corresponding to an unconscious mental representation as it is felt by the ω neurons; (i.e., the causal relation holds between two neurophysiological systems, rather than between the mind and the world). Searle's objection is thus merely question-begging.

It is easy to soothe Searle's worry that Freud's view of the mental as unconscious *an sich* may entangle one in an infinite regress. Freud held that the mental is in itself unconscious in two distinct senses. In the more delimited case, Freud believed that mental representations must be empirically distinguished from consciousness of those representations in order to preserve the intuition of mental continuity. In this context 'the mental' means 'mental representation'. What Searle calls the act of perceiving of an unconscious content is, for Freud, just the proliferation of information from the mental representation through the ω neurons, and does not require us to posit higher-order perceptions *ad infinitum*. There is also a sense in which Freud can speak of a conscious mental representation as in itself unconscious, but this pertains to his ontological claim that every mental event is a physical event and can be exhaustively described using only physical predicates. This reading no more licenses an infinite regress than does the preceding one. Strictly neuroscientific descriptions of mental events must, in virtue of their very nature, dispense with terms invoking ontological subjectivity.

XV

DONALD DAVIDSON: THE RATIONAL UNCONSCIOUS

I have shown, in earlier chapters, that Freud's theory of occurrent unconscious mental events was confronted by two rival theories: the neurophysiological dispositionalist account and the dissociationist thesis. In the preceding two chapters, I have shown how John Searle revived a sophisticated version of the dispositionalist account which, however, remains vulnerable to Freudian criticism. In the present and succeeding chapters, I will argue that Donald Davidson has revived a version of the dissociationist approach. Unlike Searle, who rightly treats his thesis as a rival to that of Freud, Davidson offers his as a philosophical underpinning for Freud's work, apparently unaware that the two versions of mental architecture are deeply incompatible. Unlike Searle, whose argument, as we have seen, is strongly reminiscent of those advanced in the last century, Davidson gives dissociationism a distinctive twist.

DAVIDSON'S THESIS

Donald Davidson's 'Paradoxes of irrationality' (1982) is explicitly described by its author as a philosophical defence of Freud's view of the mind.[156] Davidson claims that:

> Psychoanalytic theory as developed by Freud claims to provide a conceptual framework within which to describe and understand irrationality. However, many philosophers think that there are fundamental errors or confusions in Freud's thought. So I consider here some elements in that thought which have often come under attack, elements that consist of a few very general doctrines central to all stages of Freud's mature writings (290).

Davidson attributes three specific assertions to Freud that he wishes to defend philosophically. According to Davidson, Freud claims that (1) each human mind contains a number of semi-autonomous structures which can be truly categorized in terms of ordinary psychological predicates, (2) these structures resemble people in that they possess psychological traits such as beliefs and desires, but also in that these psychological items can combine to produce new events (e.g., actions) and (3) some of the psychological characteristics of mental substructures must be viewed as physical dispositions in their causal relations with other mental substructures. Davidson proposes that these three theses can be considered independently of the Freudian hypothesis of the unconscious, although they are of course compatible with this hypothesis.

Davidson develops his theory as follows. A rational explanation of an action invokes an agent's desires and beliefs, said to give rise to rational actions by combining in certain ways. These desire/belief combinations explain their resultant (rational) actions both logically and causally, along the lines of the practical syllogism. A desire/belief pair may provide an explanation for an action without this being the reason that brought about the action, in which case the logical but not the causal element is present. The rationality of an action is the congruence between cause and logical explanation.

When we come to explain irrational action, there are two extreme positions which Davidson christens the 'Plato Principle' and the 'Medea Principle'. The Plato Principle states that all actions are rational, insofar as all actions are based on desire-belief pairs. This 'doctrine of pure reason' makes it difficult to understand irrational action. If the Plato Principle holds, irrational actions must be understood as only apparently irrational. The Medea Principle holds that a rational intention can be hijacked by a non-rational (non-intentional) mental force. Davidson holds that neither of these principles can explain the occurrence of actions which are at once irrational and intentional: Plato loses the irrationality and Medea loses the intentionality. Neither alternative will suffice because irrationality of this type occurs when a mental cause brings about an action that is not its reason. Davidson emphasizes that this pattern of explanation is also applicable to other spheres of irrationality. At least one type of irrational belief, wishful thinking, consists in adhering to a belief because of desires rather than reasons substantiating the belief. Davidson also notes that the circumstances that he has set out as characterizing motivated irrationality describe necessary but not sufficient conditions.

How can a mental event be caused by some other mental item which is not also the reason for its occurring? It is not enough to invoke a purely physical, non-mental and neural cause, because Davidson's description requires the irrational event to possess a mental cause. To describe a mental event as irrational is to subsume its cause under a mental description. The mental character of non-rational causes can be preserved if we understand the mind through the model of interpersonal relations. In an interpersonal context, the desires and beliefs in one mind (that of Sasha) may result in rational actions which exploit the desires of another (Ben). The actions of Ben, who is the object of Sasha's clever machinations, are caused by mental events in Sasha's mind and yet Sasha's desires and beliefs are not the reasons for Ben's actions.

If we imagine the human mind to be divided so as to resemble two or more separate people, irrationality can be understood as caused by something resembling an interpersonal encounter. One 'part' of the mind induces another 'part' of the mind to do its bidding, and we get mental causes that are not reasons in the required sense.[157] A 'part' of the mind must possess a 'structure of reasons, of interlocking beliefs, expectations, assumptions, attitudes and desires' (Davidson, 1982:300) which is more consistent than the corresponding structure of the mind as a whole. For Davidson, then, motivated irrationality is the product of an interaction between relatively autonomous, rational mental structures.

XVI

FREUD VERSUS DAVIDSON

Davidson offers an account of human irrationality which he also describes as providing philosophical justification for Freud's 'conceptual framework'. However, closely examined, how consistent is Davidson's thesis with Freud's position?

Davidson states that:

> If to an otherwise unobjectionable theory we add the assumption of unconscious elements, the theory can only be made more acceptable, that is, capable of explaining more. For suppose we are led to realise by a genius like Freud that if we posit certain mental states and events we can explain much behaviour that otherwise goes unexplained; but we also discover that the associated verbal behavior does not fit the normal pattern. The agent denies he has the attitudes and feelings we would attribute to him. We can reconcile observation and theory by stipulating the existence of unconscious events and states that, aside from awareness, are like conscious beliefs, desires and emotions (1982:305).

FREUD AND DAVIDSON ON MENTAL DIVISION

Davidson seems to regard the notion of unconscious mental events as unproblematic.[158] His main concern is to justify notions of mental division and the non-rational interaction between relatively segregated networks of propositional attitudes. He appears to assume that once this justification has been secured, the incorporation of a notion of unconscious mental events is reasonably straightforward. I will show that given his philosophical commitments, this is not the case. Prior to this, I will delineate certain aspects of Freudian theory pertinent to the issue of mental division but logically independent of the thesis of unconscious mental events, thus highlighting the contradiction between the views propounded by Davidson and Freud.

According to Davidson, mental division is underwritten by the possibility that certain areas of the fabric of propositional attitudes may be more tightly (coherently) woven than the fabric as a whole. Mental divisions are therefore demarcated by their propositional gradient. Although this thesis does not capture even Freud's pre-topographical conception of mental division for reasons that I will shortly make clear, it does bear strong similarity to a fundamental Freudian concept initially developed in the pre-topographical phase of Freud's work and retained in the post-topographical: the notion of the 'complex'[159] or 'psychical group'. However, Freud felt that a 'complex' or 'psychical group' is not constellated by its exceptional coherence, but rather by its dissociation from the main body of the subject's mental life. As Freud and Breuer (1893) put it:

> In hysteria groups of ideas originating in hypnoid states are present and ... these are cut off from associative connection with the other ideas, but can be associated among themselves, and thus form the more or less highly organised rudiment of a second consciousness, a *condition seconde* (15).

Although Freud eventually rejected the idea that ideational groups can become dissociated simply by virtue of having occurred during a hypnoid state 'hypnoid hysteria'), coming to insist that associative dissociation came about because of the need of the subject to circumscribe a group of ideas which would otherwise provoke the experience of mental pain 'defence hysteria'), he retained the idea that complexes are created and sustained by virtue of the active severance of associative connections, a process which he termed 'defence' (Freud & Breuer, 1895). Given the causal role played by defence in Freud's system, one must conclude that any superior coherence within isolated ideational groups must derive in the Freudian framework from the manner in which these groups have become dissociated from the remainder of the subject's mental life rather than vice versa. It follows that Davidson's claim about the cause of mental division is diametrically opposed to that proposed by Freud.[160] Although both Davidson and Freud have used the concept of mental division to explain motivated irrationality, for Freud division of the mind is itself motivated, whereas for Davidson the division of the mind is a consequence of its organization, although he does not appear to exclude the possibility that this organization is founded on deeper motivational forces.

Davidson's mental divisions also might be taken as structures such as the Freudian ego and superego. It is not clear from Freudian theory whether or not these 'agencies' can be understood as demarcated by propositional coherence with respect to the overall propositional coherence of the mental apparatus. These structures, as well as the Kleinian notion of 'internal objects', are probably best understood as analogous to rather than coterminous with Davidson's mental divisions.

THE ATTRIBUTION OF UNCONSCIOUS MENTAL CONTENT

According to Davidson, the dense desire/belief networks that constitute the human mind are constituted by the normative principle of rationality. Rationality, in this sense, consists of the standards of rational thought and the appropriate relations between thought and world with respect to belief fixation and action. Rationality is thus constitutive of propositional attitude ('folk') psychology. The network of folk-psychological items is claimed to be holistic, in that 'a belief is identified by its location in a pattern of beliefs; it is this pattern that determines the subject-matter of the belief, what the belief is about' (Davidson, 1975:168). Davidson seems to imply that the principle of the interdependence of propositional items is not merely an interpretative device to facilitate the attribution of mental content: the content of intentional items is *constituted* by their position in the propositional web. Within a single mind, propositional attitudes are co-constitutive of one another. Each belief (or desire, fear, hope, etc.) is individuated by virtue of its location within a network of propositional attitudes and can be understood only in relation to a complex background of rationally related folk-psychological items shared, for the most part, with the person making the propositional attitude attribution.

The most obvious way that Davidson's model of the divided mind can be harmonized with Freud's topography, the way in which Davidson clearly envisaged it, is to postulate that, in some instances of mental division, one component of the division may be unconscious. That is, a coherent and rationally ordered structure of folk-psychological items of which the subject is unconscious comes into conflict with a counterpart structure of which the subject is conscious or preconscious. The unconscious structure determines the outcome of the conflict through causal and non-rational means.[161]

Taken as a philosophical apology for Freudian theory, Davidson's thesis fails in a manner which should by now be apparent. The attribution of rationality to the unconscious captures only preconscious and $\text{unconscious}_{\text{ego}}$ mental states, and is only imperfectly consistent with the quintessentially Freudian conception of $\text{unconscious}_{\text{irr}}$ mental states. Davidson has accommodated a modified version of Freudian theory within his own notion of mental structure rather than having provided a philosophical justification for Freud's topography.

We have seen that Freud (1915a) accepts that Charity-based methods of content attribution are appropriate and workable, if not inevitable, when considering many mental states, but also holds that, because of the intrinsically incoherent nature of $\text{unconscious}_{\text{irr}}$ states, they cannot be fully or adequately captured by this interpretative strategy. Of course, it does not follow from this that Freud claims that $\text{unconscious}_{\text{irr}}$ contents are simply irrelevant to rationality-invoking content attribution. Indeed, for Freud, $\text{unconscious}_{\text{irr}}$ states are only detectable insofar as they impinge upon rationally ordered preconscious processes.

RATIONALITY AND RATIONALISATION

Unlike Searle, Davidson's story of (possibly) unconscious mental states is bound up with his analysis of motivated irrationality. Davidson (1982) gives the following example of irrationality, borrowed from a footnote to Freud's case study of the 'Rat Man' (1909b).

> A man walking in the park stumbles on a branch in his path. Thinking the branch may endanger others, he picks it up and throws it in a hedge beside the path. On his way home it occurs to him that the branch may be projecting from the hedge and so still be a threat to unwary walkers. He gets off the tram he is on, returns to the park, and restores the branch to its original position. Here everything the agent does (except stumble on the branch) is done for a reason, a reason in the light of which the corresponding action seemed reasonable. Given that the man believed the stick was a danger if left on the path, and a desire to eliminate the danger, it was reasonable to remove the stick. Given that, on second thought, he believed the stick was a danger

in the hedge, it was reasonable to extract the stick from the hedge and replace it on the path. Given that the man wanted to take the stick from the hedge, it was reasonable for him to dismount from the tram and return to the park. In each case the reasons for the action tell us what the agent saw in his action, they give the intention with which he acted, and they thereby give an explanation of the action (294).

Later in the same paper he comments that:

It is easy to imagine that the man who returned to the park to restore the branch to its original position in the path realises that his action is not sensible. He has a motive for moving the stick, namely, that it may endanger a passer-by. But he also has a motive for not returning, which is the time and trouble that it costs. In his own judgement, the latter consideration outweighs the former; yet he acts on the former. In short, he goes against his own best judgement (294).

Still later he informs us that:

The man who returns to the park to replace the branch has a reason: to remove the danger. But in doing this he ignores his principle for acting on what he thinks is best, all things considered. And there is no denying that he has a motive for ignoring his principle, namely that he wants, perhaps very strongly, to return the branch to its original position. Let us say this motive does explain the fact that he fails to act on his principle. This is the point at which irrationality enters. For the desire to replace the branch has entered into the decision to do it twice over. First it was a consideration in favour of replacing the branch, a consideration that, in the agent's opinion, was less important than the reasons against returning to the park. The agent then held that everything considered he ought not return to the park. Given his principle that one ought to act on such a conclusion, the rational thing for him to do was, of course, not to return to the park. Irrationality entered when his desire to return made him ignore or override his principle. For although his motive for ignoring the principle was a reason for ignoring the principle, it was not a reason against the principle itself, and so when it entered in this second way, it was irrelevant as a reason, to the principle and to the action. (297)

Freud (1909) gives this account in a footnote because of its similarity to an obsessional action committed by the Rat Man. Freud states with regard to the Rat Man's action that:

Compulsive acts like this, in two successive stages, of which the second neutralises the first, are a typical occurrence in obsessional neuroses. The patient's consciousness naturally misunderstands them and puts forward a set of secondary motives to account for them - rationalises them. (192)

In the footnote, Freud describes the irrational (compulsive) action in a manner slightly but significantly different from Davidson, and includes an explanation along the lines of the passage reproduced above.

> He was walking one day in the park at Schönbrunn...when he kicked his foot against a branch that was lying on the ground. He picked it up and flung it into the hedge that bordered the path. On his way home he was suddenly seized with uneasiness that the branch in its new position might perhaps be projecting a little from the hedge and might cause an injury to someone passing by the same place after him. He was obliged to jump off his tram, hurry back to the park, find the place again, and put the branch back in its former position - although any one else but the patient would have seen that, on the contrary, it was bound to be more dangerous to passers-by in its original position then where he had put it in the hedge. The second and hostile act, which he carried out under compulsion, had clothed himself to his conscious view with the motives that really belonged to the first and philanthropic one (192-193, n 2).

Returning for a moment to Davidson's explanation, we must first inquire into the status of the principle that one should do what is best all things considered. This principle is an aspect of the norm of rationality which, Davidson believes, is constitutive of the mental.

> The issue raised a few paragraphs back, whether irrationality in an agent requires an inner inconsistency, a deviation from that person's own norms, is now seen to be misleading. For where the norms are basic they are constitutive elements in the identification of attitudes and so the question of whether someone 'accepts' them cannot arise. All genuine inconsistencies are deviations from the person's own norms. This goes not only for patently logical inconsistencies but also for weakness of the will (as Aristotle pointed out), for weakness of the warrant and for self-deception (1986:84).

Davidson includes these considerations in order to counter the charge that the apparently irrational person is not really irrational if he or she does not accept the normative principles of rationality in the first place, a state of affairs in which the incoherence between principle and action would be absent. However, if as Davidson claims, the norms of rationality are basic and constitutive, how can the irrational person 'ignore' or 'override' them, as Davidson also claims? Surely, it is a mistake to explain such irrationality in terms of one's attitude towards rationality itself. The upshot is that Davidson cannot reasonably account for irrationality in terms of a motivated rejection of the principle. It is therefore more consistent to interpret his argument as turning on the claim that, given the thesis of the all-encompassing normative force of the principles of rationality, any apparent violation must be understood as the effect of a divided mind, each component of which must conform to the norms of rationality. For Davidson, we simply cannot regard an event as mental if we regard it as falling completely outside the bounds of these norms.

In contrast to Davidson, Freud's explanation of motivated irrationality turns on the (ironically, quintessentially Davidsonian) distinction between the purpose of an action and its description. As actions only satisfy the norms of rationality under certain descriptions, it may be conjectured that the failure of an action or conjunction of actions to satisfy these norms is due to their presentation under an inappropriate description.[162] Freud believes that our development as human beings, the emotional commitments which this development engenders, the deep structure of our minds and the biological drives which motivate us, place powerful constraints upon the stories that we tell to explain our own actions. Perhaps more fundamentally, Freud claims that folk-psychological attributions of mental content to ourselves, as well as others, is 'theoretical' in nature. If this is the case, even if we accept that behavior is governed by normative principles of rationality, there is no reason to assume that this will always be captured in our descriptions of that behavior.

Let us assume, along with Davidson and others, that human behavior is normatively rational. This assumption is not, in fact, incompatible with Freudian thought as radically irrational $unconscious_{irr}$ states are states of representation which do not enter directly into human behavior. Let us also assume that the attribution of folk-psychological states is a theoretical activity. And, finally, let us assume that there are compelling psychological constraints on how we are able to ascribe and describe these states. According to Freud, if a true description of one's mental state contravenes such narrative constraints, a false description will be generated which both 'explains' the action and satisfies the constraints; (Freud uses Jones' term 'rationalization' to denote this process). Freud states that, in replacing the branch in the path, the man's self-ascription of the desire to prevent an accident was false. The fact that the man placed the branch in a hazardous position implies, says Freud (assuming the rationality of behavior), that he wished to harm a passer-by. The Freudian account explains both why the man acts in contradiction to what he represents as best all things considered, and also captures an aspect of his irrationality about which Davidson is silent: i.e., the fact that the man returns the branch to a position which he knows to be hazardous, in contradiction with his avowed intention of removing the branch from the hedge so as to prevent accidental injury.[163]

Of course, it might be argued that, in postulating a false description of the motives for an akratic act pre-empting the possibility of all things being considered, the Freudian account fails to come to grips with true Davidsonian akrasia. This may well be the case but, equally, it may well be the case that the Davidsonian conception of akratic behavior is mistaken. Freud's account must therefore be regarded as a rival account of the dynamics of those forms of behavior called akratic', the main significance of which in the context of the present discussion is to show that Davidson's story about akrasia, whatever its intrinsic virtues, does not philosophically underwrite Freud's thesis.

INTENTIONALISTIC AND ANTI-INTENTIONALISTIC EXPLANATION

Davidson's concern with rationality and ordinary irrationality lead him to take for granted some assumptions which, as we have seen, are not only incompatible with Freud's concept of unconscious$_{irr}$ processes, but also are difficult to apply to paradigmatically Freudian phenomena. In particular, Davidson's account is rationalistic: the mental is by definition characterized by complex, logically ordered desire/belief networks.

> Davidson...regards the Principle [of Charity] as being constitutive of the concepts it governs. The concepts of belief, desire, meaning and intentional action are defined by what the 'theory', the Principle of Charity, says about them. If they do not apply in accordance with the principle, there is no reason to take them as applying at all (Evnine, 1991: 113).

Davidson may be taken to mean that charity is analytic with respect to mental states (Evnine, 1991: 185). But, as Evnine points out in passing, if Charity does possess this constitutive role - if attributions of content are governed by normative, holistic considerations - then it is difficult to take Davidson literally when he claims that desires and beliefs enter into causal relations with other psychological items. Interpretative constructions do not seem to be the sort of thing that can enter into causal relations, unless we also subordinate causation to an interpretative scheme, a strategy which Davidson (1970) explicitly rejects. Davidson (1995) makes it clear that he believes propositional attitudes to be a code for indexing psychological states, just as numbers are a code for indexing temperature. If this is the case, then charity is constitutive of the indexing system - of thought and talk of mental states - rather than of mental states themselves, although the former must provide information about the functional organization of the latter. If thought and talk of causal relations between folk-psychological items are intended as idioms for describing more-or-less rational states, the extension of these idioms in order to capture irrational states interpretatively is not self-evidently legitimate. The purpose of charity is, after all, the attribution of rational patterns. Davidson is arguably attempting to extend it beyond its appropriate explanatory domain an issue raised, as we shall see, by Dennett as well as Freud.

Psychoanalysis does not normally or distinctively deal with what Gardner (1993) calls 'ordinary irrationality'. Psychoanalysis attempts to explain deeply irrational states, such as a terror of pigeons or the delusion that one is God. Deeply irrational states are 'propositionally opaque'. They 'do not exhibit the immediate intelligibility, and unity of identification and explanation which...characterises ordinary irrationality' (Gardner, 1993: 91). It is this propositional opacity which renders the problem of folk-psychological causation particularly acute. Consider the example of the man, discussed by Alexander (1962) and Mischel (1965) who compulsively lunges at lampposts with his umbrella. The man cannot tell us why he engages in this strange behavior. What are we to make of it? Let us assume that the lamppost lunging has some true explanation in terms of the man's unconscious Oedipal preoccupations. Is it that he desires to kill his father, and unconsciously believes that his lunging is a killing and the lampposts are his father? Does he unconsciously desire to lunge at lampposts in the unconscious belief that by doing so he will kill his father? Or do these scenarios involve the sexual possession of his mother rather than the murder of his father? Is his lunging intended to bring about a desired state of affairs, or does it simply represent some element of the unconscious phantasy underpinning it? The indeterminacy inherent in ordinary content attribution is constrained by the web of meaning surrounding the sentence to be interpreted in that any interpretative move systematically affects the interpretation of the entire meaning-network. In the hypothetical case mentioned above, the unconscious meaning of the lunging is specific to the context of lunging at lampposts; (i.e., systematic investigation into those circumstances in which the man lunges will tell us nothing about the unconscious meaning of his lunging at lampposts). By the same token, the unconscious meaning of lampposts is specific to the contexts in which they are lunged at. This is semantic indeterminacy with a vengeance. Although we can give an intentional-stance characterization of the cause of the compulsion, we have no means to determine just what beliefs and desires interact to bring about the result. We have too many unconstrained interpretative options. As I have already noted, Freud rejected the view that unconscious$_{irr}$ expressions come about through anything like the practical syllogism. Although episodes like compulsive lamppost lunging derive their content from the content of their unconscious causes, this process cannot be given a true description as a rational process. In taking this line, Freud is free from some of the explanatory demands that we must make of Davidson but, of course, bound by others.

Although Freud never discusses the matter philosophically, his interpretative procedure licenses a move which circumvents the problems raised by the extreme indeterminacy of interpretation noted above. Freud's term 'condensation' signifies the notion that distinct unconscious items can set off numerous associative trains which terminate in one and the same preconscious derivative; i.e., that the unconscious meaning of a derivative cannot be adequately captured by means of a one-to-one mapping of the elements of the unconscious item onto the components of the preconscious item. However, the notion of 'condensation' might also be understood as a pragmatic interpretative device designed to deal with indeterminacy. To say that a derivative is overdetermined might be to say that a complex unconscious representation is expressed in its entirety by means of the derivative. The derivative as a whole is said to map onto the unconscious representation as a whole because we are unable to determine how (or even if) there is a systematic mapping relation between their components. The use of this approach is contingent upon the interpreter possessing prior true knowledge of the unconscious cause of irrational behavior. This is, of course, practically impossible and encounters the problems of the attribution of unconscious$_{irr}$ mental content noted in Chapter Eleven.

Even if one is a realist with respect to folk-psychological entities, the notion that truly irrational events can be explained in terms of rationality seems debatable. Dennett, who is an anti-realist in this connection, expresses the view that:

> An intentional interpretation of an agent is an exercise that attempts to make sense of the agent's acts, and when acts occur that make no sense, they cannot be straightforwardly interpreted in sense-making terms. Something must give: we allow that the agent only "sort of" believes this or that, or believes this or that "for all practical purposes," or believes some falsehood which creates a context in which what had appeared to be irrational turns out to be rational after all....These particular fall-back positions are themselves subject to the usual tests of belief attribution, so merely finding a fall-back position is not confirming it. If it is disconfirmed, the search goes on for another saving interpretation. If there is no saving interpretation - if the person in question is irrational - no interpretation at all will be settled on (87 - 88).

Although it may at first blush seem strange, Freud is much closer to Dennett than he is to Davidson with respect to this issue. As I have already shown, Freud was deeply suspicious of the utility of intentional and folk-psychological accounts of unconscious$_{irr}$ mental events. At the same time, he acknowledged that we do not possess a workable alternative. Freud's solution was to use folk-psychological language cautiously and self-consciously as what Quine called an 'essentially dramatic idiom', occasionally pausing to remind the reader (and presumably himself) that the belief in unconscious folk-psychological entities amounts to a form of 'animism' whilst simultaneously attempting to develop a formal psychological vocabulary (his 'metapsychology') which does not advert to folk-psychological entities.

Dennett (1987) illustrates his contentions by means of an example which Freud might describe as a 'symptomatic act' and therefore in principle open to psychoanalytic explanation.

> At breakfast I am reminded that I am playing tennis with Paul instead of having lunch today. At 12:45 I find myself polishing off desert when Paul, in tennis gear, appears at my side and jolts me into recollection. "It completely slipped my mind!" I aver,

blushing at my own absent-mindedness. But why do I say that? It is because, as I recall, not a single conscious thought about my tennis date passed through my head after breakfast? That might be true, but perhaps no conscious thought that I was going to lunch today occurred to me in the interim either, and yet here I am, finishing my lunch (88).

According to Dennett, the proffered explanation that the appointment 'slipped his mind' is offered because he wanted to avoid considering the possibility that he was 'starkly irrational' (89). The folk-psychological account of such episodes assumes rationality.

As creatures of our own attempts to make sense of ourselves the putative mental activities of folk-theory are hardly a neutral field of events and processes to which we can resort for explanations when the normative demands of intentional system theory run afoul of a bit of irrationality (91).

It is precisely because Dennett's failure to keep his tennis appointment was a failure of rationality that it cannot, in his view, be adequately explained from the 'intentional stance'; (one must tack it on to the computational level or the level of neurophysiological realization). Dennett's diagnosis of 'stark irrationality' confronts us with an obvious problem. In such instances we can often identify what is plausibly a motive for the forgetting. Let us imagine (and we must imagine, because Dennett does not push his analysis this far) that Dennett's tennis partner was John Searle, who had recently written a highly critical review of Dennett's *Consciousness Explained* that had, in turn aroused some ill-feeling in Dennett. Intuitively, we have no difficulty attributing Dennett's forgetting to his ill-feeling. However, it does not seem reasonable to subsume the forgetting under conventional forms of intentionalistic explanation which would assert that Dennett's animosity was a reason for his lapse, a point to which I shall return below. To ignore this point is to limit the analysis of such episodes to the exclusive disjunction of either classical intentionalistic description or utter irrationality. This is precisely the sort of dilemma which Freud attempted to undercut by means of concepts of motivational explanation that do not conform to the explanatory cannon of the practical syllogism.

Of course, Davidson shows that a wholesale abandonment of intentionalistic explanation is not necessary in such instances. We can retain split-mind intentionalism, augmented by an element of non-intentionalistic mental causation. For Freud, the Davidsonian alternative is only possible if the causally efficacious subsystem is not identified with unconscious$_{irr}$ elements that are by definition refractory to rational characterization.

Let us now substitute for Dennett's example an episode of forgetting described by Freud.

> I had written a short pamphlet On Dreams...summarising the subject-matter of my Interpretation of Dreams...for the series *Grenzfragen des Nerven- und Seelenlebens* [*Frontier Problems of Nervous and Mental Life*]. Bergmann [the publisher] of Wiesbaden had sent me the proofs, and had asked for them back by return of post, as the book was to be issued before Christmas. I corrected the proofs the same night and placed them on my desk so as to take them with me next morning. In the morning I forgot about them, and only remembered them in the afternoon when I saw the wrapper on my desk. In the same way I forgot the proofs that afternoon, that evening and the following morning, till I pulled myself together and took them to a letter-box on the afternoon of the second day, wondering what could be the reason for my procrastination. It was obvious that I did not want to send them off, but I could not discover why. However, in the course of the same walk I called in at my publisher's in Vienna - the firm that had published my "Interpretation of dreams". I placed an order for something and then said, as if impelled by a sudden thought: "I suppose you know that I've written the dream-book over again?" – "Oh, you can't mean that!" he said. "Don't be alarmed", I replied; "it's only a short essay for the Löwenfeld-Kurella series." But he was still not satisfied; he was worried that the essay would interfere with the sales of the book. I disagreed with him and finally asked: "If I'd come to you before, would you have forbidden my publishing it?" – "No, I certainly wouldn't." Personally I believe I acted quite within my rights and did nothing contrary to common practice; nevertheless it seemed certain that a misgiving similar to that expressed by the publisher was the motive for my delay in sending back the proofs (1901: 160).

Several philosophers in the broadly Wittgensteinian tradition (e.g., Flew, 1954; Toulmin, 1954; MacIntyre, 1958; Siegler, 1967; Dilman, 1972) have interpreted Freud's theories as claiming that actions may be carried out because of unconscious reasons. According to this interpretation, Freud forgot to post his proofs because unconsciously he did not want to publish 'On dreams' and also unconsciously believed that, by failing to send the proofs, he would keep the book from publication. This position is consistent with that expressed by Davidson. On a Davidsonian interpretation, some subsystem within Freud's mind behaved in such a manner as to cause Freud to forget to send the proofs. According to this explanation, the subsystem (a) desired that 'On dreams' not be published and (b) believed that by causing Freud to forget to return the proofs, this desire would be realized. I will refer to this pattern of explanation as the 'intentionalistic' explanation of motivated rationality.

Shope (1970) takes issue with the intentionalistic interpretation of Freud's approach to irrationality. According to Shope, Freud does not commit himself to the view that parapraxes, like the forgetting of the proofs, are strictly intentional. According to Shope, Freud explains parapraxes as caused by the rejection (suppression or repression) of a thought prior to the slip. In other words, (1) Freud's mental subsystem *S* wants 'On dreams' to remain unpublished, (2) *S* believes that the wish that 'On dreams' not to be published will be satisfied by causing Freud's failing to return the proofs to his publisher and (3) thus *S* causes Freud's forgetting to return them.

According to this view, it was Freud's suppression of the intention not to publish the book that caused his forgetting: he did not intend to prevent the publication of the book by means of forgetting the proofs. To put this slightly differently, it is precisely because the wish to prevent the publication of 'On dreams' was suppressed that it was able to bring about Freud's lapse. Of course, Freud's forgetting did nonetheless display his reluctance.

Boudreaux (1977) criticizes Shope by finding examples from Freud which appear to be inconsistent with this interpretation. Some of the ostensibly intentionalistic examples that Boudreaux garners from Freud can be squared with Shope's hypothesis on the assumption that, when Freud describes a parapraxis as expressing an intention, he means that an intention was expressed through the parapraxis not that the parapraxis was committed in order to express the intention. When, for example, Freud states 'Since he recognised the mislaying of the keys as a symptomatic act - that is, as something he had done intentionally' (1901:141), he does not mean that the subject unconsciously intended to lose the keys, but rather that the losing of the keys expressed an unconscious intention and was caused by the rejection of that intention. Boudreaux also holds up examples purporting to show the communicative intention to commit parapraxes; for example, 'I inferred that he intended this slip to express [to Freud] the view that, like his brother, he had fallen ill through the fault of his father' (1901:80). But on Shope's view we should understand Freud as claiming that it was the rejection of his wish to tell Freud that he blamed his father for his illness which brought about the slip, not that he intended to communicate this by means of committing the slip.

On Shope's analysis, then, Freud does not explain forgettings and related manifestations of irrationality as intentional actions: the intentional stance takes us only as far as an identification of the competing motives, the presence of which provide a precondition for parapraxis. I will describe the acts caused by the disavowal of wishes as manifestations of these wishes, although within this account the wishes do not serve as reasons for their corresponding acts I use the term 'manifestation of a wish' as a mode of causation less constrained by the content of the wish than the conclusion of a practical syllogism involving the wish as a premise). I will refer to Shope's interpretation of Freud as the 'anti-intentionalistic' thesis. According to this view, it was Freud's disavowal of his wish not to publish 'On dreams' which caused him to forget to return the proofs, an act manifesting the disavowed wish. So, (1) Freud wished that 'On dreams' be published, (2) Freud simultaneously wished that 'On dreams' not be published, (3) Freud unconsciously disavowed the wish that 'On dreams' not be published and (4) Freud's disavowal caused his forgetting to return the proofs, an act manifesting the disavowed wish that 'On dreams' not be published.

In both intentionalistic and anti-intentionalistic accounts there is one point at which the story becomes unsatisfactorily vague: the point at which mental causation enters the picture. In the intentionalistic account this happens at point (3), how does the subsystem cause Freud's forgetting? Davidson models the intrapsychic situation at (3) along the following lines.

> For example, wishing to have you enter my garden, I grow a beautiful flower there. You crave a look at my flower and enter my garden. My desire caused your craving and action, but my desire was not a reason for my craving, nor a reason on which you acted....Mental phenomena may cause other mental phenomena without being reasons for them, then, and still keep their character as mental, provided cause and effect are adequately segregated (1982: 300).

How literally are we to take Davidson's analogy? If Davidson wants us to take him literally, if he is claiming that motivated irrationality stems from a mental subsystem strategically manipulating the whole person to fulfil its wishes, he implies that mental subsystems are able to represent themselves as well as the person as a whole, thus considerably exceeding the criterion that a mental division is simply a nexus of desires and beliefs which is more coherent than the mind as a whole. Davidson appears to require the interpersonal analogy to strengthen the bare notion of mental division so as to make it adequate to explain irrationality within the confines of the intentional stance.[164]

In the anti-intentionalist account, the story becomes vague when mental causation enters the sequence at (4), raising three questions which need to be addressed. Just how does the disavowal bring about the parapraxis? Why does the repudiated wish remain causally efficacious? How does the parapraxis preserve the content of the repudiated wish? Like Davidson, Shope is insufficiently explicit.

A FREUDIAN APPROACH

The example of Freud's parapraxis is not a good exemplar of unconscious causation because the two competing thoughts which, in some fashion, gave rise to the parapraxis - the desire that 'On dreams' be published and the contrary desire that 'On dreams' be withheld from publication - are both preconscious mental contents. As such, they throw no light on the problem of $\text{unconscious}_{\text{irr}}$ causation because preconscious mental contents do, in fact, conform to Davidson's strictures concerning the normative role of rationality.

For the sake of the present discussion, let us imagine that Freud's preconscious wish that 'On dreams' not be published (I will call this wish W_1) was a derivative of an $\text{unconscious}_{\text{irr}}$ mental content *Uc*. I will refer to this as the augmented account of Freud's parapraxis. To say that W_1 is a derivative of *Uc* is just to say that (a) W_1 is associatively linked to *Uc*, and (b) W_1 inherits some of the causal powers that *Uc* would possess if *Uc* were preconscious. Were this the case, then intentionalistic and anti-intentionalistic approaches would need to be able to encompass the unconscious$_{irr}$ causation involved in the activation of W_1 as a derivative of *Uc*.

Freud's thesis offers an explanation of why it is that the disavowed wish, W_1, retains its causal efficacy in spite of his rejection of it. W_1 asserts itself because of its derivative status with respect to *Uc*. It is the causal link to U that keeps the wish alive as an expression of *Uc* and brings about its non-intentionalistic manifestation. This approach conceives of the parapraxis as (1) *Uc* activates W_1, (2) W_1 contradicts Freud's wish to have 'On dreams' published (W_2), (3) Freud disavows W_1 and (4) Freud's disavowal of W_1 causes his forgetting to return the proofs, thus manifesting W_1.

The notions of actions manifesting wishes is critical for a clear demarcation of the intentionalistic from the anti-intentionalistic interpretations of Freud's position. The claim that the suppression of a wish is a key feature of the causal circumstance responsible for the expression of the wish in the form of a parapraxis does not entail that the parapraxis cannot be given a true, classically intentionalistic description. By the same token, a vague explanation of the slip couched in terms of mental causation is too weak to capture the fact that the slip displays the content of the motive. By means of what form of mental causation can a motive find non-rational expression in a parapraxis or symptomatic act in a manner that is content-preserving? The abandonment of the practical syllogism for understanding such examples leaves an explanatory gap.

Hopkins (1991, 1994) and Gardner (1993) have pointed to Freud's use of the concept of wish fulfillment to fill this explanatory gap. According to this view, once a desire has been repudiated from consciousness, it may find expression by means of a mental process which simply represents the desire as fulfilled. Such a process cannot be captured by classical intentionalistic explanation. The subject does not represent the desire as satisfied because (a) he wants the desire to be satisfied and (b) he believes that by representing the desire as satisfied he will thereby satisfy it. Rather, once repudiated, the desire is just represented as satisfied. Wish fulfillment therefore provides a content-preserving yet non-intentionalistic expressive medium.

Using this explanatory strategy we can, with Freud, explain his parapraxis as (1) Freud wishes not to have 'On dreams' published (W_1), (2)

W_1 conflicts with his wish to have 'On dreams' published (W_2), (3) Freud repudiates W_1, (4) Freud unconsciously represents W_1 as fulfilled and (5) this brings about Freud's forgetting the proofs. Of course, we have not explained the transition from (4) to (5), but this cannot reasonably be taken to detract from the cogency of the Freudian story. Even in the case of the practical syllogism, there is no account of just how the logical entailment of the conclusion by its premises determines their causal relation. These matters must, in the end, be left to neurophysiology. It is sufficient for our purposes to have proposed the sequence of mental events between which causal relations are taken to hold.

XVII

CONCLUSIONS

The present work has attempted to draw conclusions about Freud's views on several topics of concern to contemporary philosophy of mind. The main conclusions that have been reached are as follows:

With regard to the mind-body problem, Freud moved from 1895 onwards from the dominant position of psychophysical dualism to advocate a version of the identity theory.

With regard to the concept of unconscious mental events and its justification, Freud advocated the view that neurophysiological processes instantiate mental processes, opposing the competing dissociationist and dispositionalist theses. He elaborated a version of what I have called the 'Continuity argument' against the latter.

With regard to Jackson's influence upon Freud, I have shown that Freud endorsed Jackson's neuroscientific anti-localizationism, but came eventually to reject Jackson's ontological dualism.

With regard to the phenomenon of consciousness, Freud proposed that consciousness is a function of a dedicated neurophysiological system, that cognition is not a function of this system and that intrinsically unconscious cognitive processes can only issue in conscious thought by virtue of activating appropriate linguistic representations.

With regard to the realism/anti-realism debate, Freud treated entities featured in mentalistic accounts of the unconscious anti-realistically.

With regard to functionalism, I have shown that Freud's philosophy of mind was incompatible with strong causal role functionalism, but hospitable to homuncular functionalism.

With regard to the theory of unconscious thinking, I have shown that Freud used the term 'unconscious' in at least four distinct senses, and that his claim that what I have termed 'unconscious$_{irr}$' processes do not instantiate logical norms raises problems for the attribution of unconscious$_{1}$ mental contents.

With regard to John Searle's argument for the connection principle and his critique of Freud, I have shown that Searle's arguments on behalf of the connection principle are vulnerable to the Freudian Continuity argument against the dispositionalist theory of unconscious mental events, and that his criticisms of Freud are marred by misunderstanding of Freudian claims.

With regard to Davidson's defence of Freud, I have shown that Davidson's purported philosophical apology for Freudian mental topography is essentially incompatible with some of Freud's fundamental theses and therefore cannot philosophically underwrite Freud's position.

NOTES

INTRODUCTION

[1] Herzog (1988) attributes the source of the myth of Freud as anti-philosopher to his biographers Wittels (1931) and Jones (1955).

[2] For example, Freud (1873-1939: 375) wrote in 1927 to Werner Achelis, a psychologist who had written a philosophical essay on dreaming, that:

> What I have to say about your argument will not surprise you, as you seem to be familiar with my attitude towards philosophy (metaphysics). Other defects in my nature have certainly distressed me and made me feel humble; with metaphysics it is different - I not only have no talent for it but no respect for it, either. In secret - one cannot say such things aloud - I believe that one day metaphysics will be condemned as a nuisance, as an abuse of thinking, as a survival from the period of the religious *weltanschauung*. I know well to what extent this way of thinking estranges me from German cultural life.

Given Freud's scientism, hostility to metaphysics and his materialism, it is surprising that he seems to have been unaware of the Vienna Circle. According to Neider (1977), cited in Bouveresse (1995), a number of the *Wiener Kreis* philosophers had come to Vienna for the purpose of being psychoanalyzed, and Carnap, for one, was in analysis for twenty years. We know that there were links between the Vienna Psychoanalytic Society and the Vienna Circle, and that members of the Circle worked on the reformulation of psychoanalytic theory along logical positivist lines, and that both Carnap and Neurath spoke well of it (Schlipp, 1963; Frank, 1959). Furthermore, a considerable number of the Viennese analysts, including Heinz Hartmann, maintained contact with the Circle (Frank, 1959). Freud analysed Margaret Stonborough-Wittgenstein, a sister of Ludwig Wittgenstein, and presented her with a copy of the deluxe edition of 'The future of an illusion' on his flight from Vienna in 1938 (Leupold-Löwenthal & Lobner, 1975; McGuiness, 1981). There is a letter from Freud to Klara Wittgenstein in the Freud Museum, London.

[3] It is not generally known that, whilst at university, Freud and some of his friends produced a philosophical journal. Freud mentions the contents of only one issue of this journal in his correspondence with his Rumanian friend Eduard Silberstein. This letter, quoted in Chapter One of the present work, mentions that the young Sigmund Freud contributed an article criticising an article by his Friend Lipiner on the teleological argument for the existence of God.

Freud's philosophical activities during these years are alluded to in the 'revolutionary dream' ('Count Thun') recounted in 'The interpretation of dreams' (1900). McGrath (1986) makes some interesting comments about the events to which the dream may allude. Accord-

ing to Herzog (1988), Freud was dissuaded from pursuing a career in philosophy because he lacked confidence in his own abilities; (but see note 2 above).
[4] Mach was also a friend of Freud's mentor and collaborator Josef Breuer. Freud mentions Mach in a letter to Fliess on 12 June 1900 (Freud, 1887-1904:417) and in a 1912 letter to Josef Popper-Lynkeus (Freud, 1873-1939:321).
[5] Freud was opposed both to those philosophers (such as Brentano, James and Wundt) who denied the existence of unconscious mental events, and the representatives of *naturphilosophie* who advanced a mystical conception of the unconscious (Herzog, 1988).
[6] There was, nonetheless *some* support for psychoanalysis from within the philosophical community during Freud's lifetime. Two examples are Hugo Friedman a German philosopher who publicly defended Freud's view of the unconscious (Decker, 1977) and Israel Levine, a British philosopher who is discussed in the present work.
[7] Compare this with Freud's comment, made in response to Tausk's presentation on the theory of knowledge at the Vienna Psychoanalytic Society on 24 November 1909, that:

> It would be interesting to find out whether a philosophic study [of a question] would yield more than a mere translation into a language difficult to understand, or whether one could perhaps expect a further simplification and the achievement of clear results (Nunberg & Federn, 1962-75, Vol. 2: 335).

[8] In 1933 Rabbi Judah Magnes, Chancellor of the Hebrew University of Jerusalem, wrote to Freud concerning the creation of a chair. Freud replied that:

> The view that it is premature to create a chair for psycho-analysis so long as none for psychology exists invites a discussion of the relationship between the two sciences. My opinion is as follows: psycho-analysis is also psychology in the sense that it is a science of the *unconscious* psychic processes, whereas what is taught as academic psychology is confined to dealing with *conscious* phenomena. There need be no contradiction between the two; psycho-analysis could be presented as an introduction to psychology; in reality, however, the contradiction is produced by the fact that the academic circles don't want to have anything to do with psycho-analysis (Freud, 1873-1939: 414).

[9] Chessick (1980) misleadingly characterizes Freud's metaphysics as in the tradition of Leibniz and the Continental rationalists. See also (Freud, 1923a: 253; (1926a: 96) and his remarks in the letter to Max Eitingon cited in Jones (1957:140).
[10] This seems to echo Brentano's '*Vera modus philosophiae non alia nisi scientae naturalis*': 'The true method of philosophy is none other than that of natural sciences') (Haynal, 1994).
[11] Glymour (1991:144) puts this nicely: 'A big part of contemporary cognitive science,' he writes, 'is pretty much what you would expect if Sigmund Freud had had a computer.'

CHAPTER ONE

[1] Years later Freud's path crossed that of Brentano again: Brentano's sister-in-law, Anna von Leiben, was Freud's hysterical patient 'Caecelie M' described in the *Studies on Hysteria* (Haynal, 1994).
[2] Freud's first contact with Herbart's ideas seems to have been through a work by Lindner (1858) which was part of his *Gymnasium* curriculum. Later, at the University of Vienna, Freud's professor of psychiatry, Theodor Meynert, was of a Herbartian persuasion (Ellenberger, 1970). Wilhelm Wundt castigated Freud as a Herbartian (Decker, 1977).
[3] Brentano regarded Hegel, Fichte and Schelling as 'the extreme limit of degeneration' (Gilson, 1966: 69).
[4] Freud is referring here to rival accounts of the nature of light, a piece of information that he presumably picked up in his course on physiological optics. Freud purchased Helmholz's (1867) book on physiological optics while still a student and retained it until the end of his life (Davies & Fichtner, forthcoming). It was in this book that Helmholz discussed his theory of unconscious inference in visual perception.
[5] It is unlikely that Freud's methodological dualism can be attributed to Brentano's influence. Although the latter was an articulate exponent of methodological dualism, this approach seems to have been commonplace amongst psychologists and neuroscientists of the late nineteenth century (Sulloway, 1979).

CHAPTER TWO

[1] In addition to writiers mentioned elsewhere in the present text, the influence philosopher Wilhelm Jerusalem deserves mention. For a discussion of Jerusalem's impact on Freud see Kaltenbeck (1985) and Geeardyn (1997). I am indebted to Saul Haimovitch for calling my attention to Jerusalem.
[2] Kanzer (1981) speculates that a letter of 22 September 1896 refers obliquely to Lipps. The relevant passage is:

> But I am not in the least in disagreement with you, and have no desire at all to leave psychology hanging in the air with no organic basis. But, beyond a feeling of conviction [that there must be such a basis], I have nothing, either theoretical or therapeutic, to work on, and so I must behave as if I were confronted by psychological factors only. I have no idea yet why I cannot fit it together (Freud, cited in Kanzer, 1981: 395).

The books in question are *Grundtatsachen des Seelenlebens* (1883), *Psychologische Studien (1885), Ästheische Faktoren der Romanschauung* (1891), *Der Streit über die Tragödie* (1891, inscribed 2 October 1891), *Grundzüge der Logik* (1893), *Raumäestheik und geometrisch-optische Täuschungen* (1897, inscribed 6 October, 1897), *Komik und*

Humor (1898), *Das Selbstbewusstsein; Empfindung und Gefühl* (1901), *Vom Fühlen, Wollen und Denken* (1902) and *Einheiten und Relatzionen* (1902). Freud also read at least one of Lipps' papers 'Der Begriff des Unbewussten in der Psychologie' (1897) which he cites in 'The interpretation of dreams' (1900) and 'Jokes and their relation to the unconscious' (1905).

CHAPTER THREE

[1] Andersson (1962).
[2] Silverstein (1985, 1989).
[3] Solms and Saling (1986, 1990), Sulloway (1979), Leupold-Löwenthal (1998).
[4] Amacher (1965), Natsoulas (1974), Solomon (1974a).
[5] Flanagan (1984) describes him as having moved from a type identity theory to a token identity theory. Wallace (1992) regards Freud as a materialist - a dual-aspect monist or token identity theorist (with type identity theoretic leanings in 1895) from 1888 until the end of his life.
[6] Mackay (1989) seems to argue that Freud moved from psychophysical parallelism to the identity theory at some point between 1895 and 1900, Flanagan (1984) and Wallace (1992) attribute to Freud shifting *materialist* commitments. Holt (1974) believes Freud's stance was inconsistent.
[7] Freud purchased a copy of Locke's *Essay* in 1883.
[8] For example, Jackson (1887) stated that:

> Those who believe in the doctrine of concomitance do not believe that sensations, volitions, ideas and emotions produce movements or any other physical states. These expressions imply disbelief in the doctrine of conservation of energy; movements always arise from liberations of energy in the outer world, and it would be marvelous if there were an exception in our brains (86).

[9] Many other examples from the nineteenth-century literature are cited by MacDougall (1911).
[10] Of course, materialism has a long and venerable history. I do not mean to ignore nineteenth-century versions of materialism and their philosophical predecessors from Democritus and Epicurius through Hobbes and La Mettrie. Rather, I contend that materialism was by no means a dominant position in the philosophy of mind during the nineteenth century. Global assertions of metaphysical materialism carried little explanatory weight during the latter part of the nineteenth century. In fact, Pringle-Pattison, writing in Baldwin's *Dictionary of Philosophy and Psychology* (1902), wrote that:

> Materialism as a dogmatic system hardly survives in philosophical circles, although...it is no doubt influential among certain sections of the working classes, and often forms the creed of the half-educated specialist (46).

With the discovery of cerebral localization, claims that the material events in the brain are at the very least intimately bound up with mental events no longer seemed outlandish or shocking. However, it became clear that materialist claims would have to be justified *neuroscientifically*. On the whole, the neuroscientists were wisely reluctant to make claims about how the brain might give rise to mental events. This reluctance had both scientific and metaphysical grounds. Given the widespread equation of the mental with the conscious, nineteenth-century neuroscience would need to solve the 'hard problem' of how neural wetware gives rise to consciousness. This problem remains refractory for contemporary neuroscience. The primitive neuroscience of the nineteenth century was completely unequipped to deal with it. Philosophically, metaphysical dualism was assumed to be 'the only game in town', as I will describe in the present work.

[11] It should be noted that Freud wrote more than one hundred neuroscientific works, most of which were composed prior to 1896. At the time of writing, only nine of these have been translated into English. My research has been confined to these English-language translations and it is therefore possible that there are passages in the as yet untranslated works that falsify my claims.

[12] Although there has been some controversy about whether this unsigned article was in fact written by Freud, the matter now seems settled (Solms & Saling, 1990).

[13] It is sobering to notice that Solms and Saling do not recognize that their objection to Silverstein also counts against their own argument.

[14] This coheres with Freud's remarks in a footnote to Bernheim's suggestion stating that:

> It appears to me unjustifiable, and unnecessary, to assume that an executive act changes its localization in the nervous system if it is begun consciously and continued later unconsciously. It is, on the contrary, probable that the portion of the brain concerned can operate with a varying quota of attention (consciousness)' (cited in Freud, 1888d: 84, note 1).

[15] This paper bears the date 1905 in Volume VII of the *Standard Edition* of Freud's psychological works. However, in Volume I, which appeared thirteen years after Volume VII, the editor reported that Rosenzweig had discovered that the paper was, in fact, originally published in 1890.

[16] James (1890) claimed that the cerebral cortex was the 'organ' of consciousness. Freud (1920) was more specific, speculating that consciousness is a property of some module *within* the cortex.

[17] Compare the following literal rendering of the opening passage of the original manuscript with the polished text which appears in the *Standard Edition* of Freud's works (Cf. Solms, 1994: 158).

> The aim of this short book - work - to bring together the tenets of PA in most terse - concise form & to

also dogmatically

state them in most unequivocal terms.

Rejects catechism, assumes forms of questions & answers. Its intention not to compel belief or arouse conviction.

Naturally

understandable fashion

The claims - teachings - of PA based upon incalculable numbers of observations (& experiences) and only someone who has repeated those observations on himself and others is in a position to arrive at a judgment of his own upon it.

[18] There have been numerous conjectures about why Freud abandoned the 'Project'. I am in agreement with Solomon (1987) that 'as the complexity of the problems became more apparent, Freud ...saw that neurology would not provide the sought-after details in his lifetime' (139). It is interesting to note his comments on a presentation by Surgeon Major-General Hollerung to the Vienna Psychoanalytic Society on 20 October 1909. Freud said that he:

> Does not venture to combine biological and psychological thinking. In this sense, he would like to express his appreciation and admiration for the fact that the speaker found the energy to begin working on problems that may be on the agenda a century after us (Nunberg & Federn, 1962-75, Vol. 2: 280).

[19] This is a fact of the history of psychology. There is no *philosophical* reason why this sort of dispositionalism should be taken to *entail* dualism. Indeed, I shall describe John Searle's anti-dualistic dispositionalism with respect to unconscious mental items in Chapter Thirteen of the present work.

[20] A prime example, which Freud may well have had in mind when writing this passage, is Eduard von Hartmann whose immensely influential *Philosophy of the Unconscious* claimed that we 'merge into an eternal Unconscious, into a unique, omnipresent, omniscient and all-wise being' (cited in Brentano, 1874: 108). Schopenhauer also falls into this category. As Levine (1923) states: 'The conception of the unconscious in both Schopenhauer and Hartmann is essentially a metaphysical principle' (31). Hartmann's book was grandiose and poorly reasoned. James (1890) writes acerbically that 'Hartmann fairly boxes the compass of the universe with the principle of unconscious thought. For him there is no namable thing that does not exemplify it' (169).

CHAPTER FOUR

[1] This coheres with Freud's comment that psychoanalysts 'should resist the temptation to flirt with endocrinology and the autonomic nervous system, when what is needed is an

apprehension of psychological facts with the help of a framework of psychological concepts ' (1926b:257).
[2] See also McGrath's (1986:18) statement that Freud 'believed that the physiological processes in the brain and the psychological processes of the mind were not parallel and causally linked but, rather, were identical.'
[3] Compare Jones' view with the concluding 'Kantian' paragraph of Section One of 'The unconscious' (1915a).

CHAPTER FIVE

[1] These authors show that concern with the concept of the unconscious goes back at least as far as the seventeenth and eighteenth centuries with the work of men such as Leibniz, Platner and Wolff.
[2] Ellenberger (1970) is one of a number of scholars who fail to emphasize the sharp differences between various conceptions of the unconscious current during the latter part of the nineteenth century. Decker (1977) and Macmillan (1991) are two of the few scholars who remark on the uniqueness of Freud's concept.
[3] The term 'dissociation' was introduced into psychology by Pierre Janet. Janet dropped the word after his 1889 philosophy thesis, but it was introduced into the English literature by William James in 1890 (Hacking, 1995).
[4] There was a third common use of the term 'unconscious' to denote the *absence* of consciousness.

> The physiological psychologists, although equating all psychic activity with consciousness, did use the word "Unconscious". But to them it meant the absence of all thought - "zero grade" of consciousness, as Wundt said (Decker, 1977: 271).

[5] Dalbiez (1941) seems to be the only writer to clearly distinguish Freud's philosophical conception of the unconscious from its rivals, and to distinguish the two main rivals from one another. He describes Freud's concept as a 'realist' view in that it distinguishes mental events from our perceptions of those events. He describes the rival views as 'idealist' in that they fail to draw this distinction. Dalbiez describes the two main idealist views as the 'physiological theory' (my 'dispositional theory') and the 'theory of the plurality of centres of consciousness' (my 'dissociationist theory'). Levine (1923) distinguishes Freud's theory from the split-consciousness theory, writing that 'Freud's psychology should be distinguished from those theories which speak of a "subconscious" or "subliminal" self in each of us' (162). Gardner (1993), too, denies that Freud's theory is 'partitive'.
[6] Freud commented approvingly on a philosophical presentation by Hollerung to the Vienna Psychoanalytic Society on 20 October 1909 as follows:

> He [Hollerung] is an opponent of dualism, on which present-day psychology relies. One cannot speak of [this] psychology as a science; it is not feasible to ignore the

> objective, the somatic factor. That which we call psychic is only a small part of the expression of the organic system (Nunberg & Federn, 1962-75, Vol. 2: 281)

[7] See Freud (1900: 615) and (1926b: 198). A example is found in 'Organic and hysterical motor paralyses' (1893) where he remarks that 'the paralysed organ...is involved in a subconscious association....The conception of the arm exists in the material substratum, but it is not accessible to conscious associations'(171).

[8] Klein (1977) noted that Freud erroneously enlisted Maudsley's support for the concept of unconscious ideas in 'The interpretation of dreams' due to his having taken a sentence from Maudsley out of context from a secondary source.

[9] See also Freud's 1893 lecture 'On the psychical mechanism of hysterical phenomena', where he stated that:

> It is probable that in every hysteria we are dealing with a rudiment of what is called [in French] '*double conscience*', dual consciousness, and that a tendency to such a dissociation and with it the emergence of abnormal states of consciousness...is the basic phenomenon of hysteria (1893: 38-39).

[10] Freud alluded to this term again - this time critically - in his (1915a) essay on 'The unconscious'.

[11] Contemporary advocates of the dissociationist approach include Nemiah (1974, 1985) and Hilgard (1977).

[12] Hacking (1995) mentions that the British physician Thomas Wakeley, who edited *The Lancet*, suggested that double consciousness might throw light on the metaphysics of personal identity.

[13] It should not be thought that Freud later entirely abandoned the concept of a splitting of consciousness. Freud retained the view that the notion of split consciousness provides the most economical explanation for certain forms of psychopathology (Cf., Freud, 1940d). After 1895 the notion of splitting was nested within the overarching topographical approach rather than competing with it.

[14] Freud's occasionally used the term 'subconscious' in the context of his discussions of hysteria (e.g., Freud, 1893; Freud, 1895). This term had been coined by Janet, perhaps the most prominent of the French writers on hysteria, within the context of a dissociationist theory. Freud *never* used this term in works written after 1895 and actively discouraged it as misleading (1900, 615; 1915a: 170; 1926b: 197-198).

[15] Because mind and consciousness were axiomatically equated, the locution 'splitting of the mind' was often used interchangeably with 'splitting of consciousness'. See Macmillan (1991). Breuer claimed in the section to which I refer that 'the psychical activity which is so striking in the well-known cases of "*double conscience*" is present to a rudimentary degree in every major hysteria' and is 'the basic phenomenon of this neurosis'. Freud's notion of the unconscious was sometimes taken to be a theory of split consciousness. The psychologist Otto Lipmann, for instance, wrote that Freud spoke of 'another consciousness of which we ordinarily know nothing' (cited in Decker, 1977). Störring believed that Freud's unconscious was a second state of consciousness (Ibid.).

Amongst contemporary writers Castoriades (1997) makes the absurd claim that psychoanalysis 'shows...the plurality of subjects contained within the same envelope' (251).

[16] Breuer's patient 'Anna O' was described as suffering from the symptom of '*double conscience*' (Freud, 1895: 42).

[17] In light of this fact, Freud's (1923b) retrospective account is misleading. Referring to the cathartic approach adumbrated in the 'Studies on hysteria', he wrote that 'It will be seen that an essential part of this theory was the assumption of the existence of unconscious mental processes' (236). The German physician Fritz Umpfenbach also described the 'Studies' as portraying the power of unconscious ideas (Decker, 1977).

[18] Perhaps one should not make too much of this, as the term 'psychological analysis' appears in 'The neuro-psychoses of defense' (1894).

[19] Twenty years later in 'The unconscious' (1915a) and in later works Freud would ridicule the notion of an unconscious consciousness.

[20] This is strikingly similar to a passage in Maudsley's (1867) *The Physiology and Pathology of the Mind*.

> It is not merely a charge against self-consciousness that it is not reliable in that of which it does give information; but it is a provable charge against it that it does not give any account of a large and important part of our mental activity: its light reaches only to states of consciousness, and not to states of mind. Its evidence then is not only untrustworthy...but it is of little value, because it has reference only to a small part of that for which its testimony is invoked. May we not then justly say that self-consciousness is utterly incompetent to supply the facts for the building up of a truly inductive psychology? (cited in Altschule, 1965).

Freud found support for his new anti-introspectionism in the philosophical work of Wilhelm Jerusalem, as described in his letter to Fliess dated 25 May, 1895 (Freud: 1887-1904: 129).

[21] Solomon (1987) responds to this common charge as follows:

> Freud is often criticized for his philosophical naiveté, largely on the basis of his "confusing" mentalistic and biological categories and remaining ignorant of the complexities of psychophysical dualism.... Freud was not only aware of these problems, but was one of the very few psychologists or philosophers of his time (the other being William James) who began to see the serious problems in the linguistic and metaphysical conservatism that provided the inertia of Cartesian dualism in psychology (138).

CHAPTER SIX

[1] It is possible that Freud may have also encountered Hamilton's philosophy of mind in the context of Hamilton's dispute with Carpenter regarding the latter's dispositionalist theory of 'unconscious cerebration' (Altschule, 1965).

[2] It was Kris (1956) who first suggested that Hering had an influence on Freud's concept of unconscious mental events.

[3] Levine (1893-1988) became lecturer in philosophy at University College, Exeter, in 1923; later professor and head of department and, finally, dean of the Faculty of Arts (Freud and Jones, 1993). I am indebted to Lydia Marinelli of the Freud Museum, Vienna, for bringing Levine to my attention.

[4] Freud may perhaps be referring to Butler's extravagant anti-Darwinism, in the aid of which he attempted to enlist Hering's lecture.

[5] Hering is probably referring here to Helmholz's theory of unconscious inferences in visual perception.

[6] This is a gibe at von Hartmann's *Philosophy of the Unconscious.*

[7] Freud's (1900) metaphor of the unconscious as a 'another stage' (*schauplatz)* may derive from Hering's text.

[8] Gardner (1993) treats Freud's 'gaps' as gaps in *self-explanation*. This does not seem warranted by Freud's description. Although Freud says that the gaps cannot be explained psychologically without interpolating unconscious mental events, this is not the same as asserting that the gaps are explanatory gaps. Gardner's claim that 'Freud's "gaps" correspond to irrational phenomena' (227) does not cohere with Freud's example of *Einfalle* - ideas suddenly coming into one's mind -mentioned in the passage to which Gardner refers.

[9] This objection has recently revived by Searle. See Chapter Thirteen of the present work.

[10] Consideration of the linguistic argument goes back at least as far as the 'Studies on hysteria' (Freud & Breuer, 1895:223), in which Breuer asserted that the neurophysiological event corresponding to a given mental item 'is the same in content and in form' whether the item is conscious or unconscious and suggested the term 'ideational substratum' for such processes. Breuer seems to be either equivocating or fudging here, as the notion of a physical substratum for mental events is consistent with dualism while the attribution of content to neurophysiological processes presupposes materialism.

[11] It is possible to assert the equation of the mental with the conscious without avowing dualism by including the proviso that conscious mental events are identical to physical events. According to this view, there are sequences of non-mental neural events which give rise to mental neural events; (i.e., neural dispositions for mental states also possessing the property of being conscious). Although the causal process linking unconscious non-mental physical dispositions with their conscious mental physical counterparts becomes more comprehensible as a process of physical causation, it seems perverse to insist on such a roundabout theory if it is designed simply to prop up a concept of the mental as coextensive with the conscious.

[12] Earlier, in 'A note on the unconscious in psycho-analysis' (1912a), Freud had written that this approach 'is clearly at fault in denying psychology the right to account for its most common facts, such as memory, by its own means' (260)

CHAPTER SEVEN

[1] For a very scholarly account of the relationship between Freud's views and the views of aphasiologists contemporary with him see Greenberg (1997).
[2] Readers interested in this subject should consult Robert M. Young's (1970) classic *Mind, Brain and Adaptation in the Nineteenth Century.*
[3] Oddly enough, the term 'agnosia', as in 'visual agnosia' (blindsight), was apparently introduced into the neuroscientific lexicon by Sigmund Freud in his aphasia book.
[4] Wundt, the father of experimental psychology, was also a psychophysical parallelist. According to Decker (1977), this was a common position amongst turn-of-the-century psychologists. However, apparently parallelist claims must be interpreted cautiously. It seems to have often been the case that avowals of psychophysical parallelism by nineteenth-century writers were intended as avowals of *anti-interactionism* (e.g., Clifford, 1874). However, in the absence of clear *identity* claims, the rather negative anti-interactionist position easily slid towards metaphysical confusion.
[5] In fact, the 'hypothesis of concomitance' is a Leibnizian term for psycho-physical parallelism.
[6] In his concern for segregating psychological from neuroscientific vocabularies, Jackson can be seen as a philosopher in the tradition culminating in Davidson's anomalous monism. Pringle-Pattison, writing in Baldwin's *Dictionary of Psychology and Philosophy* (1901), describes this tradition as originating with Höffding who wrote in his *Outline of Psychology* that:

> We are...impelled to conceive the material interaction between the elements comprising the brain and the nervous system as an outer form of the inner ideal unity of consciousness. *It is as though the same thing were said in two languages* (cited in Baldwin, 1901: 100, emphasis added).

[7] E.g., 'A morphological account of the physical *bases of psychical states* does not suffice; we must give an anatomical account' (Jackson, 1887: 87, italics added).
[8] Charles Mercier believed psychoneural concomitance to be inscrutable. According to Mercier (1888):

> The change of consciousness never takes place without the change in the brain; the change in the brain...never without the change of consciousness. But *why* the two occur together or what the link is which connects them, we do not know and most authorities believe that we never shall and can never know (11, cited in Güzeldere, 1995).

[9] Alternatively, as Solms & Saling (1990) suggest, the 'Jacksonian' flavor of the 1888 articles 'Aphasia' and 'Gehirn' may be entirely fortuitous. Unlike the 1891 book *On Aphasia*, Freud's 1888 articles make no reference to Jackson.
[10] See Reise (1950).

[11] I have not included any references to Jackson's work that may appear in Freud's untranslated neuroscientific works.
[12] Reise (1950) notes that Freud and Rie's book on *Infantile Cerebral Hemiplegias* takes a more traditional neuroanatomical stance.
[13] Like Jackson before him, Freud seems close to a concept of token identity here.
[14] It is worth noting in passing that the prevailing view of the constitution of the mental was at this time atomistic, and that Freud invoked the atomism of the mental in the context of an argument that sounds strange from the vantage-point of contemporary philosophy. Although it is doubtful that full-blooded holistic conceptions of the mental had been mooted in the nineteenth century, Freud's atomism was at least equivocal. In Meynert's scheme simple perceptual ideas were stored as such in the brain and associated by means of association fibres. Freud argued that neither association and perception nor the neurophysiological processes underpinning them could be sharply demarcated from one another, i.e., that there is no such thing as a self-contained "simple idea".
[15] Intimations of the Davidsonian thesis that the distinction between events and their descriptions provides a route to an identity theory of mind can be found in Lashley (1923), who wrote that 'subjective and objective descriptions are not descriptions from two essentially different points of view, or descriptions of two different aspects, but simply descriptions of the same thing with different degrees of accuracy and detail, (338, also cited in Güzeldere, 1995: 117).
[16] Wallace (1992) believes that the evidence of other passages of the book renders this implausible and that *On Aphasia* was written from a materialist (identity theoretic or dual-aspect monistic) position. He also states that although the notion of psychoneural 'concomitance' is Jacksonian, the term '*dependent* concomitant' is a Freudian coinage suggesting, perhaps, a modification of Jackson's metaphysics. The fact that Freud gave the phrase in English and placed it within quotation marks suggests that he at the very least *believed* himself to be using a Jacksonian concept. As I have mentioned, Jackson often implicitly claims that mental events are dependent upon neural events.
[17] Marx (1967) notes that Freud, unlike other aphasiologists such as Küssmaul (1885, with whose work Freud was familiar), was reluctant to accept notions of *unconscious* mental correlates corresponding to the hypothesized latent modifications of the cortex, a reluctance which flows naturally from his dualism.

CHAPTER EIGHT

[1] I am greatly indebted to Natsoulas' (1984, 1985, 1989a, 1989b, 1991, 1992) superb work on this subject.
[2] Of these, only the last has been found and published under the title 'A phylogenetic fantasy: overview of the transference neuroses' (Freud, 1987) .

[3] Silverstein incorrectly holds that Freud was a psychophysical interactionist in 1915. It could be more plausibly claimed that the writing of the metapsychological essays forced Freud to grapple with the problems of mind-brain identity.
[4] Contemporary advocates of this approach include Churchland (1988), Rosenthal (1986), Armstrong (1980), Carruthers (1989) and Dennett (1991). For a careful discussion of the philosophical issues, see Güzeldere (1997).
[5] A similar if not identical epistemological point had been made by Maudsley (1867:13) who wrote that 'Consciousness gives no account of the essential material conditions which underlie every mental manifestation'.
[6] Strictly speaking, consciousness is not coextensive with ω functioning, as some ω functions - for example the discharge from ω into ψ are intrinsically unconscious.
[7] According to Klein (1977), Freud's fundamental distinction between sensation (ω) and thought (ψ) was invoked by Aristotle, Locke and Kant, who may have influenced Freud's thinking.
[8] A very similar position can be found in Maudsley (1867). Bain had proposed in 1885 that thought must be distinguished from the consciousness of thought (Altschule, 1965).
[9] A theory of the neurophysiology of consciousness relying on synchronized frequencies has been proposed by Crick and Koch (1990). However, these authors invoke synchronized frequencies as a solution to the 'binding problem' rather than postulating that afferent frequencies carry qualia.
[10] The concept of consciousness as essentially passive had earlier been promulgated by Morton Prince (1885).
[11] Freud's sensitivity to the sensory and motor aspects of speech derives from his research in aphasiology. Wernicke and Broca discovered the localization of motor and sensory aspects of speech and Wernicke distinguished sensory aphasia from motor aphasia, Taken as a theory of thought as subvocal speech, Freud's views might be compared with those of Lashley (1923) 'Consciousness is the particular laryngeal gesture we have come to use to stand for the rest' (240, cited in Güzeldere, 1995a). However, Freud might alternatively be understood as claiming that motor impulses, irrespective of their outcome, evoke afferent feedback along sensory (φ) channels (C.f. Cotterill, 1995).
[12] Freud's views on the psychological role of language bear a striking similarity to those of Kant, who may have influenced them (Brook, 1988). Similar views were also expressed by Nietzsche in section 354 of *The Gay Science* (1887).
[13] According to Gallese (Mutalik, 1998) 'mirror neurones' in the brain are motor neurones that fire when observing *someone else* perform a motor action, thus providing a neurological basis for Freud's speculations about identification. In common with other nineteenth-century neuropsychologists, Freud advanced a motor theory of speeach acquisition (Greenberg, 1997).
[14] This passage shows that the Continuity argument was already important to Freud in the 'Project'.
[15] As Natsoulas notes, Freud (1915a) believed that something like this situation explains schizophrenic thought- and speech-disorders.

[16] In light of his views on affect, Freud is clearly equating 'psychical acts' with acts of *cognition*. This view is implicit in his account of *Ucs*. As the 'true psychical reality' (1900: 613) and is found elsewhere in his writings. Klein (1977) suggests, to my mind plausibly, that Freud's conception echoes Brentano's (1874) claim that sensations are non-mental because non-intentional.

[17] Freud's thesis that conscious perception is not continuous but involves an extremely rapid alternation between 'on' and 'off' states - in effect sampling the external world - may owe something to the work of Spence (1879), who suggested this idea and, interestingly, hypothesized the process to be causally dependent on what would now be called neural spiking frequencies.

> The simplest form of consciousness, or mental life, must consist in an alteration of a state of consciousness with a state of unconsciousness.... Perhaps it would be safer, for the present, to call it a pulsation, or undulation in the brain, or a vibration of the molecules of the brain, paralleled in consciousness. This pulsation or vibration is, of course, very rapid; otherwise, we should not have to infer its existence, but would know it by perceiving the alternations of one state with another (345, cited in Güzeldere, 1995). As far as I am aware, Freud never connected his 1920 'sampling' hypothesis with his 1895 ideas about neural frequencies. For a more elaborate discussion of see Smith (1999).

CHAPTER NINE

[1] Searle (1992) denies that the principle of holism is in principle inapplicable to non-mental systems.

[2] Strictly interpreted, this remark would appear to refute my claim that Freud was an identity theorist. In light of the evidence marshaled thus far, which are taken from Freud's *explicit* discussions of the mind-body problem, it is probably best to understand this remark as loosely intended. Freud presumably uses 'physical' to mean 'non-mental'.

[3] Chessick (1980) calls this passage a crucial link between Freud and philosophy which 'skirts the edge of Schopenhauer's notion of the Will on the one hand, and of Kant's notion of the thing-in-itself on the other' (257). A number of writers have noted Freud's affinity with and references to Schopenhauer's work (Young & Brooke, 1994). The only work by Schopenhauer that Freud possessed at the time of his death was *Über die vierfache Wurzel des Satzes vom zureichenden Grunde* (1875). Freud possessed a copy of Frost's (1918) *Schopenhauer als Erbe Kants in der philosophischen Seelenanalyse* and Kaplan's (1916) *Schopenhauer und der Animismus* both of which were apparently gifts from the authors (Davies & Fichtner, forthcoming).

[4] Chessick (1980) notices the Kantian overtones of Freud's remarks, but describes this as 'curious and unintended' (287). In the same work he describes Freud's epistemology as 'clearly in the Kantian tradition', stating that 'Kant's approach was on Freud's mind to

the end' (295). See also Freud's letter to Marie Bonaparte of 21 August 1938 (Jones, 1957: 495-496), the 22 August entry in 'Findings, ideas, problems', apparently inspired by the correspondence with Bonaparte.

[5] Klein (1977) illicitly uses the *conceptual* priority of the vocabulary of consciousness as a claim against Freud's assertion of the *causal* priority of the unconscious with respect to consciousness. [6] Freud's remarks about animism in 'The unconscious' invite comparison with Churchland''s famous passage in *Scientific Realism and the Plasticity of Mind* (1981).

> The story [of folk-psychology] is one of retreat, infertility, and decadence. The presumed domain of FP used to be much larger than it is now. In primitive cultures, the behavior of most of the elements of nature were understood in intentional terms. The wind could know anger, the moon jealousy, the river generosity, the sea fury, and so forth. These were not metaphors. Sacrifices were made and auguries undertaken to placate or divine the changing passions of the gods. Despite its sterility, this animistic approach to nature has dominated our history, and it is only in the last two or three thousand years that we have restricted FP's literal application to the domain of the higher animals (211).

[7] With the expression 'taught biologically' we have introduced a new basis of explanation [of mental processes], which should have independent validity, even though it does not exclude, but rather calls for, mechanical principles' (322).

[8] Strictly speaking, folk-psychological interpretations of our mental states.

[9] I will use the terms 'instrumentalism' and 'anti-realism' synonymously.

[10] Surprisingly, Jones (1953) does not understand that this passage expresses a pre-psychoanalytic conception of the mind, offering it as an example of Freud's open-mindedness.

[11] Contrary to popular belief, Freud was not in principle opposed to biological interventions in the treatment of mental disorders. Freud wrote to Marie Bonaparte) that 'hope and future here lies in organic chemistry or the access to it through endocrinology' (Jones, 1957: 480[12] This remark is an allusion to Pierre Janet.

CHAPTER TEN

[1] This passage implies that Freud's notion of the 'mental apparatus' was intended to be taken at what is now called the *computational* level.

[2] '*Die Seele*' is Freud's standard term for 'mind' and is normally translated as such.

[3] Compare with Freud's remark, in his letter to Einstein, that 'It may perhaps seem to you that our theories are a kind of mythology and, in the present case, not even an agreeable one. But does not every science come in the end to a kind of mythology like this? Cannot the same be said today of our own physics?' (1933b).

[4] Of course, as I have already noted, Freud rejected the notion of unconscious affects, as he believed them to be in part *constituted* by their qualia.

[5] The preconscious is not called 'unconscious' 'except when we are talking loosely or when we have to make a defence of the existence in mental life of unconscious processes in general' (Freud, 1923b, 71).

[6] Freudian notions of psychopathologicity seem, on the whole, to boil down to the motivated, unconscious diversion of motivational aims from fulfilling their proper functions. However, the achievement of *sublimated* aims is considered a realization of the proper function of unconscious motives, a derived proper function.

CHAPTER ELEVEN

[1] See also Freud (1923b: 16).

[2] I am indebted to Matte-Blanco (1975, 1988) and Rayner & Tuckett (1988) for their accounts of Freud's position.

[3] The 'id' is synonymous with 'unconscious$_{irr}$'.

[4] Freud's summary list at the end of Section Five of 'The unconscious' apparently subsumes exemption from negation under exemption from mutual contradiction and therefore specifies only five items.

[5] Freud's '*trieb*' is often rendered '*instinct*' in the *Standard Edition* of his collected works. Contemporary usage favors '*drive*'.

[6] I attribute to Freud the idea that events are particulars, that causal relations hold between events and that possesses a nomological character.

[7] Freud sometimes used '*Assoziation*' ('Association') instead of '*Einfalll*'. For example in *Zur Geschichte der Psychoanalytischen Bewegung* he wrote 'nachdem ich mich, einer dunkeln Ahnung folgend, entschlossen hatte die Hypnosen mit den freien Assoziation zu vertauschen':'after I had resolved, following a vague inspiration, to substitute for hypnosis free association' (1914: 16).

[8] For defences of Freud, see Edelson (1988) and Hopkins (1986).

[9] For an interesting discussion see Freud (1905: 250-251n).

[10] Given the connectionist architecture initially proposed in the 'Project', it would be rash to commit Freud to the view that *syntactic* properties constrain such transitions.

[11] There is an elaborate discussion of this in the 'Project'. This is a neural-level account of the 'primary processes'.

[12] Paul Chabaneix (1897) wrote on the role of 'subconscious' mental processes in creativity.

[13] I use 'mind' in the broad sense of 'intentional system' (Dennett, 1986).

[14] Indeed, it for this very reason that Cavell (1993) concludes that Freud's thesis of unconscious$_{irr}$ is mistaken, substituting for it a Davidsonian split-mind account.

[15] Of course, as Grünbaum (1984) has shown, the Tally argument is highly vulnerable to methodological criticism. Fortunately, this argument does not depend on the use of the Tally argument. Any approach which establishes a systematic correspondence between stimulus and unconscious response could, in principle, serve.

CHAPTER TWELVE

[1] A very similar philosophical reconstruction of Freud has been made by continental philosophers of the 'hermeneutic' tradition, such as Ricoeur (1970, 1974, 1981) and Habermas (1971).
[2] Strangely, MacIntyre also states that 'vehement denial' and 'a flow of highly excited association' (65) is normally taken as confirming an interpretation.
[3] I.e., evidence showing the unconscious to be a real rather than a theoretical entity.
[4] Precisely the same error was committed by Habermas (1971), who also accused Freud of confusion with respect to reasons and causes. Habermas claimed that in contrast to natural scientific hypotheses, psychoanalytic hypotheses:

> Possess validity for the analyst only after they have been accepted as knowledge by the analysand himself. For the empirical accuracy of general interpretations depends not on controlled observations and subsequent communication among investigators but rather on the accomplishment of self-reflection and subsequent communication between the investigator and his "object" (261).

CHAPTER THIRTEEN

[1] The reader will note that Searle's argument regarding the unconscious is, in essence, identical to Hering's (1870) argument.
[2] The fact that this counter-argument cannot be applied to $\text{unconscious}_{\text{irr}}$ states does not effect its force, as Searle disputes the existence of *any* occurrent unconscious mental states.
[3] Of course, externalist intuitions might render this plausible. As neither Searle nor Freud make externalist claims, I will ignore this line of investigation.
[4] According to Searle (1995):

> Talk of unconscious mental states and processes is always dispositional. Talk of unconscious mental phenomena that are in principle inaccessible to consciousness is incoherent (550).

If aspectual shape is a necessary characteristic of (conscious) mentality, and if the present argument is right, it would seem that Searle's premises force the obviously absurd conclusion that the cognitive transformation of conscious mental items is itself non-mental.
[5] I exclude consideration of the attribution of *preconscious* mental states (such as one finds in Freud's 'Psychopathology of everyday life') which are closer to Searle's pattern of explanation.
[6] It might be argued that Freudian conflict is paradigmatically conflict between an unconscious attitude and a moral imperative rather than conflict between competing attitudes. However, moral principles are, in Freudian psychology, treated as attitudes, and psychical conflict of this nature are routinely described as instances of competition be-

tween unconscious attitudes and moral attitudes *in relation to their objects*. Freud does not hold that general moral principles can, as such, enter into unconscious conflict.

CHAPTER FOURTEEN

[1] Searle is also insensitive to the philosophical points upon which both he and Freud agree, such as the conceptualization of unconscious states within a broadly neuroscientific framework and the view that consciousness is an irreducible natural property of the central nervous system.
[2] It is perhaps worth noting that Searle never provides an argument to support the claim that aspectual shape cannot in principle be exhaustively characterized neuroscientifically.
[3] This error has been committed by other philosophical commentators on Freud, such as Bouveresse (1995). Freud was evidently insufficiently explicit about his theory of perception.

CHAPTER FIFTEEN

[1] Davidson's approach to psychoanalytic theory has been elaborated extensively by Gardner (1992) and Cavell (1993).
[2] Davidson is somewhat confusing on this point. Although he describes his theory in terms of relations between parts of the mind, he also seems to explain motivated irrationality in terms of the impact of one part upon the mind as a whole.

CHAPTER SIXTEEN

[1] I do not know of any place in Davidson's writings where he discusses the nature of consciousness.
[2] The term 'complex' is frequently misattributed to Jung, an error which was even committed by Freud himself. Anzieu (1986) has noted that Freud used the term 'complex of ideas' at least as early as 1892, long before Jung, and used it again in the 'Project'. Jung re-defined Freud's essentially cognitive concept of the complex as 'an emotionally coloured ideational content' (Anzieu, 1986: 80). Breuer appears to attribute the term to Janet (Freud and Breuer, 1895: 231).
[3] Although Davidson's thesis may conceivably throw light upon Freud's (1915b) otherwise puzzling claim that repressed ideas attract to themselves preconscious items with which they cohere semantically.
[4] The view that unconscious mental contents possess (or at least may possess) a rational structure is surprisingly widespread amongst those attempting to underwrite philosophically or derive support from Freudian theory. Fodor (1991), for example, writes in the

passage alluded to in note 10, that only three things of lasting importance have happened in cognitive science, one of which is:

> Freud's demonstration that postulating unconscious beliefs and desires allows a vast range of anomalous behavioral (and mental) phenomena to be brought within the purview of familiar forms of belief/desire explanation (of practical rationality). Freud thus anticipated, and roundly refuted, the charge that Granny-psychology is stagnant science (277).

[5] This is analogous to Davidson's (e.g., 1970) claim that relations between events only instantiate causal laws under certain descriptions.

[6] Dennett's (1986) distinction between beliefs and opinions corresponds quite closely to the fundamental elements of Freud's analysis. Briefly, 'beliefs' are non-introspectable, non-linguistic states which determine behavior and are inferred from behavior. Opinions, on the other hand, are sentences to which one assents. Dennett opines that akrasia and self-deception are made possible by the chasm between belief and opinion.

> My opinions can be relied on to predict my behavior only to the degree, normally large, that my opinions and beliefs are in rational correspondence.... It is just this feature of the distinction between opinion and belief that gives us, I think, the first steps of an acceptable account of those twin puzzles, self-deception and akrasia (306-307).

[7] See Gardner's (1993) discussion of how Davidson is required to exceed his bare criteria for mental division in order to make his thesis explanatory rather than just redescriptive.

REFERENCES

Alexander, P. (1962) Rational behaviour and psychoanalytic explanation. *Mind*, 71:326-341.

Altschule, M. D. (1965) *Roots of Modern Psychiatry: Essays on the History of Psychiatry*. London: Grune & Stratton.

Amacher, P. (1965) Freud's neurological education and its influence on psychoanalytic theory. *Psychological Issues*, 4(4) (Monograph 16). New York: International Universities Press.

Andersson, O. (1962) *Studies in the Prehistory of Psychoanalysis: The Etiology of Psychoneuroses and Some Related Themes in Sigmund Freud's Scientific Writings, 1886-1896*. Stockholm: Svenska Bokforlaget.

Anscombe, R (1981) Referring to the unconscious. *International Journal of Psycho-Analysis*, 62: 225-241.

Anzieu, D. (1986) *Freud's Self-Analysis*. Trans. P. Graham. London: Hogarth Press and the Institute of Psycho-Analysis.

Armstrong, D (1968) A *Materialist Theory of the Mind*. New York: Humanities Press.

Azam, E. (1887) *Hypnotisme, double conscience et altérations de la personnalité*. Paris: Ballière.

Baldwin, J. M. (Ed.) (1901) *Dictionary of Philosophy and Psychology, Vol. I*. London: Macmillan.

-- (1902) *Dictionary of Philosophy and Psychology, Vol. II*. London: Macmillan.

Barclay, J. (1964) Franz Brentano and Sigmund Freud. *Journal of Existentialism*, 5: 1-36.

Binet, A. (1889) Recherches sur les altérations de la conscience chez les hystériques. *Revue Philosophique*, 27: 135-170.

-- (1892) *Les altérations de la personalité*. Paris: Felix Alcan.

Block, N. (1995) On a confusion about a function of consciousness. In N. Block, O. Flanagan & G. Güzeldere (Eds.), The *Nature of Consciousness: Philosophical Debates*. Cambridge, MA: MIT Press.

Boring, E. G. (1933) *The Physical Dimensions of Consciousness*. New York: The Century Company.

Boudreaux, G. (1977) Freud on the nature of unconscious mental processes. *Philosophy of the Social Sciences*, 7:1-32.

Bouveresse, J. (1995) *Wittgenstein Reads Freud: The Myth of the Unconscious*. Princeton, NJ: Princeton University Press.

Bradley, F. H. (1895) On the supposed uselessness of the soul. In G. N A. Vesey (Ed.), *Body and Mind*. London: George Allen and Unwin.

Braude, S. (1991) *First Person Plural: Multiple Personality and the Philosophy of Mind*. London: Routledge.

Brentano, F. (1874) *Psychology from an Empirical Standpoint*. London: Routledge and Kegan Paul, 1973.

Broad, C. D. (1925) *The Mind and its Place in Nature.* London: Routledge and Kegan Paul.
Brodie, B. (1857) *Mind and Matter.* New York: G. P. Putnam & Co.
Brook, J. A. (1988) Freud and Kant. *Samiksa*, 42(4): 109-136.
Butler, S. (1880) *Unconscious Memory: A Comparison between the Theory of Dr. Ewald Hering...and "The Philosophy of the Unconscious" by Dr. Edward von Hartmann; with Translations from these Authors.* London: David Bogue.
Carruthers, P. (1989) Brute experience. *Journal of Philosophy*, 86(5): 258-269.
Castoriades, C. (1997) Psychoanalysis and philosophy. In T. Dufresne (Ed.). *Freud under Analysis: Essays in Honor of Paul Roazen.* New York: Jason Aronson.
Cavell, M. (1993) *The Psychoanalytic Mind: From Freud to Philosophy.* Cambridge, MA: Harvard University Press.
Chabaneix P. (1897) *Physiologie cérébral: le subconscient chez les artistes, les savants et les écrivains.* Paris: Ballière.
Challaye, F. (1933) *Nietzsche.* Paris: Mellottée Séditeur.
Chalmers, D. J. (1996) *The Conscious Mind: In Search of a Fundamental Theory.* Oxford: Oxford University Press.
Charcot, J. -M. (1887) *Clinical Lectures on Diseases of the Nervous System, Vol. III.* Trans. T. Saville. London: New Sydenham Society, 1889.
Chessick, R. D. (1980) *Freud Teaches Psychotherapy.* Cambridge: Hackett.
Churchland, P. (1986) *Scientific Realism and the Plasticity of Mind.* Cambridge: Cambridge University Press.
-- (1988) *Matter and Consciousness.* Cambridge: MIT Press.
Clifford, W. K. (1874) Body and mind. In *Lectures and Essays, Vol.II.* London: Macmillan, 1879.
-- (1878) On the nature of things in themselves. In G.N.A. Vesey (Ed.) *Body and Mind.* London: George Allen & Unwin.
Cotterill, R. (1995) On the unity of conscious experience. *Journal of Consciousness Studies*, 2(4): 290-312.
Crick, F. (1994) The Astonishing Hypothesis: The Scientific Search for the Soul. London: Touchstone.
-- & Koch, C. (1990) Towards a neurobiological theory of consciousness. *Seminars in the Neurosciences*, 2: 263-275.
Dalbiez, R. (1941) *Psychoanalytical Method and the Doctrine of Freud, Vol. II.* Trans. T. F. Lindsay. London: Longmans, Green & Co.
Davidson, D. (1970) Mental events. In *Essays on Actions and Events.* Oxford: Clarendon Press, 1980.
-- (1973) The material mind. In *Essays on Actions and Events.* Oxford: Clarendon Press, 1980.
-- (1974) Psychology as philosophy. In *Essays on Actions and Events.* Oxford: Clarendon Press, 1980.
-- (1975) Thought and talk. In Davidson, D. *Inquiries into Truth and Interpretation.* Oxford: Clarendon Press, 1984.

-- (1982) Paradoxes of irrationality. In R. Wollheim and J. Hopkins (Eds.) *Philosophical Essays on Freud.* Cambridge: Cambridge University Press.
-- (1995) Davidson, D. In S. Guttenplan (Ed.) A *Companion to the Philosophy of Mind.* Oxford: Blackwell.
-- (1986) Deception and division. In J. Elster (Ed.) *The Multiple Self.* Cambridge: Cambridge University Press.
Davies, K. & Fichtner, G. (forthcoming) *Sigmund Freud's Library: A Comprehensive Catalogue.*
Decker, H. (1977) *Freud in Germany: Revolution and Reaction in Science, 1893-1907.* New York: International Universities Press.
Dennett, D. C. (1987) *The Intentional Stance.* Cambridge, MA: Bradford/MIT.
-- (1987) Fast thinking. In *The Intentional Stance.* Cambridge, MA: Bradford/MIT.
-- (1991) *Consciousness Explained.* London: Allen Lane.
-- (1993) Back from the drawing board. In B. Dahlbom (Ed.), *Dennett and His Critics.* Oxford: Basil Blackwell.
Dorer, M. (1932) *Historische Grundlagen der Psychoanalyse.* Leipzig: Felix Meiner.
Dretske, F. (1995) *Naturalising the Mind.* Cambridge, MA: MIT Press.
Ellenberger, H. F. (1970) *The Discovery of the Unconscious: The History and Evolution of Dynamic Psychiatry.* New York: Basic Books.
Erdelyi, M.H. (1985) *Psychoanalysis: Freud's Cognitive Psychology.* New York: W. H. Freeman & Co.
Esterson, A. (1993) *Seductive Mirage.* Chicago: Open Court.
Evnine, S. (1991) *Donald Davidson.* Cambridge: Polity Press.
Fancher, R. (1977) Brentano's Psychology from an Empirical Standpoint and Freud's early metapsychology. *Journal of the History of the Behavioral Sciences*, 13: 207-227.
Fechner, G. (1848) *Nanna, oder Über das Seelenleben der Pflanzen.* Leipzig: Voss.
-- (1851) *Zend-Avesta oder Über der Dinge des Himmels und des Jenseits.* Leipzig: Voss.
Feyerabend, P. (1963) Mental events and the brain. *Journal of Philosophy*, 60: 160-166.
Field, J. C. (1922) Is the concept of the unconscious of value in psychology? *Mind*, 31: 414-423. Reprinted in G. C. Field, *Studies in Philosophy.* Bristol: J.W. Arrowsmith, 1935.
Flanagan, O. (1986) *The Science of Mind.* Cambridge, MA: Harvard University Press.
Flew A. (1956) Motives and the unconscious. In H. Feigl and M. Scriven (Eds.). *Minnesota Studies in the Philosophy of Science, Vol. I.* Minneapolis: University of Minnesota Press.
Flügel, J. C. & West, D. (1964) *A Hundred Years of Psychology: 1833-1933, With an Additional Part: 1933-1963.* New York: Basic Books.

Fodor, J. (1991) Replies. In B. Loewer and G. Rey (Eds.) *Meaning in Mind: Fodor and his Critics.* Oxford: Basil Blackwell, 1991.
Forrester, J. (1980) *Language and the Origins of Psychoanalysis.* London: Macmillan.
Frank, P. (1959) Psychoanalysis and logical positivism. In S. Hook (Ed.) *Psychoanalysis, Scientific Method and Philosophy.* New York: New York University Press.
Frattaroli, E. J. (1992) Metapsychology and consciousness. In E. E. Garcia (Ed.). *Understanding Freud: The Man and his Ideas.* New York: New York University Press.
Freud, S. (1871-1881) The *Letters of Sigmund Freud to Eduard Silberstein.* W. Boelich (Ed.). Trans. A. J. Pomerans. Cambridge, MA: Harvard/Belknap, 1990.
-- (1873-1939) *The Letters of Sigmund Freud.* Ernst L. Freud (Ed.). Trans. T. Stern and J. Stern. London; Hogarth Press and the Institute of Psycho-Analysis, 1970.
-- (1887-1904 *The Complete Letters of Sigmund Freud to Wilhelm Fliess.* (Ed. and Trans. J. M. Masson). Cambridge, MA: Harvard University Press.
-- (1888a) Aphasia. In Solms, M. & Saling, M. (Eds.) *A Moment of Transition: Two Neuroscientific Articles by Sigmund Freud.* Trans. M. Solms and M. Saling. London: Karnac Books, 1990.
-- (1888b) Gehirn. In Solms, M. & Saling, M. (Eds.), *A Moment of Transition: Two Neuroscientific Articles by Sigmund Freud.* Trans. M. Solms and M. Saling. London: Karnac Books, 1990.
-- (1888c) Hysteria. *S.E.**, 1.
-- (1888d) Preface to the translation of Bernheim's *Suggestion*, *S.E.*, 1.
-- (1890) Psychical (or mental) treatment. *S.E.*, 7.
-- (1891) *On Aphasia: A Critical Study.* New York: International Universities Press, 1953.
-- (1894) The neuro-psychoses of defence. *S.E.*, 3.
-- (1896) Further remarks on the neuro-psychoses of defence. *S.E.*, 3.
-- (1897) *Infantile Cerebral Paralysis.* Coral Gables, FLA: University of Miami Press, 1968.
-- (1900) The interpretation of dreams. *S.E.*, 4 & 5.
-- (1905) Jokes and their relation to the unconscious. *S.E.*, 8.
-- (1909a) Analysis of a phobia in a five year old boy. *S.E.*, 10.
-- (1909b) Notes upon a case of obsessional neurosis. *S.E.*, 10.
-- (1910a) Five lectures on psycho-analysis. *S.E.*, 11.
-- (1910b) The psycho-analytic view of a psychogenic disturbance of vision. *S.E.*, 11.
-- (1911) Formulations on the two principles of mental functioning. *S.E.*, 12.
-- (1912a) A note on the unconscious in psycho-analysis. *S.E.*, 12.

---

* *The Standard Edition of the Complete Psychological Works of Sigmund Freud.* James Strachey (Ed.). 24 Vols. London: Hogarth Press and the Institute of Psychoanalysis, 1953-1964.

-- (1912b) Recommendations to physicians practicing psycho-analysis. *S.E.*, 12.
-- (1912-13) Totem and taboo. *S.E.*, 13
-- (1913) The claims of psycho-analysis to scientific interest. *S.E.*, 13.
-- (1914) Zur Geschichte der psychoanalytischen Bewegung. *Gesammelte Werke: Schriften auf den Nachlass 1892-1939, Vol. X.* Frankfurt-am-Main: S. Fischer Verlag.
-- (1915a) The unconscious. *S.E.*, 14.
-- (1915b) Repression. *S.E.*, 14.
-- (1916-17) Introductory lectures on psycho-analysis. *S.E.* 15 &16.
-- (1917a) A difficulty in the path of psycho-analysis. *S.E.*, 17.
-- (1917b) A metapsychological supplement to the theory of dreams. *S.E.*, 14.
-- (1920) Beyond the pleasure principle. *S.E.*, 18.
-- (1922) Dreams and telepathy. *S.E.*, 18.
-- (1923a) Two encyclopaedia articles. *S.E.*, 18.
-- (1923b) The ego and the id. *S.E.*, 19.
-- (1923c) Remarks on the theory and practice of dream interpretation. *S.E.*, 19.
-- (1924) A short account of psycho-analysis. *S.E.*, 19.
-- (1925a) An autobiographical study. *S.E.*, 20.
-- (1925b) The resistances to psycho-analysis. *S.E.*, 19.
-- (1926a) Inhibitions, symptoms and anxiety. *S.E.*, 20.
-- (1926b) The question of lay analysis. *S.E.*, 20.
-- (1926c) Psycho-analysis. *S.E.*, 20.
-- (1927) The future of an illusion. *S.E.*, 21.
-- (1929) On a dream of Descartes. *S.E.*, 21.
-- (1933a) New introductory lectures on psycho-analysis. *S.E.*, 22.
-- (1933b) Why war? *S.E.*, 22.
-- (1939) Moses and monotheism. *S.E.*, 23.
-- (1940a) An outline of psycho-analysis. *S.E.*, 23.
-- (1940b) Abriss der Psychoanalyse. *Gesammelte Werke: Schriften auf den Nachlass 1892-1939, Vol. XVII.* Frankfurt-am-Main: S. Fischer Verlag.
-- (1940c) Some elementary lessons in psycho-analysis. *S.E.*, 23.
-- (1940d) The splitting of the ego in the process of defence. *S.E.*, 23.
-- (1941a) Psycho-analysis and telepathy. *S.E.*, 18.
-- (1941b) Findings, ideas, problems. *S.E.*, 23.
-- (1950) The origins of psycho-analysis. *S.E.*, 1.
-- (1987) *A Phylogenetic Fantasy: Overview of the Transference Neuroses.* I. Grubrich-Simitis (Ed.). A. Hoffer & P. T. Hoffer (Trans.). Cambridge, MA:Harvard/Belknap.
-- & Jones, E. (1993) *The Complete Correspondence of Sigmund Freud and Ernest Jones, 1908-1939.* R. Andrew Paskauskas (Ed. and Trans.). Cambridge, MA: Harvard/Belknap.
-- & Rie, O. (1891) *Klinische Studie über die halbseitige Cerebrallämung der Kinder.* Vienna: Moritz Perles.

Friedman, J. & Alexander, J, J. (1983) Psycho-analysis and natural science: Freud's 1895 Project Revisited. *International Review of Psycho-Analysis*, 10: 303-318.

Frost, W. (1918) *Schopenhauer als Erbe Kants in der philosophischen Seelenanalyse. Nachweis einer empirischen Anwendbarkeit der transcendentalen Methode.* Bonn: no publisher.

Gardner, S. (1991) The unconscious. In J. Neu (Ed.) *The Cambridge Companion to Freud.* Cambridge: Cambridge University Press.

-- (1993) *Irrationality and the Philosophy of Psychoanalysis.* Cambridge: Cambridge University Press.

Garver, M. M. (1880) The periodic character of voluntary nervous action. *American Journal of Science*, Third Series, 20(117): 189-193.

Geeardyn, P. (1997) *Freud's Project: On the Roots of Psychoanalysis.* Trans. P. Vandendaele. London: Rebus.

Geha, R. E. (1988) Freud as fictionalist: The imaginary worlds of Psychoanalysis. In P. Stepansky (Ed.), *Freud Appraisals and Reappraisals: Contributions to Freud Studies, Vol. II.* Hillsdale NJ: Analytic Press.

Gilson, L. (1966) Brentano on science and philosophy. In L. L. McAlister (Ed.) *The Philosophy of Franz Brentano.* London: Duckworth, 1976.

Glymour, C. (1991) Freud's androids. In J. Neu (Ed.) *The Cambridge Companion to Freud.* Cambridge: Cambridge University Press.

Greenberg, V. D. (1997) *Freud and His Aphasia Book: Language and the Sources of Psychoanalysis.* London: Cornell University Press.

Grubrich-Simitis, I. (1993) *Zurück zu Freud's Texten. Stumme Dokumente sprechen Machen.* Frankfurt-am-Main: S. Fischer Verlag.

Grünbaum, A. (1993) *Validation in the Clinical Theory of Psychoanalysis.* Madison, CT: International Universities Press.

Guttmann, G. (1998) From the sum of excitation to the cortical DC potential. In G. Guttmann and I. Scholz-Strasser (Eds.). *Freud and the Neurosciences.* Vienna: Verlag der Österreichen Akademie der Wissenschaften.

Güzeldere, G. (1995a) Consciousness: What it is, how to study it, what to learn from its history. *Journal of Consciousness Studies*, 2(1): 30-51.

-- (1995b) Problems of consciousness: a perspective on contemporary issues, current debates. *Journal of Consciousness Studies*, 2(2): 112-143.

-- (1997) Is consciousness the perception of what passes in one's own mind? In N. Block, O. Flanagan & G. Güzeldere (Eds.) *The Nature of Consciousness: Philosophical Debates.* Cambridge, MA: MIT Press.

Hacking, I. (1992) Multiple personality disorder and its many hosts. *History of the Human Sciences*, 5: 3-31.

-- (1995) *Rewriting the Soul: Multiple Personality and the Sciences of Memory.* Princeton, NJ: Princeton University Press.

Hadamard, J. (1949) *The Psychology of Invention in the Mathematical Field.* Princeton, NJ: Princeton University Press.

Hamilton, W. (1853) *Discussions on Philosophy and Literature, Education and University Reform, Chiefly from the Edinborough Review; Corrected, Vindi-*

cated, Enlarged in Notes and Appendices. Second edition. London: Longman, Brown, Green & Longmans.

Hare, R. (1952) *The Language of Morals.* Oxford: Clarendon.

-- (1984) Supervenience. *Proceedings of the Aristotelian Society.* Supplementary volume 58: 1-16.

Hartmann, E. von (1869) *Philosophie der Unbewusstsein.* Berlin: Dunker.

Haynal, A. (1994) Freud's relationship to philosophy and biology as reflected in his letters. In A. Haynal & E. Falzeder (Eds.), *100 Years of Psychoanalysis.* Geneva: Institutions Universitaires des Psychiatrie des Genève.

Heil, J. (1992) *The Nature of True Minds.* Cambridge: Cambridge University Press.

Helmholz, H. von (1867) *Handbuch der psysiologischen Optik.* Leipzig: Verlag von Leopold Voss.

Herbart, J. F. (1824) Psychologie als Wissenschaft, neugegründet auf Erfahrung, Metaphysik und Mathematik. In *Sämtliche Werke.* Leipzig: Voss.

Hering E. (1870) *Über das Gedächtniss als allegemeine Funktion der organisirten Materie.* Vienna: K.K. Hof- und Staatsdrukerei.

Herzog, P. (1988) The myth of Freud as anti-philosopher. In P. Stepansky (Ed.) *Freud Appraisals and Reappraisals: Contributions to Freud Studies, Vol. II.* Hillsdale, NJ: The Analytic Press, 1988.

-- (1991) Conscious and Unconscious: Freud's Dynamic Distinction Reconsidered. Madison, CT: International Universities Press.

Hilgard, E. R. (1977) *Divided Consciousness: Multiple Controls in Human Thought and Action.* New York: John Wiley and Sons.

Holt, R. (1974) Drive or wish? In M. Gill and P. Holzman (Eds.) *Psychology versus Metapsychology.* Madison, CT: International Universities Press.

Honderich, T. (1988) *Mind, and Brain: A Theory of Determinism, Vol. I.* Oxford: Clarendon Press.

Hopkins, J. (1991) The interpretation of dreams. In J. Neu (Ed.), *The Cambridge Companion to Freud.* Cambridge: Cambridge University Press.

-- (1994) The unconscious. In S. Guttenplan (Ed.), *A Companion to the Philosophy of Mind.* Oxford: Basil Blackwell.

Humphrey, N. & Dennett, D.C. (1989) Speaking for ourselves. *Raritan*, 9: 68-98.

Husserl, E. (1919) Reminiscences of Brentano. In L. L. McAlister (Ed.) *The Philosophy of Brentano.* London: Duckworth, 1976.

Huxley, T.H. (1874) On the hypothesis that animals are automata. In G.N.A. Vesey (Ed.), *Body and Mind.* London: George Allen and Unwin.

Jackson, J. H. (1875) On the Anatomical and Physiological Localisation of Movements in the Brain. In J. Taylor (Ed.) *Selected Writings of John Hughlings Jackson, Vol. I.* London: Hodder & Stoughton, 1958.

-- (1879) On affectations of speech from disease of the brain. In J. Taylor (Ed.) Selected *Writings of John Hughlings Jackson, Vol. II.* London: Hodder & Stoughton, 1958.

-- (1878-79) On the affectations of speech from disease of the brain (Part I). In J. Taylor (Ed.), *Selected Writings of John Hughlings Jackson, Vol. II.* London: Hodder & Stoughton, 1958.

-- (1884) Evolution and dissolution of the nervous system. In J. Taylor (Ed.), *Selected Writings of John Hughlings Jackson, Vol. II.* London: Hodder and Stoughton, 1958.

-- (1887) Remarks on evolution and dissolution of the nervous system. In J. Taylor (Ed.), *Selected Writings of John Hughlings Jackson, Vol. II.* London: Hodder and Stoughton, 1958.

James, W. (1890) *Principles of Psychology.* New York: Dover, 1950.

Janet, P. (1886) Les actes inconscients et le dédoublement de la personnalité pendant le somnambulisme provoqué. *Revue philosophique*, 23: 449-472.

Jerusalem, W. (1895) *Die Urteilsfunktion. Eine psychologische und erkenntniskritische Untersuchung.* Vienna/Leipzig: Verlag von Wilhelm Braumüller.

Jones, E. (1953) *The Life and Work of Sigmund Freud, Vol. I.* New York: Basic Books.

-- (1955) *The Life and Work of Sigmund Freud, Vol. II.* New York: Basic Books.

-- (1957) *The Life and Work of Sigmund Freud, Vol. III.* New York: Basic Books.

Kaltenbeck, F. (1985) Sigmund Freud et Wilhelm Jerusalem. *Orincar?* 4: 87-113.

Kant, I. (1786) *Metaphysical Foundations of Natural Science.* Trans. J. Ellington. Indianapolis: Bobs-Merril, 1970.

Kanzer, M. (1973) Two prevalent misconceptions about Freud's Project (1895). *The Annual of Psychoanalysis*, 1: 88 -104.

Kaplan, L. (1916) *Schopenhauer und der Animismus. Eine psychoanalytische Studie.* Vienna: Franz Deuticke.

Kaufmann, W. (1980) *Discovering the Mind, Vol. III: Freud Versus Adler and Jung.* New York: McGraw-Hill.

Kinsbourne, M. and Warrington, E. K. (1963) 'Jargon Aphasia'. *Neuropsychologica*, 1: 27-37.

Kitcher, P. (1992) *Freud's Dream: A Complete Interdisciplinary Science of Mind.* Cambridge, MA: Bradford/MIT.

Klein, D. B. (1977) *The Unconscious: Invention or Discovery?* Santa Monica, CA: Goodyear Publishing Company.

Kris, E. (1950) The significance of Freud's earliest discoveries. *International Journal of Psycho-Analysis*, 31: 108-116.

-- (1954) Introduction. *The Origins of Psychoanalysis.* New York: Basic Books.

-- (1956) Freud in the history of science. *The Listener*, 55: 631.

Küssmaul, A. (1885) Die Störungen der Sprache. In H. W. Ziemssen, (Ed.) *Handbuch der speciellen Pathologie und Therapie*, Third Edition. Leipzig: Vogel.

Lange, F. A. (1873-75) *Geschichte des Materialismus und Kritik seiner Bedeutung in der Gegenwart.* Iserlohn: Verlag von J. Baedeker.

Laplanche, J. & Pontalis, J.–B. (1980) *The Language of Psycho-Analysis.* Trans. D. Nicholson-Smith. London: Hogarth.

Lashley, C. (1923) The behavioristic interpretation of consciousness, II. *The Psychological Review*, 30(5): 329-353.

Leahy, T. H. (1978) *A History of Psychology: Main Currents in Psychological Thought*. New York: Prentice-Hall.

Leary, D. E. (1980) German idealism and the development of psychology in the nineteenth century. *Journal of the History of Philosophy*, 18: 299-317.

Lehrer, R. (1995) *Nietzsche's Presence in Freud's Life: On the Origins of a Psychology of Dynamic Unconscious Mental Functioning*. Albany, NY: State University of New York Press.

Leibniz, G. W. von (1714) *Monadology*. In *The Monadology and Other Philosophical Writings*. (Ed. and Trans. R. Latta). London: Oxford University Press, 1925.

Leupold-Löwenthal, H. (1998) Freud as a neurologist. In G. Guttmann and I. Scholz-Strasser (Eds.). *Freud and the Neurosciences*. Vienna: Verlag der Österreichen Akademie der Wissenschaften.

Leupold-Löwenthal, H. & Lobner, H. (1975) *Sigmund Freud House Catalogue*. Vienna: Löcker & Wögenstein.

Lewes, G. H. (1877) The *Physical Basis of Mind*. London: Trubner & Company.

Levine, I. (1923) *The Unconscious: An Introduction to Freudian Psychology*. London: L. Parsons.

-- (1926) *Das Unbewusste*. Leipzig: Internationaler Psychoanalytischer Verlag.

Levy, D. (1996) *Freud among the Philosophers*. London: Yale University Press.

Lindner, G. A. (1858) *Lehrbuch der empirischen Psychologie nach genetischen Methode*. Graz: Wiesner.

Lindsay, J. (no date) *Dionysos. Nietzsche contra Nietzsche*. London: Fanfrolico Press.

Linke, D. B. (1998) Discharge, reflex, free energy and encoding. In G. Guttmann and I. Scholz-Strasser (Eds.). *Freud and the Neurosciences*. Vienna: Verlag der Österreichen Akademie der Wissenschaften.

Lipps, T. (1883) *Grundtatsachen des Seelenlebens*. Bonn: Verlag von Max Cohen & Sohn.

-- (1885) *Psychologische Studien*. Heidelberg: Verlag von Georg Weiss.

-- (1891) *Der Streit über die Tragödie*. Hamburg/Leipzig: Verlag von Leopold Voss.

-- (1891) *Ästhetische Faktoren der Raumanschauung*. Hamburg/Leipzig: Verlag von Leopold Voss.

-- (1893) *Grundzüge der Logik*. Hamburg/Leipzig: Verlag von Leopold Voss.

-- (1897) *Raumäesthetik und geometrisch-optische Täuschungen*, Leipzig: Verlag von Johann Ambrosius Barth.

---- (1897) 'Der Begriff des Unbewussten in der Psychologie'. *III Internationaler Congress für Psychologie in München*. München: Verlag von J. F. Lehmann.

-- (1898) *Komic und Humor. Eine psychologisch-äesthet-ische Untersuchung*. Hamburg/Leipzig: Verlag von Leopold Voss.

-- (1901) *Das Selbstbewusstsein; Empfindung und Gefühl*. Wiesbaden: Verlag von J. F. Bergmann.

-- (1902) *Einheiten und Relationen. Eine Skizze zur Psychologie der Aperzeption*. Leipzig: Verlag von Johann Ambrosius Barth.

-- (1902) *Vom Fühlen, Wollen und Denpen. Eine Psychologische Skizze.* Verlag von Johann Ambrosius Barth.

Lycan, W. (1990) Introduction to Part II. *In Mind and Cognition: A Reader.* Oxford: Basil Blackwell.

-- (1987) *Consciousness.* Cambridge, MA: MIT Press.

Lyons, W. (1986) *The Disappearance of Introspection.* Cambridge, MA: Bradford/MIT.

MacDougall, W. (1911) *Body and Mind: A History and Defence of Animism.* London: Methuen & Co.

MacIntyre, A. (1958) *The Unconscious: A Conceptual Study.* London: Routledge and Kegan Paul.

Mackay, N. (1986) Freud, explanation and the mind-brain problem. *Psychoanalysis and Contemporary Thought, 9*: 373-404.

-- (1989) *Motivation and Explanation: An Essay on Freud's Philosophy of Science.* Madison, CT: International Universities Press.

Macmillan, M. (1990) *Freud Evaluated: The Completed Arc.* Amsterdam: Elsevier.

-- (1992) In T. Gelfland and J. Kerr (Eds.), *Freud and the History of Psychoanalysis.* Hillsdale, NJ: Analytic Press, 1992.

Mancia, M. (1983) Archaeology of Freudian thought and the history of neurophysiology. *International Review of Psycho-Analysis,* 10: 185-192.

Manson N.C. (1995) *Extending the Mental: Philosophical Assessments of Approaches to the Unconscious in Freudian Theory and Empirical Psychology.* Unpublished Master of Philosophy thesis, University College, London.

Marr, D. (1982) *Vision.* San Francisco: W. H. Freeman and Company.

Marx, O. (1967) Freud, and aphasia: An historical analysis. *American Journal of Psychiatry,* 124: 814-825.

Matte-Blanco, I. (1975) *The Unconscious as Infinite Sets.* London: Duckworth.

-- (1988) *Thinking, Feeling and Being.* London: Routledge.

Maudsley, H. (1867) *The Physiology and Pathology of Mind.* New York: D. Appleton and Co.

McGinn, C. (1990) *The Problem of Consciousness.* Oxford: Basil Blackwell.

McGuiness, B. (1981) Freud and Wittgenstein. In B. McGuinness (Ed.), *Wittgenstein and his Times.* Oxford: Basil Blackwell.

Mercier, C. (1888) *The Nervous System and the Mind.* London: Macmillan.

Meyer, R. M. (1913) *Nietzsche. Sein Leben und sein Werke.* Munich: C. H. Beck'sche Verlagsbuchhandlung (Oskar Beck).

Mill, J. S. (1865) *An Examination of Sir William Hamilton's Philosophy and of the Principal Philosophical Questions Discussed in His Writings.* Toronto: University of Toronto Press, 1979.

Millikan, R. G. (1984) *Language, Thought and Other Biological Categories.* Cambridge, MA: Bradford/MIT.

-- (1993) *White Queen Psychology and Other Essays for Alice.* Cambridge, MA: Bradford/MIT.

Mischel, T. (1965) Concerning rational behaviour and psychoanalytic explanation. *Mind*, 74:71-78

Monk, R. (1990) *Ludwig Wittgenstein: The Duty of Genius.* Oxford: The Free Press.

Mutalik, P. (1998) Sweet music in Bremen. *Journal of Consciousness Studies,* 5(5-6): 734-738.

Natsoulas, T. (1984) Freud and consciousness I: Intrinsic consciousness. *Psychoanalysis and Contemporary Thought*, 7: 195-232.

--- (1985) Freud and consciousness II: Derived consciousness. *Psychoanalysis and Contemporary Thought*, 8: 183-220.

--- (1989a) Freud and consciousness III: The importance of tertiary consciousness. *Psychoanalysis and Contemporary Thought*, 12: 97-123.

--- (1989b) Freud and consciousness. IV: A propedeutic for functions of consciousness in hypercathected speech-imagery. *Psychoanalysis and Contemporary Thought*, 12: 619-662.

--(1991) Freud and consciousness: V: Emotions and feelings. *Psychoanalysis and Contemporary Thought*, 14: 69-108.

--(1992) Freud and consciousness VI: A present-day perspective. *Psychoanalysis and Contemporary Thought*, 15: 305-348.

Neider, H. (1977) Gespräch mit Heinrich Neider: Persönliche Erinnerungen an den Wiener Kreis. *Conceptus*, 1.

Neisser, U. (1967) *Cognitive Psychology.* Englewood Cliffs, NJ: Prentice-Hall.

Nemiah, J. C. (1974) Conversion: Fact or chimera. *International Journal of Psychiatry in Medicine*, 5: 443-448.

-- (1985) Review of A. Roy (Ed.), 'Hysteria'. *Psychosomatic Medicine,* 47: 303-305.

Nietzsche, F. (1887) *The Gay Science.* Trans. W. Kaufmann. New York: Vintage Books, 1974.

-- (1928) *The Antichrist.* Trans. P. R. Stephenson. Illust. Norman Lindsay. London: Fanfrolico Press.

Nunberg, H. & Federn E. (Eds.) (1962-75) *Minutes of the Vienna Psychoanalytic Society, 4 Vols.* New York: International Universities Press.

Papineau, D. (1993) *Philosophical Naturalism.* Oxford: Blackwell.

Place, U. T. (1956) Is consciousness a brain process? In C. V. Borst (Ed.) *The Mind/Brain Identity Theory.* London: Macmillan.

Poincaré, H. (1913) *Last Essays.* Trans. J. W. Bolduc. New York: Dover Publications, 1963.

Prince, M. (1885) *The Nature of Mind and Human Automatism.* Philadelphia: J. B. Lippincott Company.

Putnam, H. (1960) Minds and machines. In S. Hook (Ed.), *Dimensions of Mind.* New York: Collier.

-- (1975) The meaning of "meaning". In K. Gunderson (Ed.), *Minnesota Studies in the Philosophy of Science, Vol. VII: Language, Mind and Knowledge.* Minneapolis: University of Minnesota Press.

Quinton, A. (1972) Freud and philosophy. In J. Miller (Ed.), *Freud: The Man, His World, His Influence.* London: George Weidenfeld and Nicolson.
Rayner, E. and Tuckett, D. (1988) An introduction to Matte Blanco's reformulation of the Freudian unconscious and his conceptualisation of the internal world. In I. Matte-Blanco, *Thinking, Feeling and Being.* London: Routledge, 1988.
Reise, W. (1950) Freudian concepts of brain function and brain disease: their sources, scope and evaluation. *Journal of Nervous and Mental Disease*, 127: 287-307.
Ribot, T. H. (1885) *Les maladies de la personnalité.* Paris: Felix Alcan.
Ricoeur, P. (1970) *Freud and Philosophy.* New Haven, CT: Yale University Press.
Rieber, R. W. (Ed.), (1980) *Wilhelm Wundt and the Making of a Scientific Psychology.* New York: Plenum Press.
Romanos, G. D. (1986) *Quine and Analytical Philosophy.* London: MIT.
Rosenthal, D. (1986) Two concepts of consciousness. *Philosophical Studies,* 94(3): 329-359.
Rubenstein, B. (1965) Psychoanalytic theory and the mind-body problem. In N. S Greenfield and W. C. Lewis (Eds.), *Psychoanalysis and Current Biological Thought.* Madison: University of Wisconsin Press.
Russell, B. (1921) *The Analysis of Mind.* London: Allen and Unwin.
Sacks, O. (1998) Sigmund Freud: the other road. In G. Guttman and I. Scholz-Strasser (Eds.). *Freud and the Neurosciences: From brain Research to the Unconscious.* Vienna: Verlag der Österreichen Akademie der Wissenschaften.
Sartre, J-P. (1943) *Being and Nothingness: An Essay on phenomenological Ontology.* Trans. H. Barnes. New York: Philosophical Library, 1956.
Scavio, M. J., Cooper, A. and Clift, P. S. (1993) Freud's devaluation of Nietzsche. *Psychohistory Review*, 21(3): 295-318.
Schacter, D. (1988) On the relation between memory and consciousness: dissociable interactions and conscious experience. In H. Roediger and F. Craik (Eds.), *Varieties of Memory and Consciousness.* Hillsdale, NJ: Lawrence Erlbaum.
Schiffer, S. (1981) Truth and the theory of content. In H. Parret and J. Bouveresse (Eds.) *Meaning and Understanding.* New York: Walter de Gruyter.
Schlick, M. (1925) Extracts from *Allgemeine Erkenntnislehre.* In G. N. A. Vesey (Ed.) *Body and Mind.* London: Trubner and Company.
Schlipp, P. A. (1963) *The Philosophy of Rudolf Carnap.* London: Cambridge University Press.
Schopenhauer, A. (1875) *Über die vierfache Wurzel des Satzes vom zureichenden Grunde. Eine philosophische Abhandlung.* Leipzig: F. A. Brockhaus.
Searle, J. R. R. (1992) *The Rediscovery of the Mind.* London: Bradford/MIT.
-- (1995) Searle, John R. In Guttenplan, S. (Ed.) *A Companion to the Philosophy of Mind.* Oxford: Blackwell.
Sellars, W. (1956) Empiricism and the philosophy of mind. In H. Gunderson (Ed.) *Minnesota Studies in the Philosophy of Science, Vol. VII: The Foundations of Science and the Concepts of Psychology and Psychoanalysis.* Minneapolis: University of Minnesota Press.
-- (1963) *Science, Perception and Reality.* New York: Humanities Press.

Shamdasani, S. (1994) Introduction to Flournoy, T. *From India to the Planet Mars: A Case of Multiple Personality with Imaginary Languages.* Princeton, NJ: Princeton University Press.

Shallice, T, T. (1992) *From Neuropsychology to Mental Structure.* Cambridge: Cambridge University Press.

Shope, R. (1970) Freud on conscious and unconscious intentions. *Inquiry*, 13:149-159.

Silverstein, B. (1985) Freud's psychology and its organic foundation: Sexuality and mind-body interactionism. *Psychoanalytic Review*, 72: 203-228.

-- (1986) 'Now comes a sad story': Freud's lost metapsychological papers. In P. Stepansky (Ed.), *Freud Appraisals and Reappraisals: Contributions to Freud Studies, Vol. I.* Hillsdale, NJ: Analytic Press.

-- (1989) Freud's dualistic mind-body interactionism: implication for the development of his psychology. *Psychological Reports*, 64: 1091-1097.

Silverstein, S. & Silverstein, B. (1990) Freud and hypnosis: the development of an interactionistperspective. *The Annual of Psychoanalysis,* 18: 175-190. New York: International Universities Press.

Smart J. J. C (1959) Sensations and brain processes. In C.C.V. Borst (Ed.) *The Mind/Brain Identity Theory.* Cambridge, MA: Bradford/MIT.

Smith, D. L. (1999) Sigmund Freud and the Crick-Koch hypothesis. *International Journal of Psycho-Analysis.* In press.

Smith, L. (1986) *Behaviorism & Logical Positivism: A Reassessment of the Alliance.* Stanford: Stanford University Press.

Solms, M. (1994) Review of I. Grubrich-Simitis' Zurück zu Freud's Texten. Stumme Dokumente sprechen machen. *International Journal of Psycho-Analysis*, 75: 153-159.

-- & Saling, M. (Eds.) (1990) A *Moment of Transition: Two Neuro-scientific Articles by Sigmund Freud.* Trans. M. Solms and M. Saling. London: Karnac.

-- & Saling, M. (1986) On psycho-analysis and neuroscience: Freud's attitude toward the localizationist tradition. *International Journal of Psycho-Analysis*, 67: 397-416.

Solomon, R. C. (1974a) Freud's neurological theory of mind. In R. Wollheim (Ed.), *Freud: A Collection of Critical Essays.* Garden City, NY: Anchor Press/Doubleday Books.

-- (1974b) Freud and 'unconscious motivation'. *Journal of the Theory of Social Behavior, 4*: 191-216.

Spehlmann, R. (1953) *Sigmund Freuds neurologische Schriften.* Berlin, Göttingen and Heidelberg: Springer Verlag.

Spence, P. (1879) Space and time considered as negations. *Journal of Speculative Philosophy*, 13(4): 337-346.

Spencer, H. (1855) *The Principles of Psychology.* Longman's: London.

Spiegelberg, H. (1982) *The Phenomenological Movement: A Historical Introduction.* The Hague: Martinus Nijhoff.

Stewart, W. (1969) *Psychoanalysis: The First Ten Years, 1888 - 1898.* London: George Allen & Unwin.

Storr, A. (1985) The sanity of true genius. In *Churchill's Black Dog and Other Phenomena of the Human Mind.* London: Collins, 1988.
Strachey, J. (1957) Appendix C to Freud's 'The unconscious': 'Words and things.' *S.E,.* 14: 209-215.
Sulloway, F. (1979) *Freud, Biologist of the Mind: Beyond the Psychoanalytic Legend.* New York: Basic Books.
Szasz, T. S. (1972) *The Myth of Mental Illness.* New York: Paladin.
Taine, H-A. (1870) *De l'intelligence.* Paris: Hachette.
Titchener, E. B. (1917) A *Text-Book of Psychology.* New York: Macmillan.
Toulmin, S. (1954) The logical status of psycho-analysis. In M. Macdonald (Ed.), *Philosophy and Analysis.* Oxford: Basil Blackwell.
Vaihinger, H. (1911) *The Philosophy of 'As If'.* Trans. C. Ogden. New York: Harcourt Brace, 1935.
Vesey G. N. A. (1965) *The Embodied Mind.* London: George Allen & Unwin.
Villaret, A. (Ed.) (1888/1891) *Handwörterbuch der gesamten Medizin (2 vols.).* Stuttgart: Ferdinand Enke Verlag.
Wallace, E. (1988) Mind-body: Monistic dual-aspect interactionism. *Journal of Mental and Nervous Diseases,* 176:4-21.
-- (1990) Mind-body and the future of psychiatry. *Journal of Medical Philosophy,* 15: 41-73.
-- (1992) Freud and the mind-body problem. In T. Gelfand and J. Kerr (Eds.), *Freud and the History of Psychoanalysis.* Hillsdale, NJ: Analytic Press.
Watson, J.B. (1913) Psychology as the behaviorist views it. *Psychological Review,* 20: 158-177.
-- (1927) The unconscious of the behaviourist. In *The Unconscious: A Symposium.* New York: Alfred A. Knopf.
Whitehead, A. N. (1928) *Process and Reality.* Cambridge: Cambridge University Press.
Whyte, L. (1979) *The Unconscious Before Freud.* London: Julian Friedman.
Wilkes, K. V. (1988) *Real People: Personal Identity without Thought Experiments.* Oxford: Clarendon Press.
Wittels, F. (1931) *Freud and his Time.* New York: Liveright.
Williams, L. P. (1989) André-Marie Ampère. *Scientific American.* 260:72-79.
Wittgenstein, L. (1982) Conversations on Freud; excerpt from the 1932-3 lectures. In Wollheim, R. and Hopkins, J. (Eds.) *Philosophical Essays on Freud.* Cambridge: Cambridge University Press. Reprinted from C. Barrett (Ed.), *Wittgenstein: Lectures and Conversations.* Berkeley: University of California Press, 1966.
Young, C. & Brooke, A. (1994) Schopenhauer and Freud. *International Journal of Psycho-Analysis,* 75(1): 101-118.
Young, R. M. (1970) *Mind, Brain and Adaptation in the Nineteenth Century.* Oxford: Oxford University Press.

INDEX

18682133R00134

Printed in Great Britain
by Amazon